Instructor's Manual

to accompany

The Marketing Game!

Third Edition

Charlotte H. Mason
Kenan-Flagler Business School
University of North Carolina at Chapel Hill

William D. Perreault, Jr.
Kenan-Flagler Business School
University of North Carolina at Chapel Hill

McGraw-Hill
Irwin

Boston   Burr Ridge, IL   Dubuque, IA   Madison, WI   New York   San Francisco   St. Louis
Bangkok   Bogotá   Caracas   Kuala Lumpur   Lisbon   London   Madrid   Mexico City
Milan   Montreal   New Delhi   Santiago   Seoul   Singapore   Sydney   Taipei   Toronto

McGraw-Hill Higher Education

*A Division of The **McGraw-Hill** Companies*

Instructor's Manual to accompany
THE MARKETING GAME!
Charlotte H. Mason and William D. Perreault, Jr.

Published by McGraw-Hill/Irwin, an imprint of the McGraw-Hill Companies, Inc., 1221 Avenue of the Americas, New York, NY 10020. Copyright © 2002, 1995, 1992 by Charlotte H. Mason and William D. Perreault, Jr. All rights reserved.

11 QSR QSR 0

ISBN-13: 978-0-256-13989-1
ISBN-10: 0-256-13989-X

www.mhhe.com

Table of Contents

Contents

PART ONE

Introduction to The Marketing Game!

Part One of this manual provides an introduction to *The Marketing Game!* including a section on changes in the third edition, an overview of the Instructor's Manual, a summary of the special features of the game, and suggestions for using the game in a variety of class situations.

NEW AND IMPROVED: AN UPDATE FOR OLD FRIENDS

CHAPTER 1, HOW TO USE THIS MANUAL

CHAPTER 2, SPECIAL FEATURES OF THE MARKETING GAME!

CHAPTER 3, SUGGESTIONS ON USING THE MARKETING GAME!

The Marketing Game: An Introduction and What's New

This introduction is divided into two parts:
- The first part is a brief introduction to what *The Marketing Game!* is about and why it has been successful for so long. It is primarily for those who are not familiar with earlier editions.
- The **second part is an overview of what's new and improved** in this edition of *The Marketing Game!* It is primarily for old friends who have previously used earlier editions.

This new edition of *The Marketing Game!* reflects the experiences of hundreds of adopters and many thousands of students. In developing the third edition, our strategy was to enhance the student software and the instructor's simulation software to make it faster and easier to setup and use, and to add new options and flexibility, while preserving the very effective essence of the earlier editions. If you're new to *The Marketing Game!*, you have arrived at a time when it has never been easier to use for you or more effective for your students. If you've been using the game for years, you'll find that the changes and enhancements are what you've hoped for—but at the same time you don't have to relearn a new simulation or give up the pedagogical successes you've experienced in the past.

WHAT IS THE MARKETING GAME?

A Brief Overview

The Marketing Game! is a competitive marketing strategy simulation. Students assume responsibility for developing a firm's marketing strategy. A set of reports (in the student text) set the stage with realistic descriptions of the firm's current situation, the nature of the market and competition it faces, and the responsibilities of the marketing manager. The reports are written to the student in his or her role as a manager, not as participant in a computer simulation.

The student (working independently or if the instructor prefers with other students as part of a management team) analyzes the firm's opportunities and makes decisions in a number of strategy decision areas—to develop an *integrated* marketing plan that should satisfy a target market and earn a profit for the firm. The Plan is submitted to the instructor and, along with Plans submitted by competing firms, is processed by *The Marketing Game* (TMG) simulation software. It produces a report for each firm that details the financial and marketing results of the firm's Plan for that period, and provides other information such as the marketing budget for the next period and marketing research reports purchased by the firm. The simulation also produces reports for the instructor that summarize and diagnose the performance of each firm.

Each firm analyzes the report based on its plan and what competitors have done, and then develops a new plan for the next period. The simulation can continue for as many decision periods as the instructor prefers. Firms compete in industries of four firms each, and there can be any number of industries. So, *TMG!* works well in large or small classes and for short or long periods of time.

The Marketing Game! can be run based on "paper" plans and reports, but it is designed to take advantage of communicating via electronic files. Both plan files and report files are password protected and (as is discussed in more detail later) this makes it extremely convenient and time efficient for the instructor (and speeds up feedback to students).

A Flexible Design Allows the Instructor to Select the Level of Difficulty

The Marketing Game! works well in a variety of learning and teaching situations—and with students who have different levels of knowledge and experience—whether the students are just learning about marketing or are seasoned executives.

This flexibility is possible because the game is not based on just one simulation, but several simulations within one integrated framework. It has been specially designed so that the instructor can select the number of decision areas—and, if desired, increase the number of decision areas (and thus the difficulty level) over time.

The instructor also has a variety of optional ways to "set up" or adjust the market environment to meet specific teaching and learning objectives. For example, the instructor can easily alter the economy (say to increase or decrease demand), or in a short term (like a summer school session) the instructor may increase the speed of the product life cycle.

The flexibility of the game is one reason it has become one of the most widely used marketing simulations in the world. Flexibility is a true comparative advantage of the game and why it works well whether it is used with senior executives in management development programs, with undergraduate and graduate students in the first marketing course, or with students in electives such as marketing strategy and product management.

Pedagogy that Reinforces Marketing Learning

- **A Dynamic Market in the Growth Stage Provides Opportunities to Succeed**

The Marketing Game! is designed to ensure that high involvement learning and real pedagogical benefits are realized. It is set in a dynamic market environment. Thus, a poor decision early in the competition does not frustrate the learning process or leave a student/manager with poor results from then on. New decision periods bring opportunity for new successes. And firms with early successes can't coast on their laurels, but must constantly "earn" their customers' business. Thus, there is ample opportunity to learn from both successes and mistakes.

The Marketing Game! reinforces the need to develop a competitive advantage and offer a target market a superior marketing mix. The market situation changes over time as competitors adjust their strategies and customer preferences evolve. The game brings the competitive nature of marketing decision making to life.

- **Good Decisions Produce Good Results**

In addition, this is not a narrowly defined market in which success by one firm dooms others to failure. There are a number of different types of opportunities to pursue. Each firm can develop its own effective and profitable marketing strategy. As in the real world, the marketing manager in the game decides whether to compete head-on with other firms or pursue a target market with less competition. Either way, however, good decisions produce good results. As simple as that sounds, it is perhaps the single greatest strength of this simulation—and where so many other simulations fall short. *There's nothing worse than a simulation that generates high involvement but that reinforces sloppy thinking.*

- **Success by One Firm Does Not Doom Others to Failure**

The Marketing Game! is a competitive simulation, but it is not based on the idea of "zero sum" competition—where one competitor can win only if all of the others lose. While many other simulations rely on the assumptions of zero sum competition, we believe that approach fails to consider the pedagogical reasons for using a simulation in the first place. It simply doesn't make sense to assume that if one student participant does a good job that another must be doing a bad job. In *The Marketing Game!*, good work and smart decisions are reinforced with good outcomes—and that reinforces the learning process for everyone involved.

- **Reinforces Profit Implications of Marketing Plans**

The Marketing Game! encourages students to really think about the profit implications of marketing decisions. A marketing budget for each firm in each period highlights the trade-offs among marketing expenditures that marketing managers must make when developing a marketing strategy. A "smart" marketing strategy must be based on a marketing mix that is consistent with target market needs—but that doesn't mean that it must be a high-cost strategy. The text includes budget planning and marketing strategy forms that help develop skills in analyzing alternative marketing plans. These can be used alone or in combination with the accompanying TMGPlan software, which produces a pro forma based on a firm's Plan and other information provided by the student.

The Marketing Game! gives the instructor the option of allocating a "discretionary budget" to firms in addition to their regular marketing budget for each period. Student managers for a firm can spend the discretionary budget all at once in one decision period, save it for a later period, or dispense it in different periods. This option encourages students to think about the issues of "investing in marketing" and the short and long term trade-offs in spending (for example, spending on promotion for a current product vs. more rapid [but more costly] development of a new product).

- **The Marketing Game! Offers a Realistic Setting**

The game is based on realistic markets and realistic marketing relationships. The "case materials" in the student text are based on developments in the information technology market and provide a logical motivation for the marketing strategy context in which students work.

The text for *The Marketing Game!* is directed to students in their role as marketing manager for a firm—*not* in their role as students. It is written as a set of company reports, memos, policies, and the like. In that way, *every decision is well motivated*. Even the reason for having marketing plan "decision forms" is motivated—as part of the firm's annual planning process. The result is a consistent focus on the market and marketing decisions that need to be made. This also eliminates the artificiality typical of many simulations. The students are not subjected to digressions about this or that contrived rule of a computer program. When that happens in other simulations, students worry more about beating the computer than about developing competitive advantage with an effective marketing strategy.

Part of the genius of the game is that the underlying mathematical model on which the simulation is based is sufficiently sophisticated to reflect the important interrelationships among marketing decision variables. Success comes from integrated, well-thought out strategies ... not on some simplistic trick or "correct answer."

Fast and Easy to Administer, even with Large Classes

The Marketing Game! offers many learning and teaching benefits, and it achieves those benefits without requiring a major time investment by faculty. This edition of the game takes convenience to a whole new level with password-protected files (covered in more detail later). In brief, however, they make it extremely easy to gather inputs from students and to distribute reports.

A major benefit of the simulation is that it produces diagnostic reports that make it easy for an instructor to quickly see what a firm is doing in the market and whether there is some consistency to the logic behind a plan.

The game has continuously improved since the first edition. The simulation produces results that make sense. As a result the instructor is not put in the position of trying to explain to students why some strange outcome has occurred. In addition, the software is designed to prevent clerical input errors by students and to minimize the impact on other firms in an industry if some student hasn't done a sensible job developing a strategy and plan decisions.

The "cover story" in the student text takes into consideration that the instructor may have a variety of individual preferences about how the game will proceed, and how matters such as submission of Plans will be handled. This Instructor's Manual provides simple checklists and summaries of how to organize for the game and suggestions about the benefits and limitations of different approaches.

The Instructor's Manual also provides everything that the instructor might want to use the game, whether it's a computerized set of supplementary objective test questions, a PowerPoint slide show, a website, ideas for projects, or technical explanations of how the simulation model works. The basic philosophy is simple: it's the instructor's course, and the game is designed to make it easy for the instructor to do things his or her own way.

Both the student software and the instructor software for the third edition of *The Marketing Game!* has been completely redesigned to make it even easier and faster to manage the game. The changes in the software, along with other improvements in the new edition, are highlighted in the next section.

WHAT'S NEW IN THE THIRD EDITION OF THE MARKETING GAME?

The third edition of *The Marketing Game!* (TMG) offers major enhancements over past editions. Many improvements are in response to suggestions from the many faculty and students who have played the game in the past, and other changes are innovations that allow faculty and students to take advantage of advances in information technology, including the Internet. In combination, the changes make *The Marketing Game!* the best marketing simulation--and the easiest and fastest to administer--ever developed. Among the major changes are:

- All of the software now features a Windows-based user interface with familiar features such as menu bars and selection buttons, status bar "hints" at the bottom of the screen, printer setup dialogs, and extensive context-sensitive help for improved ease of use.

- An easy-to-use Simulation Command Center provides a greatly streamlined process for verifying the presence of necessary files and running the simulation. In most cases, you will be able to run the simulation *for all industries* at the same time by clicking just two buttons. For example, in tests running the simulation with 56 teams (14 industries), it takes less than one minute to produce all of the reports.

- The new TMGtoXLS program exports data from all firms, periods, and industries to a consolidated database file that is in the standard Microsoft Excel™ file format; this makes it easy for the instructor to use Excel to do supplementary graphs, statistical analyses, and diagnostic summaries after any decision period or at the end of the competition.

- Thirteen multimedia tutorials on the TMG Instructor CD-Rom introduce key features of the software with narrated, full-motion "screen movies" and demonstrate exactly what to do. Eight of these multimedia tutorials focus on the TMGPlan student software, and are also provided on the TMG Student CD-Rom that comes shrink-wrapped with the text.

- TMG now features password protection and advanced encryption of Plan files and (optionally) Report files. This allows secure electronic submission and distribution of TMG files. A major benefit of this new feature is that it relieves the instructor of the logistical issues of collecting individual Plan files or of individually distributing Report files. All students can submit their electronic Plans to a central location and pick up Reports from that location—because they can't see any other student's materials without the password. For example, students can simply download their Reports from a TMG website. The exhibit below expands on these ideas.

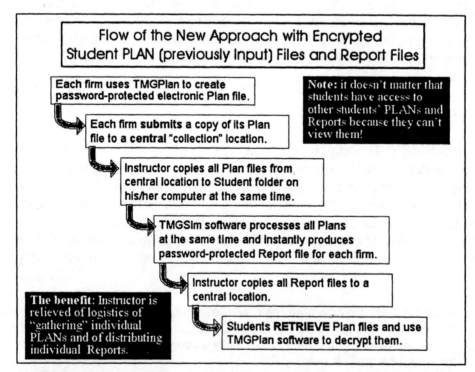

Flow of the New Approach with Encrypted Student PLAN (previously Input) Files and Report Files

Each firm uses TMGPlan to create password-protected electronic Plan file.

Note: it doesn't matter that students have access to other students' PLANs and Reports because they can't view them!

Each firm **submits** a copy of its Plan file to a **central "collection"** location.

Instructor copies all Plan files from central location to Student folder on his/her computer at the same time.

TMGSim software processes all Plans at the same time and instantly produces password-protected Report file for each firm.

Instructor copies all Report files to a central location.

The benefit: Instructor is relieved of logistics of "gathering" individual PLANs and of distributing individual Reports.

Students **RETRIEVE** Plan files and use TMGPlan software to decrypt them.

- A TMG website template is provided to instructors. It can be used as is and along with other features is set up to handle downloading Reports to students.

Alternatively, the Instructor's Manual clearly explains how to adapt the website template to add other features; even a real novice can do it.

- A new program, TMGFTP, makes it easy for students to submit Plan files or retrieve Report files over the Internet ... in just seconds with a few clicks. The program also offers a feature to make it very easy for the instructor to create custom configuration files specific to the situation at a particular school. For example, a custom configuration file can conceal any password needed for a Plan to be uploaded and also where the Plan is saved. The program provides the student with a verification report (that can be printed or saved to a file) that confirms that the Plan has been delivered and is ready for the instructor to run the simulation. This is in addition to other more basic possibilities that arise from having encrypted files. See the exhibit below for other options.

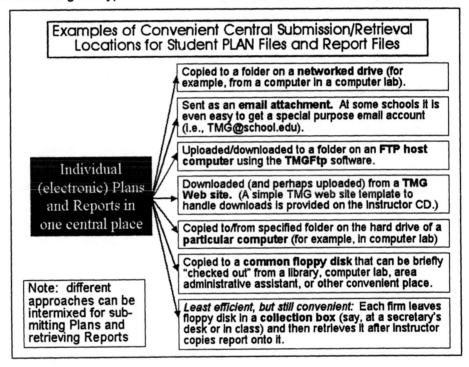

Examples of Convenient Central Submission/Retrieval Locations for Student PLAN Files and Report Files

Individual (electronic) Plans and Reports in one central place

Copied to a folder on a **networked drive** (for example, from a computer in a computer lab).

Sent as an **email attachment.** At some schools it is even easy to get a special purpose email account (i.e., TMG@school.edu).

Uploaded/downloaded to a folder on an **FTP host computer** using the **TMGFtp** software.

Downloaded (and perhaps uploaded) from a **TMG Web site.** (A simple TMG web site template to handle downloads is provided on the Instructor CD.)

Copied to/from specified folder on the hard drive of a **particular computer** (for example, in computer lab)

Copied to a **common floppy disk** that can be briefly "checked out" from a library, computer lab, area administrative assistant, or other convenient place.

Least efficient, but still convenient: Each firm leaves floppy disk in a **collection box** (say, at a secretary's desk or in class) and then retrieves it after Instructor copies report onto it.

Note: different approaches can be intermixed for submitting Plans and retrieving Reports

- A completely updated scenario replaces the former multimedia and P.I.M. products with products that focus on voice recognition and wireless communication technologies that are not yet available on the market. On the other hand, care has been taken to preserve the structure and "motivation" for plan decisions that was provided in the previous edition. This makes it easy for the instructor to simply switch to the new product market names and still rely on knowledge developed in running the simulation in the past.

- Refinements and "tweaks" to the underlying simulation model fine-tune the matching of marketing mixes and target markets. For example, customers are now more price sensitive.

- There is a simple, flexible, and powerful new facility to setup the game at the beginning of the simulation or change it along the way. It makes it fast and easy to create or modify the TMG simulation environment. Instructors who want to run TMG in different classes or sections can easily create and save different setup files, and then load the one that's relevant with the click of a button.

- A comprehensive online Help facility offers quick answers to questions about the software. Context-specific help is available at every point in the process for both students and instructors. The instructor's help file also offers guidance in setting up and administering the game.

- An integrated file viewer makes it very easy to select, view and print Report files from within TMG programs. The instructor's file viewer also automatically transforms encrypted files to standard text format.

- A new PowerPoint electronic slide presentation makes it easy for the instructor to introduce the game in class.

- Sample student Plan files for several industries and at each level of difficulty are provided and make it easy for an instructor to experiment with the simulation before using it in a class the first time.

- An electronic version of the Instructor's Manual makes it easier to answer questions or find information.

- Computer viruses have become a real threat to secure computing, but *The Marketing Game!* Plan files were designed with a file structure that makes it nearly impossible for someone to either accidentally or intentionally attach a virus when submitting a Plan to the instructor.

1. *How to Use This Manual*

FAST START SUMMARY

The first thing that you should know is that **this manual is available in digital form (as a PDF file) on the TMG Instructor CD-Rom**. You can skim through this printed version to get an overview of any topic, but if you need a reference resource on some particular details you can instantly find them with an electronic search of the digital manual. Similarly, the software has extensive help files (including context-specific help features) that make it easy to get whatever information you might need while using the software.

The second thing you should know is that the diagram on the inside cover (and repeated on the next page) provides a "big picture" overview of the general flow of *The Marketing Game!* It also highlights some of the options available to you. Taking a moment to review the diagram will do a lot to orient you. At first it may look like a lot of detail, but what you'll find is that the software speeds you through each step.

In this manual, in the multimedia tutorials (on the CD-Rom), and in the help files that accompany the programs we provide detailed directions, suggestions, and ideas about using *The Marketing Game!* But, some people like to do things first and read the directions later! If you're one of them, the "Fast-Start Directions" on the next few pages are for you. In fact, for most instructors it's not a bad approach with *The Marketing Game!* While there are a variety of options if you want them, the basics are really straightforward. So, you can get things started quickly and then selectively check the manual or help files for more information when and if you need it. However, if you prefer more of a review just skip over this initial section for now (except for the diagram on the next page)--and then skim through the rest of the chapter to see what sections of the manual you'll want to read before getting things started.

- ## Overview of Activities for *The Marketing Game!*

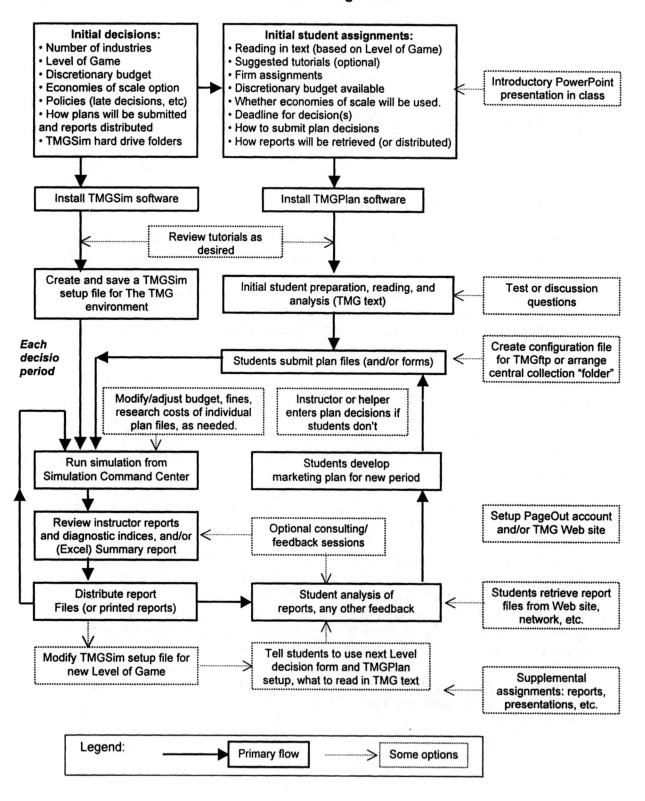

Fast-Start Directions

Remember that this is just a quick overview. In the materials that follow you'll find more guidance on any topic.

1. **Prepare for *The Marketing Game!***
   a. Decide how many "industries" you want to run. Each industry consists of exactly four competing firms. Thus, the total number of firms should be a multiple of four. Industries are referred to by letters—i.e., industry A, industry B, etc. Firms are numbered from 1 to 4 within industries. So, a firm is identified by the combination of the industry letter and firm number (for example, firm A1). One student can be the manager of a firm, or you can assign marketing management teams (e.g., about 4 students per team works well). Assign each student to a firm (firm A1, A2, A3, A4, B1, etc.)
   b. Decide what level of the game to use at the start. Level 1 is usually the best starting level with an introductory course and Level 2 is usually best with an elective or graduate course.

2. **Give students their first assignment.**
   a. Tell students
      i. Their firm assignments,
      ii. The Level of the Game,
      iii. What their discretionary (reserve fund) budget will be; the default setup value is $200,000, but you can increase or decrease it if you wish.
      iv. If you will be using the economies of scale option; the default is to NOT use it.
      v. The deadline for the first decision,
      vi. What to read before making a decision.
         1. For Level 1 (i.e. the least difficult game level), assign chapters 1-4 and 6 in the student manual.
         2. For Level 2, assign chapters 1-3, 5 and 6 in the student manual.
         3. When you are ready for Level 3, assign Chapter 7.
   b. Tell students to install the TMGPlan software, check out the tutorials (if they wish) and create a Marketing Plan Decision file for the appropriate level and turn it in (for example, on a floppy disk labeled clearly with the firm number and industry or as an attachment to an email message; these are good "general purpose" approaches, but other approaches are covered in Chapter 4.)

3. **Create folders on your hard drive for your files.**
   a. Use Windows Explorer to create folders (directories) on your hard drive for
      i. your TMG instructor (master) files,

    ii. student files (if you plan to have students submit their plan [decision] files on individual disks you do not need a separate folder), and

    iii. unencrypted report files (if you plan on using password-protected report files, which is recommended).

    iv. Check the root directory of the Instructor CD-Rom for a README.TXT file for any new information not in this manual.

4. Install the TMG software and run the TMGSim program.

    a. Insert the TMG CD-Rom in the CD-drive; follow instructions that appear. If the install procedure does not start automatically when you insert the CD, on your Windows desktop taskbar click: Start>Run>Browse>d:\setup.exe>Ok, where d: is the letter for the CD-drive in your computer. Review tutorials if you wish.

    b. Start the TMGSim program by clicking Start>Programs>TMG>TMGSim.

    c. Click the Create New Setup button. At the Create New Setup screen enter the number of industries, change Level (if not Level 1), click/change buttons to set paths for folders, and enter a descriptive label. Then click the Fill in the Setup button. Click Save and return to main.

    d. At the main screen, click the Run Simulation button. Select output options (encrypted reports is a good choice), click Select All Industries, and then click Run Simulation.

    e. Check industry reports. Click View reports. Select an instructor report (for example, REPORTa.TXt for industry A). Print copy of instructor reports if desired. See Chapter 7 for information about the diagnostic indices.

5. Distribute reports to students.

    a. If students submitted plan files on disk, and student path was set to floppy drive, reports will be written to floppy; see chapter 4 for other ideas about distributing reports.

6. Additional decision periods.

    a. Repeat steps 4d, 4e and 5 when the next decisions come in.

    b. When (if) you're ready to change the level of the game, tell the students to switch to use the appropriate decision form—and modify the setup for the new level before moving on to 4d, 4e, and 5.

    c. Whenever desired, you can use the View Reports button (on the main screen) to view the SUMMARY report that summarizes the key decisions and results up through the current decision period for an industry. Or, run the TMGtoXLS program (see the help file for details) to export TMG Summary data (a total of 111 variables for each firm and decision period) to a consolidated file (for all industries) in the standard Microsoft Excel™ file format.

INTRODUCTION TO THE CHAPTERS

If you've got the time, you may find it helpful to read through this manual—skimming over those sections that seem to be of little interest for your particular situation. There are many ideas and suggestions and some will be useful to you. Depending on your particular interests, however, it may be useful to read some chapters or sections of chapters sooner and hold off on the others until later. So, in this section, we will briefly describe the purpose and/or contents of each chapter. We'll share some ideas about which chapters are most critical—and when in the course each is most likely to be useful.

Chapter 2: Special Features of The Marketing Game!

This chapter is an overview of the special features and innovations of *The Marketing Game!* Instructors who want to see how the game compares to other simulations—and those who want a summary of the pedagogical issues considered when the game was developed—will find this chapter useful. It can also be helpful background for introducing the game to your class. However, you can use the game without reading this chapter.

Chapter 3: Suggestions on Using The Marketing Game!

This chapter discusses issues related to using the game in different courses. For example, it shares some ideas about what (difficulty) level of the game to use depending on the level of your course, the timing of decisions, whether to use student teams or individual decisions, and the like. The focus of the chapter is on the relationship between decisions about how to use the game and objectives you have for your course. This chapter also provides some suggestions about reading assignments from the text.

This chapter will be especially useful for instructors who have not used a marketing simulation before. Others will probably want to skim over this material and read more carefully those sections that apply to the type of course they are teaching. The sections on the level of the game to use, the timing of decisions, and on the use of the student software should be especially useful to anyone who is using the game for the first time.

Chapter 4: Getting Organized for The Marketing Game!

This chapter, and the one that follows, are the "core" chapters on setting up and running the game. This chapter provides ideas on various approaches for handling inputs (how students submit their marketing plan decisions) and outputs (how students get their reports). It also discusses the options available when you setup the environment of *The Marketing Game!* It will be useful reading for anyone who is using *The Marketing Game!* for the first time.

Chapter 5: Running the Programs

The instructor programs for *The Marketing Game!* are flexible and easy to run—and they all feature extensive online help systems. At any point in the process you can press the F1 key to get context-sensitive help and guidance. Even so, it may be useful to get an overview of the different options that are available and the specifics of what the programs do. That is the focus of this chapter.

Any first time user of the game will want to take a look at the first part of this chapter. It is especially useful because it overviews the flow of running the game. The rest of the chapter provides more detail on specific features. It makes sense to skim this material—so that you have some idea what is covered. But, you don't need to worry about all the detail that is presented. If you need the details, they're handy in the online help system whenever a question comes up.

Chapter 6: The Starting Position

This chapter explains the competitive situation at the start of the game. It is also useful because it explains the contents of the instructor's report. The material on the special instructor reports is especially helpful—as these reports make it easy to tell exactly where a firm stands. Users who are already familiar with *The Marketing Game!* can just skip this section.

Chapter 7: Diagnosing a Firm's Position

The Marketing Game! provides an innovative diagnostic report that makes it easy to tell where each firm is strong and where it is weak relative to other firms in the industry. *This report can also be used to tell whether a firm's strategic decisions fit together as a logical whole.*

It makes sense to spend some time with this short chapter. Once you get familiar with how to "read" the index numbers given in this report, you can usually tell exactly what a firm is doing without wading through all of the details of its decisions and the results. This index system is designed to save time—and it really works well. So a few minutes on the front end will pay off with time saved later.

This chapter also provides some brief information about the TMGtoXLS program, which exports TMG summary data for every period, firm and industry to a consolidated database in standard Microsoft Excel™ spreadsheet file format. If you're an Excel user, this file makes it quick and easy to create Excel graphs, do statistical evaluations, and prepare evaluations after any decision period or at the end of the game. More detail about TMGtoXLS appears in Appendix H.

Chapter 8: Student Software

This chapter focuses on the student software. This software makes it very easy for students to evaluate the likely financial and budget implications of a marketing plan. It enables students to submit the marketing plan decisions form electronically (i.e., as a Plan file) and to work with reports after the simulation has been run (i.e., to print reports, view password-protected reports, or save a password-protected report in standard text format). It simplifies administration of the game to have students prepare their plans in digital formats, especially for large classes. The student software is now easier than ever to use in your courses. The CD-Rom has its own auto install and setup procedure, the software has its own extensive online help; and, for students who want them, there are multimedia (full motion video clips) tutorials.

Chapter 9: PowerPoint Slide Show and Transparency Masters

This chapter focuses on the PowerPoint electronic slide show that is provided (in different formats for different versions of PowerPoint) on the Instructor CD-Rom. There is very little text material, with the exception of a brief explanation of the different files available on the CD-Rom. The PowerPoint slides are in full color, and a PowerPoint viewer is provided for instructors who do not have their own copy of PowerPoint software. However, for instructors who would prefer to use an overhead projector, this chapter includes a complete set of (black and white) transparency masters produced from the PowerPoint slide show.

These slides can be used to supplement any introduction of the game that you want to make in your class. There are many slides so you can select the ones that best fit your needs.

Another use of the slides is as a "tie-in" in lecture portions of a class. The game can be used to illustrate various points and concepts being discussed.

Chapter 10: Ideas for Supplemental Assignments

This chapter provides some ideas for supplemental assignments that can be used with the game. If you are not interested in using supplemental assignments you can skip this chapter altogether.

Chapter 11: Test and Discussion Questions

This chapter provides both objective questions and discussion questions (as well as answers) that can be used to test student understanding of the details of the game. All of the questions are available in electronic form (with their own test generator software) on the Instructor CD-Rom, so this chapter also provides some brief information about installing and using the Diploma test generation software.

In addition to both true-false and multiple-choice questions, we have included a number of essay or discussion questions that can be used for exams, or for class discussion. Some instructors like to include a few such questions on tests—to make certain that everyone is paying attention to the game. Others may want to hand out questions to students for use in a self-test exercise. Obviously, however, you do not need to look at these questions to get started with the game.

Chapter 12: Concluding the Game and Grading

This chapter provides some ideas about ways to conclude the game as well as suggestions for evaluating student performance. It is not necessary to go through this is advance. But, that might be helpful—especially if you are trying to decide what to put in your syllabus for the end of the game.

Chapter 13: Overview of the Effects of Decision Variables

This chapter provides a concise, non-technical overview of some of the most important relationships in the simulation model. It is useful to read this chapter before handing results back to the students. It's not absolutely necessary, but it can help you in giving advice and in answering student questions.

Chapter 14: The Model Structure

This chapter is similar in purpose to the previous chapter, but it is much more detailed. It provides a more in depth discussion of the structure and logic of the underlying simulation model. While we have tried to make this presentation clear and have avoided a complex mathematical presentation, the model itself is quite sophisticated and, as a result, some of the sections in this chapter are more technical in nature. However, it is not necessary to read this chapter at all—and, if you do read it, you can skip over some of the technical details that are not of interest to you.

In other words, this chapter is provided for instructors who want to know more about the inner workings of the competitive simulation. While this information can be useful, it is certainly not necessary unless you are so inclined.

Appendix A: Resources on the Instructor CD-Rom

The Instructor CD-Rom provides a number of digital resources in addition to the instructor software. This appendix briefly overviews the materials available on the CD-Rom and tells you where on the CD-Rom to find more complete information.

Appendix B: Website Resources for The Marketing Game!

If you would like to have a separate website for *The Marketing Game!,* or if you would like to easily add TMG materials to a course website, we provide a number of useful resources. These range from ready-to-use website pages that can simply be copied to a folder on your school's web server to information about how easy it is to have your own website on McGraw-Hill's PageOut web server.

Appendix C: Commonly Asked Questions and Answers

This appendix lists a number of the most commonly asked questions and their answers. Most of the items in this appendix are also dealt with elsewhere in this manual or in the student text—but it is useful to have them collected in one place. Many of the questions are phrased from the perspective of a student and reflect the concerns and issues that students have. Most of those questions (and the responses) are also provided on the TMG website (and on the website template), both of which are on the Instructor CD-Rom.

Appendix D: Blank Forms

This appendix contains copies of each of the blank forms that are included in the Student Manual, and in addition provides a copy of a sample form for instructors who use teams and want to get peer evaluations.

Appendix E: Sample Memos

This appendix contains copies of sample memos that can be used to inform students about two issues on which the Student Manual is intentionally vague (because they involve setup option choices for the instructor). The memos explain the discretionary budget (and level) and the economies of scale option.

Appendix E: Feedback from Users

We have worked hard to make *The Marketing Game!* an interesting and challenging learning experience for your students, and a game that is simple and free of hassles for you to administer. However, we, like you, are marketers—and we are interested in your comments and suggestions on *The Marketing Game!*

Appendix G. Installing the Software from a Floppy Drive

If the computer you want to use to run *The Marketing Game!* does not have a CD-drive, you can use a floppy disk drive to install the programs (except for TMGTutor, because its video files are too large to fit on floppies).

Creating installation disks is simple—and you do it with **a few clicks in the TMGDisks program, which is in the root directory of the Instructor CD-Rom.** All you need is a few floppy disks (2 to 4, depending on which programs you want to install) and temporary access to a computer that does have a CD-drive. Just run the TMGDisks program and have it copy some files from the CD-Rom to the floppies. As with the other TMG programs, **there is online help** with the TMGDisks program. And there's nothing to it.

Appendix H. TMGtoXLS and Exporting TMG Data to an Excel Spreadsheet file

The TMGtoXLS program is a simple utility that extracts information from the summary files (for all TMG industries, firms and decision periods) and exports it to a single file formatted so that it can be directly read by the Microsoft Excel™ spreadsheet program (Vers. 5 or later). This appendix provides more detail on TMGtoXLS, including an annotated list of all of the variables in the file. The same information is available in the help file for TMGtoXLS.

CONCLUSION

The Marketing Game! is flexible and offers many options—so that the game will fit the teaching/learning objectives you set for your class. We have tried to develop this Instructor's Manual in that same spirit. It is very complete on those aspects that will be of interest to every instructor, and other information is organized so that it is available and clear when and if you want it.

2. *Special Features of The Marketing Game!*

INTRODUCTION

In general, one of the main advantages of *competitive* market simulations is that they provide a high involvement learning experience for students. Yet, different simulations vary significantly. And the features of a particular simulation may be a limitation or a strength depending on the instructor's specific preferences and objectives.

Unfortunately, with many simulations it is difficult to sort out the advantages or disadvantages that might be most critical until after the simulation has actually been used in a class. For example, a critical limitation of the logic underlying the simulation model may be hidden from view—and only become apparent after several decision periods. Or, hassles in administering the simulation may surface only after it is too late to do anything about the problem.

In developing *The Marketing Game!* over a fifteen year period, we have worked to overcome the limitations of other simulations—and at the same time provide you with flexible options. The chapters in this Instructor's Manual provide substantial detail about the various options that are available—and ideas about when the different features are likely to be most useful.

In this chapter we overview the key features of *The Marketing Game!*—and ways in which it differs from other games. It also highlights some of the choices that are available to you.

A COMPETITIVE SIMULATION RATHER THAN A STUDENT-AGAINST-COMPUTER SIMULATION

The Marketing Game! is a *competitive* simulation. A student, or team of students, manages a firm's marketing program and competes against other firms.

This is distinct from simulations in which a student makes decisions and competes against a computer "model."

We have been asked why we don't create a version of *The Marketing Game!* that involves student-against-computer interactions, so it makes sense to address this directly. The issue here is straightforward. In most real life marketing situations there is not a single "correct" marketing strategy that is always best. To the contrary, a large part of the job is for the marketer to figure out which opportunities "fit" the company's resources and objectives, and that depends not only on the firm's own strengths and limitations and customer needs but also on what competitors are doing or will do in the future in the market. If two or more firms copy each other and do the same thing, they just move toward perfect competition and there is no real competitive advantage or superior customer value. So, if one wants to really reinforce the idea that a key responsibility of marketing is to figure out what customers to target and how to differentiate the firm's offering to both provide superior customer value and also to earn profits, you need to do it in a competitive situation.

It is possible in a student vs. computer situation to have the computer create a set of competitors, but if one is developing such a computer program there must be a design decision (from the very outset): will the computer-created "competitor(s)" always be the same (and basically pursue the same sort of strategy), or will the algorithm create "smart" competitors that change and take into consideration how they should respond given the student's decisions? In either event, the computer program must establish some sort of "correct answer." Usually, the definition of what is correct—and what actions by a student evoke what responses—is quite narrow in focus. So, from a pedagogical standpoint, we believe that a student vs. machine simulation makes the most sense when the objective of the exercise is for the student to learn about a specific aspect of marketing (that is, learning about a particular marketing tool or framework) rather than an objective that focuses on the integration of marketing ideas. To really reinforce issues concerning the competitive nature of marketing strategy there must be competition.

By contrast, one can create a truly competitive simulation without specifying a single correct answer. This doesn't mean that the simulation ignores what makes sense and what doesn't. Rather, it means that the "model" is of the overall market environment—and that the environment is developed to reflect what we know about actual markets. In this case, there is not a "model" of how a competitor should or will act under certain circumstances. Rather, each competitor faces the same challenge of understanding the market, finding opportunities, and establishing a differential competitive advantage.

DIAGNOSTIC REPORTS FOR THE INSTRUCTOR

Many simulations leave the instructor to wade through an impossible mass of printouts to try to figure out what students have done right or wrong. *The Marketing Game!* eliminates all of that. Each period you get a concise diagnostic report. The report shows a set of indices for each firm in the industry as well as the industry overall. These indices allow you to compare firms in different strategic decision areas—and to evaluate how well the various elements of a firm's overall plan fit with each other. By spending a few minutes with this report, you can see where a firm is strong, and where it is weak. This is especially helpful when students come by seeking advice (or therapy!). You don't need advance preparation time to be able to deal with the students effectively and quickly. A quick glance at the report helps you pinpoint what the firm has done— and helps you determine if students understand areas where they are strong or weak.

In addition, at any point in the game you can get a summary report that overviews the marketing plan decisions and performance of different firms – and the industry overall – over time. A single page summarizes up to ten periods for a firm. If you're the sort of person who wants to delve into more depth—for example to do more detailed comparisons among firms or industries, the TMGtoXLS program makes it a snap to export all of the data in the Summary file to standard spreadsheet file format.

These reports and resources—separately and in combination—save you time and also make it possible to do a better job of evaluating student performance and, as needed, providing them with feedback.

In addition, this manual provides clear explanations of the simulation model and how it works. You can see for yourself how decisions interact and how competition comes into play. And, if you wish, you can read about the technical details of the model. You are not left to try to second-guess a "black box." Even if you personally don't want to read the details of how the simulation model works, there is probably some comfort in knowing that hundreds of other faculty have done that over the years and come away with the judgment that the model is not only rich in its logic but also reinforces the learning and concepts that students (and marketing managers) really need to understand.

YOU SELECT THE LEVEL OF DIFFICULTY

The Marketing Game! is not just one simulation, but several simulations within one integrated framework. It has been specially designed so that you can easily select the number of decision areas—and increase the number of decision areas at any point as the game progresses. This is an important feature and puts you in control. The game is flexible so that you can use it to achieve the objectives you set for your class. In fact, it is because of this flexibility that you can use the game effectively for courses at different levels—and start, make changes, or stop at different points in the course.

You decide what level of the game makes the most sense for your students. For example, in the first marketing course you might start students with 13 basic decision areas. Then, as they learn more about marketing strategy planning, you can increase the number of decision areas. Or, in an advanced elective course (for example, marketing strategy, marketing problems, product management) you might start the game at a more advanced level—with students making decisions in more than 28 areas and coordinating a marketing program that involves different products, marketing mixes, and target markets.

The advanced levels of the game add more detailed decisions in the different strategic areas of marketing planning. But at every level students are challenged to develop consistent, market-oriented strategies.

In addition, at any level of difficulty, *The Marketing Game!* setup procedure makes it easy for the instructor to select among several important options to modify the simulation environment. For example, by changing the default economic index the instructor can introduce economic cycles, or by introducing economies of scale in production the instructor can make the profitability trade-offs between different market segments more challenging.

REALISTIC EXPOSURE TO MARKETING STRATEGY PLANNING

The Marketing Game! is based on real products and a realistic marketing environment. The realism is consistent—throughout the student text and in the computer model itself.

The text for *The Marketing Game!* is directed to students in their role as marketing manager for a firm—not in their role as students. It is written as a set of company reports, memos, policies, and the like. In that way, every decision is well motivated. Even the reasons for having marketing plan "decision forms," passwords, and electronic Plan files are motivated—as part of the firm's annual planning process.

The result is a consistent focus on the market and marketing decisions that need to be made. This also eliminates the artificiality typical of many simulations. The students are not subjected to digressions about this or that contrived rule of a computer program. When that happens in other simulations, students worry more about beating the computer than about developing competitive advantage with an effective marketing strategy.

The simulation model itself is also realistic. It is sufficiently complete that it avoids unrealistic assumptions. As a result, there is not a trick answer that drives the outcome of the market competition. A student (or student team) can develop any of a number of possible strategies, and any of them can work well—as long as the strategy makes sense as a whole (i.e., the marketing mix fits the target market and considers the strengths and weaknesses of competing firms). Thus, with *The Marketing Game!*, instructors are not left in the uncomfortable position of trying to explain to a student why a set of decisions that would appear logical in "the real world" don't work in the simulation. Good decisions produce good results—and poor decisions do not.

PEDAGOGICAL CONSIDERATIONS

Focuses on Target Marketing

The Marketing Game! is designed to encourage creative target marketing. There are many different possible market opportunities. The market includes both business segments and final consumers. The different segments respond in different ways to different product features, prices, and promotion. And there are different channels of distribution—with different types of dealers—to reach the target markets.

Success by One Firm Does Not Doom Others to Failure

The market environment has been carefully designed to provide a variety of different market opportunities. Competition may limit the potential of some opportunities, but a student isn't implicitly forced to go head-on against other competitors for the same market opportunity. This is extremely important in motivating and reinforcing learning, effort, and involvement. Because it is not a "zero sum" game, success by one firm does not doom others to failure.

The Market Environment Is Dynamic

Ongoing effort and learning is also encouraged because *The Marketing Game!* is set in a dynamic market environment. It starts in the growth stage of the product life cycle, and the market evolves and changes over time. This means that the design of the simulation takes into consideration the learning that occurs—as students develop a better understanding of their marketing management responsibilities and opportunities. In the early stages, there is more market growth, and more opportunity for a "success" experience—even if some aspect of marketing strategy needs refining. But, over time the competition gets tougher.

There is some realistic carryover from one period to the next, but the dynamic market environment means that each new decision period offers new opportunities. This encourages consistent effort over time. One firm can't get off to a lucky start and then "cruise" for the rest of the course—with other firms frustrated that there is no way to catch up. From beginning to end, students are reinforced for learning from the good (or not-so-good) effects of their previous decisions.

Students Must Work with a Budget

In the game, as in the real world, student-managers develop plans within a marketing budget. They must make trade-offs among the costs and benefits of serving different target markets. This is a contrast to the "more is better" philosophy of many simulations in which the firm that spends the most money the fastest ends up dominating everyone else. Such an approach ignores the importance of having a well-integrated strategy and discounts the profit consequences of ineffective overspending.

Focus Is on the Effect of Marketing Decisions, Not Random Events

Many simulations dilute the marketing learning that can take place by incorporating an excessive overlay of complex inventory rules, depreciation on production equipment, or other factors that are beyond the control of marketing managers. When factors such as these introduce intricate accounting rules and indirect effects that drive the results of a simulation, students are not able to see the relationship between their marketing decisions and the results they produce. *The Marketing Game!* was designed to avoid this pitfall. Students must operate within a budget, consider the costs of their decisions, develop products that are within feasible production limits, and the like. But the focus is on marketing and on the effect of well thought-out marketing plans on the success of a firm.

YOU DON'T NEED TO BE A COMPUTER EXPERT

It has been a priority to make the computer aspects of using *The Marketing Game!* "instructor friendly," convenient, and easy. The software for the game was specifically designed for PCs (rather than converted from a main-frame environment). It is designed to prevent errors and hassles. If an instructor (or student) makes a mistake, the software explains the problem and suggests what to do to correct it.

Getting started is also simple. The CD-Rom handles the installation of the software. The new setup procedure for the simulation takes just a minute or two … and the tutorials provide complete step-by-step illustrations. In most cases, you simply specify the number of industries and click to select a few other options–and you are ready to go. The tutorials provide step-by-steps demos, if you want them.

The routine computer work for each decision period is extremely simple and fast. Even with a very large number of firms, when students submit their Plan files it takes only a few minutes to run the simulation and produce reports. Further, the student software checks inputs *as they are entered* to help identify and eliminate input errors, so you don't run into problems because some student submitted "bad decisions."

STUDENT SOFTWARE HELPS STUDENTS AND THE INSTRUCTOR

The Marketing Game! Student Manual includes a CD-Rom with student software, including help files and multimedia tutorials. The student software makes it easy for students to submit their marketing plan decisions in electronic form—whether it is on a disk, as an attachment to an email message, or uploaded to a folder on a network computer. In addition, this software creates a pro-forma financial summary based on the firm's decisions. Using this feature, students can easily evaluate alternative sets of decisions.

The student software relies of familiar Windows features—like status bar hints, online context-sensitive help, menu bars, and buttons. It is very easy to use. Printed instructions appear as an appendix in the Student Manual. But the program is completely self-explanatory. Like the Instructor software, the student software features automatic checking of input decisions for errors such as infeasible product features, negative prices, or sales commissions beyond the permissible range.

The pro forma analysis can speed calculations and give students experience with the type of spreadsheet analyses done by practicing marketing managers. But similar analyses can also be encouraged without the software—because the Student Manual includes budget planning forms and exercises that help students see how to analyze the financial implications of their decisions.

Depending on your preferences, students can submit their marketing plan decisions as a computer file or on printed forms. If they submit their decisions electronically, the instructor software easily and quickly "gathers" the information all at once (for as many industries as you have) for analysis by the simulation. Or, if you wish, the same program can be used to quickly enter decisions from printed forms, or to review or modify decisions on the screen. Either way, the software is easy to use. In fact, if for some reason you prefer not to have students submit plan files in electronic format, a secretary, teaching assistant, or other helper can easily enter the decisions (and also run the simulation).

FEEDBACK TO STUDENTS

The Marketing Game! provides reports for each firm after each decision is submitted and analyzed. These routine reports—and optional marketing research reports that the students can purchase—provide a wealth of relevant information for marketing planning and control.

The game simulation software (TMGSim) produces the reports very quickly. In fact, when you put student decision files in a folder on your hard drive the decisions for 15 four-firm industries can be processed—and reports created— in about a minute. As a convenience to the instructor, the reports can be saved in a password-protected (encrypted) format. That way, the instructor doesn't have to worry about printing reports or distributing disks. Rather, all of the reports can be left at some convenient central location (on a computer in a lab, for download from a website or folder on a network server, on a disk that is checked out from a library desk, etc.) because a student can only view a report if he/she knows the password for the plan from which the report was created. If you wish, students can use the TMGftp software to download their reports from a network computer, or you can use the provided website that includes a preconfigured report download page. Then the students use their TMGPlan software to view and print the reports.

Alternatively, if you want to print reports yourself, they are preformatted and ready to view and print with the TMGSim file viewer (which prints to your default printer or allows you to select any other printer set up on your computer or school's computer network. If you wish to provide supplementary analysis of your own, it's easy because the TMGtoXLS program outputs key TMG summary data to a database file in standard Microsoft Excel™ spreadsheet format.

INSTRUCTOR SUPPORT

Our objective is for *The Marketing Game!* to be the flexible basis for a successful teaching and learning experience. We have worked to provide the instructor with time saving conveniences—so that teaching time can be devoted to improving the quality of what students learn, not to resolving computer or administrative problems. This manual provides support in many forms: overhead transparency masters for class presentations, suggestions for related assignments and projects, questions to test student knowledge of the game environment, suggestions on ways to organize to use the game, and ideas on how to make the most effective use of the game in different types of classes.

These components—combined with other innovative features such as the diagnostic reports and easy to use computer programs—are provided to give you choices. Our hope is that you will find it easy to use these materials to achieve the objectives you have set for your students and your course.

3. Suggestions on Using The Marketing Game!

INTRODUCTION

Because of its innovative design, *The Marketing Game!* can be used effectively in different courses—and to meet different types of teaching objectives. The game is flexible, so you can use it to suit your purposes.

In this chapter we offer suggestions for using the game in different courses. We organize most of the discussion by "type" of course. But, we also recognize that two courses that have the same title may be very different—depending on such factors as the instructor's approach, the number of students in the course, other opportunities for "hands on" marketing planning in the curriculum, students' level of preparation and experience, the length of the term, and the amount of time the instructor has to devote to the course.

In light of the varied factors involved, we offer a few general comments before getting into ideas related to specific courses. These general considerations should be relevant regardless of the specific course or course objectives.

Level of the Game

In *The Marketing Game!* you select the number of strategic areas in which students make decisions. You can start at level 1—with the fewest decision areas—or at level 2 or level 3 with more decisions. If you start at level 1 or 2, you can move up a level as the game progresses and as students show ability and skill in planning and refining their strategies. A larger number of decision areas makes the game more complex and challenging.

Even at level 1—with the fewest decision areas—there is a significant challenge because the student must consider all the basic elements of marketing strategy planning. The student must analyze the broad product-market and select one or more segments as a target market. The effect of competitors' current or likely strategies should be considered, too. Decisions in each area of the marketing mix must be made. The costs of the marketing mix decisions must be analyzed—to stay within a budget. And, particularly important, the decisions must be blended so that they make sense as a whole. For example, a firm might have done a good job selecting features for a product that meet the needs of a particular market segment, but the positive effect of having the right product will be diminished if the firm does not have enough sales representatives calling on dealers in the channel where those target customers prefer to shop. And a too low price might mean that unit sales are high but that the firm produces little profit or even a loss.

At more advanced levels there are more strategy decisions. For example, at level 1 the firm must decide how many sales reps it needs, and how many to assign to each distribution channel. At level 2, the firm also must decide what commission percent to pay those sales reps—and how much of their time is to be spent on supporting activities. The added number of decision areas makes it all the more important for firms to have a well thought out, integrated, overall strategy. At level 3, with two products, all of the elements of the overall marketing program must work together well if a strong competitive position is to be established.

Reading Assignments in the Student Text

What material you assign for students to read in *The Marketing Game!* text will depend on the level(s) of the game that you use. A summary of text reading assignment by level in the game is provided in the table below.

• Summary of Reading Assignments by Marketing Game Levels		
How You Want to Handle Level(s)	Text Reading Assignment	Optional:
Start at Level 1	Chapters 1-4 and 6	Appendix A
...then move to Level 2	... add Chapter 5	
...then move to Level 3	... add Chapter 7	
Start at Level 2	Chapters 1-3 and 5-6 (i.e., skip Chapter 4)	Appendix A
...then move to Level 3	... add Chapter 7	
Start at Level 3	Chapters 1-3, 5-7 (i.e., skip Chapter 4)	Appendix A

To get started (regardless of level) you will want your students to read Chapters 1 through 3. These chapters overview the market situation and the basic decisions that need to be made at any level of the game.

If you start the game at level 1, you should also assign Chapter 4. It explains the marketing plan decision form for level 1.

Alternatively, **if you are starting the game at level 2 or level 3, your students can skip Chapter 4 and read Chapter 5 instead.** It expands on the material in Chapter 3 somewhat—explaining some new areas of responsibility for the marketing department—and then explains the marketing plan decision form for level 2 (also relevant to level 3).

If you are starting the game **at level 3**—so that students can introduce a new product whenever they are ready—**you should also assign Chapter 7**—which overviews the new market opportunity related to the second product. There is not a separate chapter to explain the marketing plan decision form for level 3. But, it really doesn't need further explanation because it is like the decision form for level 2, except that it includes decisions for two products.

If you start at level 1 and then move to level 2, you should assign Chapter 5 when you move to level 2. Similarly, if and when you want the students to move to the level 3 decision form you can assign Chapter 7.

If you want students to prepare a budget for a proposed marketing plan, have them read Chapter 6. This chapter is only a few pages, but it helps them see how the financial summary comes together. This chapter also explains the budget planning form. This may be especially useful for students in the first marketing course or, more generally, for students who have not had much experience in working with marketing cost and revenue data.

If you want your students to use the student software, you will probably assign Appendix A. It gives directions on using the student software to enter their decisions and to see pro forma financial summaries

The text is written to be involving. While there is quite a bit of detail, the detail is not overwhelming. Rather, it is like the detail that one sees in a long case study. It is motivated by the circumstances—not simply detail for its own sake. As a result, students can read the material in the text quickly. You probably won't need to suggest that they go back over the chapters again once the game has started. They will quickly do that on their own—looking for additional insights about the market.

Additional Student Handouts in the Instructor's Manual

The third edition of *The Marketing Game!* offers a variety of advanced setup options that you may choose to use or not. Two of these concern the discretionary budget and economies of scale in production.

The Student Manual alludes to the fact that the president of the firm is considering giving the marketing department a discretionary budget (i.e., a discretionary cash reserve fund that the student may spend at any time during the game) in addition to the period-by-period budget. The manual also reviews the possibility that the firm will invest in new equipment that may make economies of scale in production possible (which has the effect of reducing unit costs with increases in cumulative production).

However, these issues are not explained in detail and students are told that the president will let them know if the president decides to move ahead with either decision. Therefore, we have included two handouts in the Instructor's Manual (and the electronic versions of the handouts are on the Instructor CD in the folder named \Memos).

If you choose to use either of these options, you can print copies of the appropriate handout(s) to distribute to your students, or if you wish the website is preconfigured to download a memo on these issues. These handouts are found in an Appendix, and in Chapter 4 there are full descriptions of these setup options. As discussed in more detail in Chapter 14, the scale savings ultimately taper off.

Individual or Team Decisions

You may want to have decisions submitted by individuals, or alternatively, by teams. This decision affects the instructor workload, the student workload, and the dynamics of the game.

In general, student teams offer many advantages. From a practical perspective, it reduces administrative time when you use teams of three to five students. But there are also pedagogical benefits to students. The interactions that take place in student teams can significantly enhance the learning experience. The students help each other see alternative points of view—and in effect take responsibility for teaching each other. The chance to develop skill in communicating business ideas to others on the team can be important later in the students' careers. In addition, having several people involved can result in better decisions. Finally, the group approach encourages development of the interpersonal skills that are relevant in working with teams in the business world.

Of course, there is another side to this. A team effort involves shared responsibility and shared effort. The game is more demanding if each individual student has the responsibility to make decisions alone. Some students—especially those at advanced stages—value the opportunity to see the results of their individual creativity and work. They like the idea of rising or falling based on independent judgment.

You may decide—for any course—to go either way. But keep in mind that there really is quite a bit of work—especially at the higher levels—if one person is doing everything alone. This approach is likely to work best if the student has sufficient elapsed time between decisions to do a careful and complete analysis—and if the game is a key part of the course so that the time the student can allocate to the game is substantial.

Timing of Decisions

Timing issues focus on (1) when the game is started in the course, (2) how frequently decisions are submitted, and (3) how long the game runs. The game is really very flexible with regard to each of these areas, but there are a few general guidelines that can be helpful in course planning.

- **Number of Decision Periods**

The game should span enough decision periods that a student (or student team) has the opportunity to obtain feedback and refine or modify a marketing plan. Most instructors run between 6 and 12 decision periods, but this is very flexible and a matter of personal preference as well as teaching/learning objectives, so it warrants some discussion.

It will usually take students a few decision periods to get a clear idea of where they are trying to go, and it may take a firm several periods to fully implement a planned strategy. Of course, you can expect a "faster start" once decisions actually begin if there is more up-front time allocated prior to decisions for teams to plan strategies, analyze markets, evaluate possible alternative strategies—and carefully think through the marketing concepts.

In a technical sense, there is no "minimum" number of decision periods that is required. However, four decision periods is probably the practical minimum. Six decision periods is much better and will give students a good chance to develop their ideas and begin to refine their plans. Additional decision periods offer the opportunity for more learning and a greater sensitivity to the challenges of competitor analysis. If the level of difficulty is increased during the game, there should be enough decision periods remaining that students can make decisions in the new areas in a long-run strategy planning framework. This is especially critical when moving up to level 3. Since level 3 allows the introduction of a new product, at the very least three decision periods should be remaining.

There is no need to limit the game to a particular number of decisions. Although 6-12 decisions periods is common, you can run the game for twenty or more decision periods—depending on your objectives. One issue to consider is the type of market environment in which you want students to compete.

The game starts with the first product at the early stages of the product life cycle. Although different segments are growing at different rates, there is more growth in the earlier periods of the game, and after 10 periods the growth due to increases in the size of the segments stops. Demand (and sales) in specific segments may continue to grow beyond that time if firms offer marketing mixes that are particularly effective in meeting customer needs—but the basic growth trend in the market subsides. This means that after the 10th decision period the market for the *first* product tends to be in the mature stage of the product life cycle. Further, once the first firm in an industry introduces a second product, that product will face a growth market for about 10 periods. You may want to consider this in planning your course. The total number of decision periods—and when firms are first allowed to introduce a second product (level 3)—will determine whether or not firms are competing in growth markets with both products, in a growth market with one product and a mature product with another, or in a mature market stage with both products.

- **Interval between Decisions**

The interval to use between decisions is largely a matter of instructor preference—and will depend in part on when the game is introduced in a course. Longer elapsed time between decisions gives the possibility for more thorough analysis—but more closely spaced decisions can make the whole process—and competitive environment—more intense. This approach really highlights that successful marketing strategies are dynamic.

Of course, the time interval between decisions need not be fixed or consistent. One useful idea is to start with less frequent decisions—and then progressively space them more closely together toward the end. This works well in an introductory course. Students get involved in market analysis and planning early—but more of the decision-making responsibility falls after they have developed a stronger understanding of the course concepts.

In-Class Time

The game can be used as the focus of substantial in-class discussion, or alternatively be treated strictly as an out-of-class assignment.

For example, when used with the introductory course, it may make sense to allocate some portion of a class period to introducing the game, giving instructions, and the like. But, after that, the game can be treated largely as an out-of-class assignment. It will only be necessary to occasionally provide additional instructions, discuss what is happening, and the like. On the other hand, some instructors like to allocate some in-class time for the game, especially when students are working in teams.

At another extreme, the game may be the central focus of the course—but involve relatively few class meetings. For example, the course might meet for some period of time to get the competition underway, but then the students might not meet together as a class for quite some time. Rather, the instructor might set times to meet with individual firms (or set times to be available if students want a meeting) and then only get together as a whole class for special sessions—say a set of "wrap up" presentations in which each firm presents its strategy and the logic for what it was doing.

Of course, there are some effective uses of in-class time related to the game. The game can be used as a context or living case around which the instructor can develop lectures or class discussions of general concepts (product life cycle issues, positioning, segmenting, etc.). Further, in some cases the instructor may want to address particular areas that seem to be related to performance in the game. For example, if it appears that each firm is doing basically the same thing—and thus competing head-to-head—the instructor might want to use this situation to highlight the various ways a firm can seek a competitive advantage. Finally, students appreciate some in-class time for short team meetings—even if it is just enough time for them to work out a schedule for their next out-of-class meeting. This can be especially helpful early in the game when everyone is getting organized.

Using Related Assignments

The game lends itself to related assignments: one or more reports focusing on analysis of the opportunities and challenges of targeting different segments, written elaborations of the logic for the current or longer-run marketing plan, justifications of the series of past decisions, a written competitor analysis that dissects the likely rationale for another firm's actions or predicts what the competitor will do next, oral presentations to a "board of directors," written statements of objectives, and the like. Additional ideas for related projects are given in Chapter 10.

While additional assignments can be useful, they are not necessary. Making decisions, analyzing the results, and being involved in the dynamics of the market competition is itself a significant learning experience.

A decision to use supplementary assignments with the game is typically going to be made based on a time trade-off. If the game is the central point of a course, there is usually time to add supplementary exercises or assignments that help to broaden the learning experience—for example, by adding a dimension that focuses on written or oral communication. On the other hand, if the game is one part of a broader course focus, there often is not time for extended supplementary assignments.

When the game is being used in a course that involves significant time commitments by students to other new learning, we recommend limiting the number of supplementary game-related assignments. That way, students can focus on doing sound analysis and making good decisions. Keep in mind that carefully developed decisions may involve much work and analysis—especially as the game moves along and students develop a deeper understanding of the concepts involved. It may be best—at least until you have used the game a few times—to resist the temptation to load on too many assignments. Our experience has been that the effort students put into the game—as with other simulations—has a way of expanding to consume all available time.

Using the Student Software

The Marketing Game! student text comes with a CD-Rom. We recommend that students use the software to prepare a Plan file for their decisions for each period. This not only eliminates the need for the instructor to take the time to type in decisions, it also eliminates the possibility of mistyped inputs by the instructor. However, even if you don't use the disk input option, students can use the pro forma option in the student software to help evaluate alternative marketing plans. For example, no "engaged" student should turn in a plan that costs more than is available in the marketing budget for that period—because the software computes spending against the budget for the student. The student software is described in more detail in Chapter 8 of this manual (which is in large part redundant with Appendix A in the Student Manual).

THE FIRST MARKETING COURSE

Although this course varies widely, this is usually where students get their first in-depth exposure to marketing concepts, learn how to evaluate market opportunities, and learn how to design a marketing strategy to seek a competitive advantage. Whether the students are undergraduates or MBAs, there is a lot to learn.

As a result, in the first course *The Marketing Game!* is typically used to supplement/complement other major course components—like text readings, lectures, problems, and cases. Because of this, an instructor may not want to devote a major portion of class time to the game—especially if the course is offered at a school that has a short term.

The game does not demand significant in-class time. The instructor can get things moving, and then use short segments of class as needed to give instructions, distribute performance results, or provide general feedback. Here, a common approach is to get the game started (perhaps with an introductory lecture based on the PowerPoint slide show), and then have students make their decisions as part of their out-of-class assignments.

In the first marketing course, it will usually be best to emphasize level 1 or 2 of the game. If your students seem to be making good decisions and developing good strategies, then you may want to move to the next level. If you move to level 3, you should allow at least three decision periods at that level.

An important decision is when to start the game. There are two basic approaches. One is to start the game relatively early in the course, and have it continue until the end with time (for example, a week or so) between each decision. Another alternative is to start the game in the later half of the course—after students have had more exposure to the marketing mix topics in class. In that case, decisions will probably be submitted more closely together—perhaps even every class period. There are different advantages to each approach.

Introducing the Game Early in the Course

By introducing the game early it can serve as a "living laboratory" throughout the course. The competitive environment of the game stimulates students. It gets them involved in the material. They are motivated to learn and understand new concepts as they are introduced. After all, new concepts and ideas have immediate applicability—in the next decision period. In addition, if students are involved in the game from early in the course the instructor can use various situations in the game as examples of the concepts being discussed.

Administratively, there are some advantages to starting the game early and having the game decision periods more spread out. First, students usually have a less hectic schedule early in the term—and that means that they can devote more time to getting off to a good start with the game. At the end of the term, some of those good intentions dissolve under the pressure of assignments from a number of classes. In addition, a longer period between decisions reduces the demands on the instructor to immediately run decisions and quickly get feedback to the students. In contrast, if the decisions are "batched"—say at the end of the course—there may not be much slack time between when decisions are submitted and when you will want to give students their feedback.

Of course, starting the game early in the course thrusts students very quickly into decision-making—usually before they have covered the details of blending the marketing mix. However, we have found that this is not a major problem—especially if students have had at least a good solid introduction to the ideas behind market segmentation and market opportunity analysis—and to the logic of blending the 4Ps to meet the needs of a specific target market.

Another approach is to start game-related assignments—reading of the text, forming groups, etc.—early in the course but then hold off until about a third of the way through the course before the first decision is due. This has the advantage that students have covered more of the course material—and they are more likely to see that a key challenge is to make everything work together as a systematic whole. Further, if they know the game is coming up they will be likely to spend more time thinking through their first set of decisions.

This approach leaves time for fewer decision periods—especially if a week or two elapses between each decision. But it usually leaves enough time for students to work through 8 to 12 decision periods. With that many decisions, they can learn a lot from the game—and still have had a chance to make a few mistakes, identify the problem, and recover before the end of the term.

Introducing the Game Late in the Course

The main advantage of introducing the game late in the course is that students have a more complete understanding of the concepts and ideas involved. In this way, the game serves as an integrating mechanism and wrap up for the course.

What is "late" may depend on the length of the term. There are really two issues to consider. One is how many class periods remain, and the other is the elapsed time that students will have between decision periods. Time pressure in making decisions can add to the excitement—but too little time to make good decisions has the potential of creating frustration.

When much of the work of the game is loaded at the end of the course, you may want to consider reducing the amount of work on other new assignments. It may even make sense to save some class time to give student teams a chance to meet, go over their results, ask you questions, and get meetings scheduled to make the next decision. In that kind of situation, students can handle two, three or even more decisions a week.

Special Consideration with a Case-Oriented First MBA Course

The "core" marketing course in an MBA program is often quite different from the undergraduate course. Although the basic concepts of marketing do not change, the students tend to be more mature, more experienced, and often more highly motivated. Classes are often more oriented toward discussion and case analysis.

The game can be very effective when used along with cases in an MBA course. Cases are especially popular in the first MBA course because they are integrative, decision oriented, and practical. The responsibility is on the student to come to class prepared and ready to present recommendations and analysis relevant to the case. Yet, cases are snapshots or vignettes at a cross-section in time. Most cases do not give the student the opportunity to actually see how their recommendations or ideas would have worked out. And what looks like a good short-term solution might have bad long-term results, or vice versa. Furthermore, cases often don't spell out any specific financial limits or budgets— so students' recommendations may be based on the assumption that it's ok to spend any amount of money to reach your objective (not smart!). The learning experience afforded by the game offsets these limitations of cases—while still offering a high involvement learning experience that is integrative and practical. It is also a very good way to highlight the control aspects of marketing—a topic that is often difficult to bring to life unless students themselves make decisions and then see the results of those decisions.

Student analysis and preparation of a long, detailed case can be quite time consuming. Part of what takes so long is digesting all the detail about the new situation. In contrast, the focus over time with the game is on developing deeper insight and making better decisions—not on relearning the basic context. This is important in thinking through the scheduling of work. Specifically, if the game is going to be used in combination with cases, it makes sense to schedule game decisions to be due on days when the caseload is lighter.

Another way to look at this is in terms of the mix of work involved. Carefully developed plans for the game are likely to involve quite a bit of analysis—especially when the students are ambitious MBA students. Some cases tend to be very analysis oriented, and others tend to be more qualitative in nature.

One way to balance the workload is to select a mix of cases—some that are more focused on the numbers and others where the analysis is more qualitative. Then, the decision dates for the game can be coupled with the more qualitative cases. The students will be doing their analytical work in making the game decisions, and then deal with the particulars of the case to refine their qualitative analysis skills.

USING THE GAME IN ADVANCED COURSES (INCLUDING EXECUTIVE PROGRAMS)

There are three basic approaches for using the game in advanced courses. In one approach, the course (or a major portion of it) focuses on the game competition. There may be one or more major related assignments, but the student's main responsibility is to do a good job with—and learn from—the game experience.

A second approach involves a blend of the game and other (only indirectly related) special learning experiences—such as a project with a local business, case analyses, a major paper, or special readings.

The third case is more similar to the way in which the game is used in the first marketing course. There are other major text, lecture and/or discussion components of the course and the game is used to supplement/complement those components.

Each of these approaches is discussed individually in the sections below.

When the Game Is a Major Focus

The Marketing Game! works well as the major focus of an elective course such as marketing strategy, marketing problems, marketing management, or competitive analysis.

One advantage of the game is that it allows a great deal of flexibility. Advanced students often have many pressures on their time. They are quite willing to work hard and devote time to a course—but have trouble scheduling all of the different things they need to do when they need to do them. Since the game can be administered without a heavy reliance on regularly scheduled class meetings, it can be very attractive to students (or, for that matter, faculty who have irregular time pressures).

When the game is the major focus of an advanced course, it is good to move toward the higher levels of the game. It may still be advisable to start with level 1 for a few decision periods—to get the competition going and to give students a chance to get accustomed to market analysis and the planning process. If the game will ultimately move to level 3, we recommend advising students of that in advance. That way they can spend more time up front developing the strategy for multimedia so that they will be in a good position to introduce a second product—when they are ready.

An important feature of the game is that not every firm in an industry needs to introduce a second product at the same time—or at all. Students have the opportunity to evaluate the financial demands of establishing a strong position with a "base" product to help generate the cash flow (budget) to be able to introduce a second product. Thus, even if you start the game at level 3, you may want to tell the students that they should not consider introducing a second product any earlier than the second or third decision period. [Note: they can, however, request the customer preferences marketing research report for the second product without producing or trying to sell any of that product – to do this, a team should request market research report 3 for the second product and leave the rest of the second product entries blank. It makes sense to start with this information so they can do a better initial job of developing the product. The text is intentionally more vague about the needs and preferences of customers for the second product than it was for the VRD market.]

When the game is the major focus of the course, it is useful to consider one or more related assignments. Written or oral assignments can add a different dimension to the game and enrich the students' experience. The particular type of assignment will obviously depend on how much time is available and on your objectives. But, one very powerful assignment that warrants special consideration in this type of class is the "presentation to the board." This may come during the progress of the game, or near the end.

The idea is to assemble a small group (perhaps including faculty colleagues, local business executives, or even more advanced students) to listen to a presentation by the student (or group) and to ask questions. If the presentation is at the end of course—after the game competition has been completed—the presentations can be to the other students. This prompts some interesting dialog, especially if competitors in an industry see a firm's actions as not having matched up well with its "post hoc" justification!

The special diagnostic reports and summaries make it relatively easy and fast for an "outsider" serving on the board to get a handle on what a firm has done—and how it fits relative to others in an industry.

This can be a challenging experience for students, but it is also a good learning opportunity. Such a presentation might follow submission of a written report. If videotape facilities are available, you may consider having the presentations taped—so students can do a "post mortem" on the session. [Note: we have had some success collaborating with faculty in our communications area with class presentations. The marketing instructor evaluates the content of the presentation and the communications instructor evaluates the "quality of the presentation/communication." We had students develop PowerPoint slides for their presentations because many hadn't practiced with PowerPoint—but recruiters emphasized that it was a skill they expected.]

Using the Game with Other Learning Components

Another way to add variety to an elective course—and expand its focus—is to combine use of the game with other types of learning components—such as cases, readings, or projects. For example, *The Marketing Game!* combined with a text of marketing cases can serve as a particularly effective combination for an elective course to follow an introductory marketing course.

In a course that involves the game and one or more other major components, you need to decide how to "space" the different course components. One approach is to spend part of the course on the game, and the rest on the other components. Alternatively, you can intermix the components throughout the course.

Although this decision is largely a matter of personal preference, there are advantages to intermixing the different assignments over time. This gives students some variety and may allow for more time between decisions for the game. This can encourage students to develop and analyze their plans more carefully.

The decision whether to use teams or have individual students make decisions for a firm may in part be based on the mix of other class components—and the role of teams in those components. If other assignments—like projects with local businesses—are team oriented, you might want to use the game based on individual effort (or with only a few students on a team). Or, if other assignments are largely based on individual effort—as might be the case with a major term paper--there may be special value in using teams for the game.

Using the Game to Supplement Text and Lecture-Oriented Electives

Using the game in elective courses that have a traditional text and or lecture focus involves many of the same considerations that are relevant to using the game in the first marketing course—except that you will probably move toward more advanced levels more rapidly. It is also useful to think about ways to capitalize on the flexibility of the game to help achieve specific objectives of the course.

For example, in a product management course you might want to use the game with teams—to highlight the organizational aspects of product (or brand) management. Specifically, you might give students the option to introduce the new product "at will." The students might be encouraged to organize so that part of the team is managing the existing product, and the others are planning for the new product introduction. Then, once the new product is introduced, there can be a manager for each brand, and perhaps other specialists who look at specific sub areas (personal selling, advertising, sales promotion) that will affect both brands.

Or, in a promotion management course, you might have students develop more detailed plans for each aspect of the promotion blend in the game (i.e., personal selling, sales promotion, advertising) as that topic is covered in the class. One way to reward an effective plan (or, more generally, excellent performance on a course related assignment) is to give the student's firm an extra budget allowance for its next decision in the game. (Note: you can increase or decrease a firm's marketing budget by using the adjustments button on the marketing plan decision form that opens when you select the modify a plan button from the main screen of TMGSim.) Having a larger budget gives the firm more flexibility—and the opportunity to build an even stronger marketing program.

Using the Game with Executive Programs

The Marketing Game! is very successfull when used in executive program courses. In one-week or two-week long programs--that typically pack a lot of material on different topics into a short elapsed time--the game offers continuity as participants see their firm and industry develop. Furthermore, the competitive, interactive, "hands-on" nature of the game generates enthusiasm among executive program participants. If time is limited so that relatively few decision periods can be run (e.g., say 5 periods), the accelerated product life cycle setup option (which is explained in detail in Chapter 4) creates a market that evolves more quickly.

The Marketing Game! is also being used with a wide variety of "in-house" company training programs. In some instances, participants have had predominately marketing backgrounds or responsibilities. In other instances, the game has been used to give employees not directly involved in marketing a better appreciation of the various components of marketing strategy and planning. **Please keep in mind that a separate license agreement is required to use *The Marketing Game!* software for training programs in a company or firm other than in a college or university.** For details please contact the authors.

Note that TMG can be used when executive program students are not in residence. They can email their decisions (or use TMGftp to submit them) and get their reports back the same way or as a download from a TMG website.

CONCLUSION

This chapter has reviewed a number of different ideas for using the game in different courses. In closing, however, it is important to emphasize that there are no rigid or "right" answers about the best way to use the game. To the contrary, it has been designed to be flexible—so that you can use it in a way that matches your needs and your objectives for your course and your students.

PART TWO

Organizing and Running the Game

Part Two of this manual provides the basics for organizing and running *The Marketing Game!*

4. *Getting Organized for The Marketing Game!*

INTRODUCTION

This chapter contains instructions and suggestions for setting up to use *The Marketing Game!* Topics include the choice of the number of industries, choices among input and output options, and deciding what options to select in setting up the simulation environment. This chapter and the next—Chapter 5–Running the Programs—focus on the instructor's software. Use of the student software is briefly described in Chapter 8 (but also discussed in detail in Appendix A of the student text).

DETERMINING THE NUMBER OF FIRMS AND INDUSTRIES

Each group of *exactly* four firms comprises an industry. Each industry is identified by a code letter from A to Z. Thus, as many as 26 industries with a total of 104 firms can be managed with a single set up file.

(Note: There is NO LIMIT on the total number of industries you can run with *The Marketing Game!*. However, if you are simultaneously running more than 26 industries some firms will need to have similar industry identification letters and firm numbers. Thus, it is *absolutely critical* that decisions forms, output reports, and data disks for the duplicate industries be clearly labeled and kept separate! A simple approach to help with this is to think not only about "industries" and firms within an industry but also industries within an "economy." Then, students who are competing in different economies will have different instructions for submitting plan files and/or retrieving reports.)

The number of firms and industries will depend in part on whether individual students or teams of students manage firms. Whether to use teams or not, and how many students form a team, is likely to depend on how many students there are in total, whether the course is introductory or more advanced, and the instructor's objectives. These, and other pedagogical considerations, are discussed in detail in Chapter 3.

SELECTING INPUT AND OUTPUT OPTIONS

The Marketing Game! provides you with the choice among a wide variety of approaches/options for inputs and outputs. The input options determine how firms' decisions will be loaded or entered in the computer. The output options determine how firms' results (reports) will be returned to students.

For example, you can have students turn in their decisions on forms and return printed results to them, have students submit their Plan files on disks (or via some other digital method, such as via a network computer folder) and then return their result report on disk or through some other electronic approach, such as a download from a website. In this section we'll review a number of the possibilities and some of the key advantages and limitations of each approach.

Whichever method you select, it's a good idea to have students keep or submit a paper copy of the decisions form. The best method in a given situation will depend on the instructor's preferences, but those preferences are usually influenced by the number of firms competing in the game and by the level of technology available to the instructor and students. You can also intermix methods ... using one approach for submitting decisions and another for distributing (or having students retrieve) reports. There are five basic options, listed below, in descending level of effort for the instructor (and ascending level of supporting technology required).

Submitting Input	Distributing Output
Paper Plan forms	Printed reports
"Sneakernet" method (floppy disks)	Floppy disks
E-mail file attachments	E-mail file attachments
Copied to a floppy or a computer or network folder at a central location	Retrieved from a floppy or a computer or network folder at a central location
File Transfer Protocol (FTP) & TMGftp program	File Transfer Protocol and TMGftp Program
	Website

Paper-Based Method, Submitting Input and Distributing Output
Submitting input
1. Firms complete plan input forms (found in the Student Guide) and submit these printed forms to the instructor.
2. The instructor (or an assistant) uses TMGSim to enter the firms' plans before running the simulation.

Distributing output
1. The instructor runs the simulation, requesting that TMGSim write all output for an industry to a single report file.
2. The instructor opens the industry report in the viewer and prints it. It includes the separate industry report files. Then the instructor distributes them.

Advantages
- Students do not need access to computers.

Disadvantages
- Instructor or a helper is responsible for all data entry.
- Students and instructor must be in close physical proximity (unless forms and reports are faxed).
- Instructor (or department) pays for printing.
- If teams are used, it's usually inconvenient to make copies of reports for each student, so students deal with the logistics of exchanging copies of the report (and a breakdown by one student in the chain can cause hassles).

"SneakerNet" Method with Floppies, Submitting Input and Distributing Output

Submitting input
1. Firms run TMGPlan to create plan files on floppy disk, and then submit these floppy disks (with a clear label indicating the industry letter and firm number) to the instructor (or to a central collecting point, like a box in a computer lab or on a secretary's desk).
2. The instructor specifies the floppy disk drive as the path for student files in TMGSim.

Distributing output
1. The instructor runs the simulation, requesting that TMGSim create separate output files for each firm.
2. TMGSim writes a report file to each firm's floppy disk, and the instructor distributes these disks to the firms. Alternatively, with encrypted reports all of the report files can be copied to a single floppy disk and then left in a library, computer lab, or other convenient place for students to copy their own files from it. Because reports are encrypted, a student can't view someone else's report.
3. Firms use TMGPlan's File Viewer to view and print their reports.

Advantages
- Students do not need access to a network.
- Students can create pro forma statements and revise their plans in TMGPlan before submitting them.
- Floppy disk is an inexpensive and easy medium for data exchange.

Disadvantages
- Instructor must load each floppy disk twice during simulation processing-- once to read the input file and once to write the report file.
- Floppy disks tend to be less reliable than a hard drive.
- Students need to be urged to use virus-checking software; TMG files resist viruses but if there are other files (including hidden files) on the disk then a virus could be a problem for the instructor.
- Students and instructor must be in close physical proximity.

E-mail Method, Submitting Input and Distributing Output

Submitting input
1. Firms run TMGPlan to create plan files, and then e-mail them to the instructor as attachments; if teams are used, the person who sends the file should copy all of the other members of the firm in the e-mail.
2. The instructor saves/copies these attachments to a folder on a disk drive.
3. The instructor specifies this folder as the path for student files in TMGSim.

Distributing output
1. The instructor runs the simulation, requesting that TMGSim create separate output files for each firm.
2. The instructor selects the email from a firm that was used to submit a report, clicks "reply to all", and then attaches the report file for that firm as an e-mail attachment.
3. Firms use TMGPlan's File Viewer to view and print their reports.

Advantages
- Students and instructor may be geographically dispersed, since all files are electronically exchanged.
- Files are very small, so it is easy to send them as an attachment and they don't take long to send or retrieve, even with a dial-up email connection.
- This is a fast and convenient approach, and if teams are involved each student gets his or her own copy of the report.
- There is no time required for printing or sorting reports and no expense.
- Students can create pro forma statements and revise plans before submitting them.
- Students can obtain proof of the date and time that they sent the file by including themselves on the distribution list for their e-mail message.
- Any student with e-mail access can use this method.

Disadvantages
- Saving attached plan files to disk, and attaching reports to e-mails, can take some time if there are a large number of firms. Depending on the e-mail package, there may be opportunities to partially automate the process with the "reply to all" approach (if teams are being used and all

students' addresses are on the email message that submitted the plan file), distribution lists, or macros.

FTP Method, Submitting Input and Distributing Output

Submitting input

1. Firms run TMGPlan to create plan files, and then use the TMGftp program (or some other FTP program if the instructor prefers) to copy these files to a folder on a server designated by the instructor (or automatically configured by the TMGftp configuration file).
2. The instructor copies all student files via FTP to a private folder.
3. The instructor specifies this folder as the path for student files in TMGSim.

Distributing output

1. The instructor runs the simulation, requesting that TMGSim create separate, encrypted output files for each firm.
2. The instructor copies all of the report files via FTP to a folder on a server where firms can retrieve/download their reports—with the TMGftp program or some other FTP software.
3. Students use FTP to download their files, and then use the File Viewer of TMGPlan to view and print their reports.

Advantages

- Students can create pro forma statements and revise plans before submitting them.
- Students and instructor may be geographically dispersed.
- Collection and distribution of files is very quick and simple for the instructor.
- Students can submit files from anywhere that they have Internet access, and can retrieve reports very quickly at their own convenience.
- The TMGftp program uses configuration files that automate uploading and downloading for students and provide complete security with respect to location of files, password names, etc.; it also provides a "verification" report that confirms that a plan file was submitted and when; see notes below.

Disadvantages

- Students must have access to a computer that has Internet access (i.e., at home via dial-up or in a computer lab, etc.) and the school must have an FTP server.
- While password-based file encryption keeps firms from viewing one another's plan files and reports, a firm could still overwrite another firm's plan file if they specify the wrong industry or firm number (but see "Other Notes" below for more comments on this issue).

- Instructors may want students to e-mail files or submit printed versions of plan files as a backup method in case of a problem, such as a server that is down.

Other Notes
- The help file for the TMGftp program provides complete information about using this approach. It is easy to use, even for an instructor who has no experience with or knowledge about FTP. There is even a section with a "script" and suggestions about information you need and how to ask for help from computer network staff (if that's needed).
- The TMGftp program takes care of security issues for you and offers a variety of simple-to-select options. However, if you are using other FTP software, for greatest security it is a good idea to have students upload their plan files to one folder—with only write access. Then, have students download report files from another folder—with only read access. Your school's IT or computer support department should be able to assist you with setting up the necessary permissions within FTP.
- Note that with the TMGftp program each student does not need his or her own log-on and password to get access to the FTP server/folder. All students can use the instructor's log-on because proprietary information can be completely concealed in a TMGftp encrypted configuration file.
- When a student starts the TMGftp program, the very first step is to enter the industry and firm number information. Then, the program will only upload or download files for that specific firm. However, if a student intentionally or unintentionally uses the wrong firm id information, an uploaded plan file could overwrite a previously uploaded plan file with the same file name.

Website Method, Distributing Output

1. The instructor requests that TMGSim create separate, encrypted output files for each firm; be certain to use encrypted files so that a student can only access his or her own report.
2. The instructor copies these encrypted files to a shared folder on the web server.
3. The instructor installs a website for the course, including a page with links to these files. A simple website is included on the instructor's CD, and it is already programmed to handle report downloads.
4. Students download their files from the website, and then use the File Viewer of TMGPlan to view and print their reports.

Advantages
- Students simply use a Web browser to obtain their reports.
- Students can get their reports quickly and at their convenience ... for example, they don't have to wait for the next class or make a special trip.

- Distribution of files is very quick and simple for the instructor.

Disadvantages
- The instructor must install the website on a webserver (or, if McGraw-Hill's Page-Out website hosting service is used, obtain a password and copy the TMG website template into a personal folder). This is not difficult, but it does take some time to go through the steps involved. However, once a website is setup all that is required is to copy the new reports to the website folder. This overwrites the old reports and, because the file names are the same each period, the same download links work fine to download the reports for the current period.

A Note about Uploading to a Website:
There are a variety of approaches for uploading files to a website, but what approach can be used often depends on the Web server and software that runs it. As a result, the TMG website and website template do not provide for uploads. You may want to check with computer support people at you school to see if they have already implemented an upload procedure for websites. Alternatively, the TMGftp makes it easy to setup an upload system for plan files; it can be used for downloads as well or downloads can easily be handled with the TMG website.

Network Folder Method, Submitting Input and Distributing Output

Submitting input
- Firms run TMGPlan to create plan files, and then save (or copy) these files to a shared folder designated by the instructor on a computer lab's network drive (one which can be accessed by a drive letter, as though it were a local disk drive).
- The instructor copies all student files to a private folder.
- The instructor specifies this folder as the path for student files in TMGSim.

Distributing output
- The instructor requests that TMGSim create separate, encrypted output files for each firm.
- The instructor copies these files to a shared folder on a network drive.
- Students copy their files from this folder, and then use the File Viewer of TMGPlan to view and print their reports.

Advantages
- Students can create pro forma statements and revise plans before submitting them.
- Students and instructor simply use Windows Explorer to copy files to and from the necessary locations.
- If added security is needed, the TMGftp program can be used to transfer student files to and from the network drive.

- Collection and distribution of files is very quick and simple for the instructor.

Disadvantages
- While password-based file encryption keeps firms from viewing one another's plan files and reports, a firm could still overwrite another firm's plan file if they specify the wrong industry or firm number (but see "Other Notes" below for more comments on this issue).
- In case of a problem, firms have no evidence of uploading a particular plan file (unless they are using TMGftp, which provides a verification report). Instructors may want students to e-mail files or submit printed versions of plan files as a backup method in case of problems.
- Shared-drive access must be available to students, and appropriate file security must be set up in advance; here again, the TMGftp program simplifies these issues.
- In many cases, direct access to the shared drive will be available only by accessing the local intranet. This will often mean that the students and instructor cannot be geographically dispersed.

Other Notes
- The help file for the TMGftp program provides complete information about using this approach. It is easy to use, even for an instructor who has no experience with or knowledge about network folders. There is even a section with a "script" and suggestions about information you need and how to ask for help from computer network staff (if that's needed).
- The TMGftp program takes care of security issues for you and offers a variety of simple-to-select options. However, if you are using other FTP software, for greatest security it is a good idea to have students upload their plan files to one folder--with only write access. Then have students download report files from another folder--with only read access. Your IT department should be able to assist you with setting up the necessary permissions within FTP.
- Note that with the TMGftp program each student does not need his or her own log-on and password to get access to the network folder. The instructor's log-on (or one established for all members of the class) can be used because proprietary information can be completely concealed in a TMGftp encrypted configuration file.

Checking for Viruses

An unfortunate reality is that computer "viruses" are widespread, and can wreak havoc. A virus on one firm's data disk can spread to the computer used to run the game, and then to the data disks of other firms. While some viruses are relatively "harmless," others can cause unpredictable effects, and still others are destructive.

We have designed the TMG Plan files so that it is virtually impossible to attach a virus to them. Thus, you can avoid virus risks almost completely if you have students submit plan files as the only attachment to an email message or if plan files are copied to a network drive or uploaded via TMGftp. Similarly, **if you are going to have students submit their plan files on floppy we strongly urge that you have them submit a disk that has no files on it other than the single plan file.** If there are other files, even hidden files or system files, they can serve as a host to computer viruses.

Even with this precaution, it is wise to use good virus-checking software with up-to-date virus definitions. When we use floppy disks for input we also ask students to run the disk through virus checking software installed on the computers in the school's computer lab. It is more up to date and better maintained than individual student's computers!

Ask your computer support personnel to make virus-checking software available in your computer labs–*and remind students to use it!*

ADVANCED SETUP OPTIONS (OPTIONAL)

The Marketing Game! features several advanced setup options which allow the instructor additional control over the game's decisions and environment. Although we initially envisioned a "Level 4," we decided instead to make these advanced features optional. That way they can be individually selected at any level (1 through 3) of the game.

All of these advanced setup options can be set by industry. Once you choose one of these options in the TMGSim SETUP procedure, you can specify that all industries will be the same, or you can vary each option across different industries.

Budgets, Budget Adjustments, and the Discretionary Reserve Fund

In *The Marketing Game!*, each firm's net contribution to profit determines its marketing department budget for the following period. As contribution increases, so does the budget. A firm's basic budget for the period is given on the report from the previous period.

There are two approaches for modifying the budget specified by the TMGSim program in the report. One approach results in an adjustment to the budget just for the next period. The other approach involves use of a discretionary (reserve) budget that will carry over to future periods if it is not spent in the current period. The dollar amount of the discretionary reserve fund is a setup option. **The default amount of the discretionary reserve fund is $200,000.**

- **Adjusting a Firm's Budget for the Current Period**

The "modify a plan" button on the main screen of the TMGSim program allows the instructor to open and modify a firm's plan, and this includes making *adjustments* (either up or down) to the firm's budget for the game period about to be run. This can be useful for dealing with "exceptional" items. For example, the instructor can charge a team for marketing research (or advice), levy a fine (say, for turning in a decision late), or increase the firm's budget by a certain amount (for example, based on a proposal for something specific the firm wants to do).

- **The Discretionary Reserve Fund**

The Discretionary Reserve Fund option allows the instructor to specify a dollar amount that will be available to each firm for use at any time throughout the game. Although different reserve fund amounts can be set for different industries, all firms within a given industry will have available the same specified amount. Firms may spend it all it once, a little each period, or not at all. Interest income (at a rate of 6%) on any unspent reserve funds is added to the firm's financial summary.

The default reserve fund amount is $200,000. However, it is a simple matter during the setup to increase this amount or eliminate it altogether. If the reserve fund amount for an industry as given in the setup is greater than 0, the financial summary reports will include the interest income and the amount of remaining reserve funds available will be given under the budget for the next period. The amount of reserve funds can be changed at any time during the game.

Availability of a reserve fund adds some flexibility, but also more complexity, to the firms' decision and planning process. With a fixed budget, firms focus on how to allocate their budget across the different spending categories. However, with a reserve fund, firms must also decide whether to spend ("invest") some of the reserves now and how much, or whether to save them for later. Firms must tradeoff the likely benefits of spending the reserve fund in one big "splash" or several, smaller increments. There is also more uncertainty about competitors' actions since it is more difficult to forecast their spending.

Giving students a reserve fund (or increasing the reserve fund amount) is especially useful if you intend to move to Level 3 of the game where students have the option to introduce a second product. Since the R&D costs to develop the new product can be substantial, without a reserve fund students often feel unduly constrained if they must stay within their budget. The availability of funds over and above their budget gives students more flexibility in when (and whether) to enter the new market.

At the end of this chapter you will find a memo (written to the firm from the president) announcing the availability of a discretionary reserve fund. If you choose this option, you can fill in the appropriate reserve fund amount, and distribute copies of this memo to your students. (A word-processing file for the memo is on the Instructor CD-Rom.)

Production Economies of Scale

In *The Marketing Game!,* the cost to produce each unit depends on the features of the product. Higher levels of the features result in a higher unit production cost. Under the production economies of scale option the unit production cost is also affected by cumulative production volume. Specifically, if this option is chosen, the unit costs will decrease from the "base" unit cost by 3% for every 100,000 units produced up until about 1 million units in cumulative production, then the incremental cost savings taper off to 1% per 100,000 and above 2,000,000 units costs are level again. Note, *once this option is enabled, all units produced contribute to cumulative production* – regardless of any changes to the product's features. Also, be aware that the student manual is not at all specific about the rate at which economies of scale will "run out." On the other hand, that typically won't come into effect unless you run a very large number of periods.

This option may be activated at any time during the game. Units produced before the option is chosen have no effect on unit costs – only units produced while this option is in effect contribute to lower unit costs. If this option is chosen, the cumulative production volume (since the option went into effect) will be reported on each firm's production summary.

Note: the pro forma financial summary produced by the student TMGPlan software computes unit cost using the base unit cost, without taking into account any production economies of scale. **Thus, if you use the option, you may want to advise your students that the TMGPlan pro formas will be conservative since the unit product costs may be overstated.**

At the end of this chapter (and on the Instructor CD-Rom as a word processing file) you will find a memo (written to the firm from the president) announcing the purchase of new production equipment that allows unit costs to decline with cumulative production. If you choose this option, you will distribute copies of this memo to your students. The TMG website is configured to download the memo.

Economic Environment

Using this option, the instructor can modify the overall economic environment of an industry. This leads to either an increase or decrease in industry demand. Compared to the "normal" economic environment, it is possible to increase or decrease total demand by as much as 15%.

This option may be changed at any time during the game. However, once changed, the effect will continue until it is changed again. This option does not appear anywhere on the firms' reports, but is reported at the beginning of the instructor's report. The normal value is 100 – values less than 100 mean that demand is suppressed, values greater than 100 indicate an increase in demand.

Accelerated Product Life Cycle

IMPORTANT WARNING! If you choose the accelerated product life cycle option, it should be set only prior to the first decision period. **Do NOT change it after the simulation is underway.**

Occasionally, an instructor may want to use *The Marketing Game!* when there is only time for a limited number of decisions. In a "typical" situation where between 6 and 10 (or more) game periods are simulated, the market environment evolves such that segment preferences gradually shift over time and industry growth begins to taper and eventually flatten as the product life cycle enters maturity. If the simulation runs for fewer periods, these changes may not become evident.

Under the accelerated product life cycle option, consumer preferences shift more rapidly and overall industry demand will tend to reach the "mature" (and possibly decline) stages earlier. It makes sense to consider this option when, say, only 4 or 5 decision periods can be run.

5. *Instructor Software and Running the Simulation*

INTRODUCTION

This chapter covers the two main instructor programs on the TMG Instructor CD-Rom. First, it provides instructions about running TMGSim, the main simulation program. TMGSim also incorporates the TMGPlan program (student software), which is discussed in Appendix A of the student text and incorporated (with a few additional features) in the instructor software. This chapter also provides information about the TMGftp program and the custom configuration creator form in that program.

Two other instructor programs that offer optional capabilities are discussed in Appendix G and Appendix H. The TMGDisks program (discussed in Appendix G) and its help file are found in the root directory of the CD-Rom. This program creates installation disks if you want to use the TMG software on a computer that does not have a CD-Rom drive. The TMGtoXLS program (discussed in Appendix H) extracts data from the TMG summary files and exports it to a file in standard Microsoft Excel™ spreadsheet format. If you like to use Excel to create graphs or perform calculations this gives you an easy way to do supplement work with data created by the TMGSim program.

We have worked to make the software easy to install, use and understand. Online help files provide context specific information as you work with the software. And this manual provides detailed explanations—in case you want the detail. But, if you still have questions about installing or using the software—or if you run into any problems—our publisher is there to help you. Simply call (toll-free) 1-800-634-3963 and ask for software support.

A NOTE ABOUT SYSTEM REQUIREMENTS

The CD-Rom packaged with your Instructor's Manual provides all of the applications software you will need to run the game. *The Marketing Game!* software is designed to run on computer systems using Windows 95 or more recent versions of Windows. The TMGSim software only requires about 3 megabytes of memory beyond what is required to run Windows, so it should run even on older machines with a minimal amount of memory, although on older machines with limited memory it is probably smart to close other applications while you're running TMG.

The TMGTutor program requires a multimedia PC. The tutorials on the CD-Rom are AVI format video clips. This is a very common digital video standard for Windows computers. To use the videos the computer needs to have a soundboard and speakers (or headphones) and a CD-Rom drive. However, it is possible to copy the video files to the computer hard drive and run them that way. (For more information on running TMGTutor videos from a hard drive, see the TMGTutor help file).

GETTING ACQUAINTED WITH THE SOFTWARE

There are several different ways to become acquainted with the software. Basically, these fall into the following categories:

- Go through some or all of the tutorials (with the TMGTutor program);

- Read this chapter to get an overview;

- Just install it and experiment with it, relying on the help system for guidance when you need it;

The approach you select is a matter of personal preference and personal style. But it is perhaps useful to share a few recommendations about how to proceed.

Just Install the Software and Let It Guide You

In general, for most people the best approach will be to look at one or two of the tutorials to get a sense for how the software is designed, and then just install it and use it.

We think that you will find the software easy to install and use--and it will be obvious what to do at any given point. In fact, if you try to do something that isn't consistent with the way the programs work a message window will open and give you additional guidance.

Rely on the Help System

Further, the online-help system is very complete and organized to make it easy to get to general information or detailed context-specific instructions--depending on your needs at a particular time. In light of that, for most people the best approach is to install the software and experiment with the programs. You're not going to hurt anything if you make a mistake.

Take a Look at a Few Tutorials

On the other hand, the TMGTutor program offers an easy way to get a handle on the software and how to use it. Its tutorial videos show you the actual screens that appear while using the program and take you through the main steps for creating a plan, setting up the simulation environment, and running the simulation. A good approach is to view a few of the videos to get a sense for how the programs are designed. Then, you can go back later and look at tutorials related to specific steps if you need assistance.

- **Tutorials Primarily for Students, and Tutorials for Instructors Only**

The first eight tutorials focus on the student software (especially TMGPlan) and how students use it. On the other hand, you can do the same things within the TMGSim software. Further, some tutorials, like the one on how to use the help system, apply to both the student and instructor software. So these eight tutorials are also included on the Instructor CD-Rom. By contrast, the last five tutorials focus on using the TMGSim program and running the simulation; they are available only to the instructor.

Or, if You Wish, Read to Get an Overview

Some people prefer to read documentation first and then work with the software. This chapter meets that need. While some sections of this chapter go into significant detail, **you do not need to try to absorb the details**. To the contrary, that's not productive. The help files for the programs include all of the information provided here (and more). So, the printed information is provided mainly as a convenience and to provide you with an overview. The chapter is structured to provide overviews at different levels of detail. There are sections that go into detail about each feature of each screen. However, there are also sections that provide a quick reference guide to specific tasks.

- **Quick Reference Guides on Specific Tasks**

The quick reference guides in this chapter (and available in the help file) are really just checklists of the sequence of steps that you take to perform a task. They provide some structure/guidance without getting into a lot of detail. As such, they are intended for people who want a road map but don't want to wade through explanations of all of the possibilities.

INSTALLING THE SOFTWARE

The installation of the instructor software is automated with a Windows setup procedure that is on the TMG Instructor CD-Rom. In most cases, all you need to do is (1) close any programs that my be open on your desktop and then (2) insert the TMG Instructor CD-Rom in the CD-Rom drive on your computer, wait a few seconds while the installation procedure automatically loads, and then follow the instructions that appear on the screen.

As this suggests, with most computers when the CD-Rom is detected in the drive a program will automatically start. You will have the choice to install the software or view the multimedia tutorials or both. If you choose to install the software first, the TMGTutor program will be installed on your hard drive; however, to view the tutorials you will need to put the CD-Rom in your CD-Rom drive.

However, some computers are not configured to detect a CD-Rom or to automatically start installation procedures. If, after you have inserted the CD-Rom, the CD-drive is no longer active (usually there's an indicator light that shows that the drive is active, but even if there is not you can usually hear the drive spinning when it is active) and the installation procedure screen has not automatically appeared, all you need to do is:

1. Click the Start button on the task bar, which is usually at the bottom of the screen.

2. Click Run, and then when the dialog window opens click Browse and select your CD-Rom drive and the Setup.exe file, and then click the Ok button.

3. Follow the instructions that appear on the screen.

We recommend that you allow the installation procedure to install the software in the default location, which is on your hard drive in a TMG folder under the Windows Program files folder. **That way, you will be able to conveniently start the various TMG programs (or open the TMG help files) from the Program files menu**. The paths for the default installation folders for the programs and associated help files are as follows:

C:\program files\TMG\TMGSim\TMGSim.exe
C:\program files\TMG\TMGPlan\TMGPlan.exe
C:\program files\TMG\TMGTutor\TMGTutor.exe
C:\program files\TMG\TMGftp\TMGftp.exe

ONLINE HELP AND STATUS BAR HINTS

Status Bar at Bottom of Screen Gives Hints

At the bottom of the TMG program screens there is a status bar that displays hints about using the program. As you move the cursor over different items on the screen the hint will change to provide information specific to the item under the cursor. This makes it easy to get a quick overview of features and what they do.

Complete On-Line Help System

The TMG programs also have complete online help systems. At any point you can click the Help button and a help window will open. Another way to get help is to click on the background portion of the screen and then press the F1 key. When that help window is open there are several ways to find additional information. When you are through looking at help, close the help window by pressing the Esc key or click the small x in the upper right corner of the help window.

Context-Specific Help

If the F1 key is pressed when the cursor is in an edit box or a button is highlighted/selected, context-specific help for that item is displayed. To highlight an edit field, click on it with the mouse. Alternatively, you can press the Tab key until the item of interest is highlighted; you'll see that the tab (and highlighting) moves systematically through all of the elements on the screen. To get help about a specific button on the screen, press the Tab key until that button is highlighted and then press the F1 key. (You must use the Tab key rather than a mouse click to highlight a button because if you click the button it will activate).

Navigating within the Help System

Once the help window is open you can move around in the help file in a number of ways. The most obvious is that you can click your mouse on a highlighted (hyperlinked) term and immediately move to that part of the help file.

On the button bar at the top of the help window there is a button marked with the symbol "<<". If you click that button you will move back one screen in the help file. Similarly, the ">>" button moves you forward one screen.

You may also find it useful to use the Back button. If you press it once it will take you back to the screen you most recently viewed. If you press it again it will take you to the screen you viewed before that one, and so on.

Another powerful tool available to you is the Index button that appears on the button bar at the top of the help window. Click the Index button and a tabbed dialog box opens. You can select and display a help page from the list that appears. Alternatively, you can click the Find selection and enter a word or term for which you want more information. The program will search through the whole help file and show you a list of pages where that term appears. Then, all you have to do is select the page of interest and then press the Display button.

Other Useful Help Features

There are other features of the Windows help system that may be helpful to you. For example, you can print a help page or copy it to the Windows clipboard. You can also set a bookmark so that you can instantly link back to the bookmarked pages. In addition, you can look at a "history list" that tracks the pages in the help file that you've reviewed, and if you select a page from that list you go back to it. You can even add your own notes (annotations) at different places in the help file. When you go back to that same page later you can click on the small paperclip image (the icon that indicates that there is an annotation) and your notes will reappear.

The best way to become familiar with these features is to try them out ... by clicking the different buttons on the button bar at the top of the help window. Of course, if you'd rather read about it than do it you can also look at Help on Using Help, covered next.

Help on Using Help

If you want more information on how to use the Windows help system, click Help on the menu bar at the top of the screen and then click Help on Help, or alternatively when the help file window is open press the F1 key.

Note: you can close help and return to the program by pressing the Esc key or by clicking the small x in the upper right corner of the help window.

CREATING TMGSIM FOLDERS/PATHS FOR INPUT AND OUTPUT FILES

Any time that you run TMGSim, the software needs to know where the various files used by or created and saved by the software are located. So, it's useful to know about this **before running the software**, and to use Windows Explorer to create folders to hold the relevant files. Then, when you start TMGSim, all you need to do is select the path for the folders you have created as part of the setup procedure.

The software for previous editions assumed that you would be using floppy disks for most input and output, but with the redesigned programs in this edition it is often faster and more convenient to do the processing from a folder on the hard drive. *The Marketing Game!* TMGSim program now uses three different folders, and they are overviewed below. After the overview, you will find a reference table that lists and describes all of the main files used throughout *The Marketing Game!*

The Folder for Student Files

The first folder is the location of the student files. If you want to receive each separate Plan file from students on an individual floppy disk, and return the corresponding report file on the same floppy disk, just select the floppy drive you want to use as the student folder. Then, as the processing of industries proceeds, you will be prompted to insert the floppy for the appropriate firm.

Alternatively, *you may want to create a separate folder (or subfolder) on your drive for the Plan files and report files for each decision period.* Then, before you run the simulation for a particular period, you can just change the student path to the folder for the current period. That way, you will have a backup of all of the students' plan files and report files for each decision period.

The student files folder/path and the unencrypted report files path may not share the same removable drive, due to requirements during simulation processing.

The Master Folder

The second folder is the master folder for the instructor's files, including all of the files used to run the simulation. It is best to establish one master folder for the duration of the game and stick with it.

The Unencrypted Reports Folder

The third folder is for unencrypted report files that are produced as an intermediate step if you select the encrypted reports option on the TMGSim Command Center Screen.

- **Restriction on Paths Placed on Removable Drives.**

The unencrypted report files path and the student path may not share the same removable drive. If you have two removable drives, one path may point to each; otherwise, at least one of these two paths must be on a hard drive.

Overview of TMG Folders, Programs and Key Files

TMGSim is the main instructor program, and TMGPlan is the main student program, for *The Marketing Game!* However, there are other optional programs (TMGftp and TMGTutor) and files that it's useful to know about. So, for convenience, they are all overviewed in the table below.

• Reference Table for TMG Programs, Folders, and the Main Files			
TMG 3rd Edition key programs and files	File Description	Folder	Corresponding file in TMG 2nd ed.
Setup.exe	**Program installer for all of the TMG software**	CD-Rom root directory	None
TMGSim.EXE	**Instructor simulation program**		TMG.BAT
TMGSim.hlp	help file for TMGSim	\TMG\TMGSim	
TMGSETUP.CFG	Default name for TMGSim setup file, but user may specify a name	\TMG\TMGSim or master	SETUP.INI
PLANif.TMG	Marketing plan decisions file for Firm number f in Industry letter i	STUDENT	INPUTSif.DAT
REPORTif.TMG	Password-protected Report	STUDENT	None

- **Reference Table for TMG Programs, Folders, and the Main Files**

TMG 3rd Edition key programs and files	File Description	Folder	Corresponding file in TMG 2nd ed.
	file for Firm f in Industry i (encrypted format)		
REPORTif.TXT	Report file for firm f in industry i (standard text format file)	REPORT	Same
SUMDELi.TXT	Summary file for Industry i, in comma delimited text file format	MASTER	Same
SUMMARYi.TXT	Summary file for Industry i, in text format	MASTER	Same
HISTORYi.TMG	History file for Industry i	Master	HISTORYi.DAT
HISTip.BAK	History backup file for Industry i, Period p	Master	Same
INDSUMi.TMG	Summary file data structure (program use only), for Industry I	Master	INDSUMi.DAT
SUMMARYi.TMG	Industry i, summary file	Master	SUMMARYi.DAT
(No longer needed)	Industry i, inputs file	Master	INPUTSi.DAT
TMGLog.txt	A log/record (mainly of file input and output) of the most recent TMGSim session(s)	Master	None
TMGPlan.EXE	**Student marketing plan software**	\TMG\TMGPlan	PLAN.BAT
TMGPlan.hlp	Student software help file	\TMG\TMGPlan	None
Plandef.CFG	Student program setup file	\TMG\TMGPlan	None
PLANif.TMG	Marketing plan decisions file for Firm f in Industry i	(student computer)	INPUTSif.DAT
ProForif.TXT	ProForma for Firm f in Industry i in text file format	(student computer)	ProForif.txt
TMGLog.txt	A log/record of the TMGPlan session	(student computer)	None
TMGTutor	**TMG tutorial player software**	\TMG\TMGTutor	None
TMGTutor.hlp	TMGTutor help file	\TMG\TMGTutor	None
'tutorial name'.avi	Tutorial video files in AVI digital video format	CD-Rom folder \Tutorial	None
TMGftp.exe	**TMG program for ftp upload of Plan files and download of encrypted report files**	\TMG\TMGftp	None
TMGftp.hlp		\TMG\TMGftp	None

• Reference Table for TMG Programs, Folders, and the Main Files			
TMG 3rd Edition key programs and files	File Description	Folder	Corresponding file in TMG 2nd ed.
TMGftp#.cfg	Custom configuration file, where # is 1 (default) or an integer from 2 to 99	\TMG\TMGftp	
TMGtoXLS.exe	TMG program to extract data from summary files and export it to a file in Microsoft Excel file format.	TMG\TMGtoXLS	None
Summary.XLS	Excel file (version 5.0 format, readable in version since 5.0)	Master	None

TMGSIM QUICK REFERENCE GUIDES

The online help system provides a number of quick reference guides if you want a check list type reminder about how to use the TMGSim program for some particular task. The available quick reference guides cover the topics listed below, and for your convenience they are duplicated in this manual.

- Create a setup environment
- Type in marketing plans
- Modify a plan file
- Create a pro forma statement
- Enter fines, additional charges, and budget changes
- Run the simulation
- View reports generated by the simulation

Quick Reference – Create a Setup Environment

To create a new setup environment in which all industries have identical values, follow these steps:

1. On the Main Screen, set up valid paths for student files, master files, and unencrypted report files (by clicking the "change" button for a path and then setting the correct drive and folder in the Set Path Window).
2. From the Main Screen, click the "Create a TMG Setup file" button.
3. On the Create New Setup Screen, fill in desired setup values for Industry A, or simply accept the default values.
4. Enter the number of industries.
5. Enter a descriptive label for the setup file.
6. Click the "Fill in values" button.
7. At the Setup Values Screen, click the "Save/Go to Main" button; when the save file dialog opens, save the setup file with the default name in the program folder, or alternatively in the master folder to which it applies.

Quick Reference – Type in Marketing Plans

To type in a series of marketing plans for firms, follow these steps:
1. Organize the written marketing plans you want to enter in ascending order (i.e., A1, then A2, A3, A4, B1, B2, and so on).
2. On the Main Screen, make sure you have entered a valid path for student files.
3. From the Main Screen, click the "Type in marketing plan(s)" button.
4. At the Starting Industry/Firm Window, enter the industry letter and firm number of the first firm for which you will enter a plan (in the example above, this would be industry A and firm 1).
5. Enter the level of the Marketing Game for which plans are to be entered.
6. Click the "OK" button.
7. On the Marketing Plan Decisions Screen, enter the firm's marketing plan decisions.
8. Click the "Save" button.
9. In the Password Entry Window, enter a password, and re-enter it for confirmation.
10. Click the "OK" button.
11. You will see a file saved confirmation message. Note that the industry and firm entry boxes will be set to the next firm in sequence (note that this is a difference between the instructor software and the student version of the plan software), and the decision entry boxes will be emptied.
12. If you wish to enter a plan for the next firm in sequence, simply enter the firm's decisions and click the "Save" button.
13. If you wish to skip one or more firms in sequence, you can change the industry and/or firm entry boxes (these edit fields are not activated in the student plan software), and then enter the firm's decisions and click the "Save" button.
14. When you are done entering and saving firms' marketing plans, click the "Cancel" button to return to the Main Screen.

Quick Reference – Modify a Plan File

To modify a firm's marketing plan, follow these steps:
2. On the Main Screen, make sure you have entered a valid path for student files.
3. From the Main Screen, click the "Open/modify existing plan" button.
4. On the Industry/Firm Window, enter the industry letter and firm number of the firm whose plan you wish to modify.
5. Enter the level of the Marketing Game for which the plan is being modified.
6. Click the "OK" button.
7. If the level in the plan file does not match the level you specified, respond to the warning message, either staying with the level you specified, or switching to the level from the plan file.

8. On the Marketing Plan Decisions Screen, make changes to the firm's marketing plan decisions.
9. Click the "Save" button.
10. In the Password Entry Window, click the "OK" button.
11. Click the "Cancel" button to return to the Main Screen.

Quick Reference – Enter Fines, Charges, and Budget Changes

To make special adjustments to a firm's budget or expenses, follow these steps:
1. On the Main Screen, make sure you have entered a valid path for student files.
2. From the Main Screen, click the "Open/modify existing plan" button.
3. On the Industry/Firm Window, enter the industry letter and firm number of the firm whose plan you wish to adjust.
4. Enter the level of the Marketing Game for which the plan is being adjusted.
5. Click the "OK" button.
6. If the level in the plan file does not match the level you specified, respond to the warning message, either staying with the level you specified, or switching to the level from the plan file.
7. On the Marketing Plan Decisions Screen, click the "Adjustments" button.
8. On the Marketing Plan Adjustments Screen, make the necessary changes.
9. Click the "OK" button.
10. Back on the Marketing Plan Decisions Screen, click the "Save" button.
11. In the Password Entry Window, click the "OK" button.
12. Click the "Cancel" button to return to the Main Screen.

Quick Reference – Run the Simulation

To run the simulation for all industries for a decision period, follow these steps:
1. On the Main Screen, make sure you have a valid setup environment; if you don't load the setup file you have previously created and saved, you will need to create a new one (see the quick reference above for instructions); if you want to increase the level of the game or change the path for a folder or alter any other setup option, modify the setup file.
2. Then, from the Main Screen, click the "Run simulation" button.
3. On the Simulation Command Center Screen, review the Industry Status panel to make sure missing files will not prevent any industry from being processed.
4. Click the "Select All Industries" button.
5. Verify that the Simulation Period box is set to the correct value.
6. Click the "Run selected industries" button.
7. When the simulation is complete, you will receive a confirmation message.
8. Click the "Return" button to return to the Main Screen.

Quick Reference – View Reports Generated by the Simulation

After you run the simulation, it's a good idea to briefly review the reports produced. These will include firms' financial summaries, and also a set of instructor-only reports. You can review them by following these instructions:

1. Start the TMGSim program if it is not already running. If the report you want to view is on a removable disk, insert the disk containing the file before starting the program.
2. Click the "Review or print a report" button from either the Main Screen or the TMG Command Center Screen.
3. The Open Dialog box will show you report files available in your Master files directory if this is the first time you have selected the Viewer since you started TMGSim. Otherwise, it will show you unencrypted report files in the last directory you accessed in the Viewer.
4. If the file you want to open is in a different directory, select the directory.
5. If you want to view an encrypted report file or a pro forma file, click on the "Files of type" menu and select the type of report you want to see.
6. Double-click on the name of the report file you want to view.
7. The report will be displayed in the File Viewer window. You can browse and search text by using on-screen buttons and the menu bar, or click the print button if you want a printed copy.

DETAILED INFORMATION ON TMGSIM

The TMGPlan program consists of a series of screens to perform different functions. The major screens are listed below, and then in the sections that follow there is more detail on each screen. Remember that all of this information is available in the online help system.

- Main Screen. Displays status of your setup environment and allows you to select other functions.
- Create New Setup Screen. Collects first-level information to create a new setup environment.
- Setup Values Screen. Allows you to view and customize the setup environment.
- Marketing Plan Decisions Screen. Allows you to create or modify the plan file containing all individual decisions for your firm's marketing plan for this decision period.
- Marketing Plan Adjustments Window. Allows you to enter fines, additional charges, and budget changes for a firm.
- Inputs for Pro Forma Screen. Collects information that is not part of a firm's marketing plan but that is necessary to compute the Pro Forma Statement.
- Pro Forma Estimates Screen. Displays the Pro Forma Statement.
- File Viewer Screen. Allows you to decrypt, view, print, and save report files.

- Simulation Command Center. Used to run the simulation.

Main Screen

The Main Screen is the first screen you see when you start TMGSim. This screen shows you the status of your setup environment, allows you to load or modify a setup file (or create a new one), and provides access to all TMGSim functions through the menu bar and a series of selection buttons. We will review a number of features of this screen, including:
- Setup Status Display
- Default Folder Settings
- Selection Buttons
- Menus

- **Setup Status Display, Main Screen**

Your setup environment is saved in a file called TMSETUP.CFG. The very first time you run TMGSim, there is no TMSETUP.CFG file. When this file exists in the folder from which TMGSim is started and runs, TMGSim automatically reads it at start up. Alternatively, you can load a previously saved setup file by clicking the Load button.

The upper left section of the screen gives you information about the status of the setup environment. If your setup environment is valid, information about it will be shown in green; information about an invalid setup or one with incomplete values will be shown in red.

Four types of status information are provided:
- The name (label) for the setup file, if one has been loaded—either automatically by the program or by you (by clicking the load setup button).
- The number of industries.
- A summary of the nature of setup, particularly the level and whether or not it is a default setup.
- The status of the required path names for the folders (so that TMGSim knows where to read and save the different types of files it needs in order to run the simulation).

There are buttons to create a setup file, modify one that has already been loaded, or load one that has been previously saved.

TMGSim File Paths. TMGSim requires several different types of computer files in order to run the simulation and perform other functions. In order to maximize flexibility in the way these files are stored, you have the opportunity to provide three Windows folders in which these files can be saved. Any two (or all three) of these folder names may be the same, in which case the folder will be used for multiple purposes. However, it is often preferable to separate the different types of files into different folders because it makes it easier to keep similar types of files together and it can reduce clerical errors in copying files.

File paths may be set on the Main, Create New Setup, and Simulation Command Center screens. Here is a brief review of each path/folder:

- Student files path. Student plan files, report files, and pro forma files are stored in this folder, or if you select a floppy drive you will be prompted to insert each firm's floppy at the appropriate time. To change the path currently specified, click the "Change" button to go to the Set Path Window. It's a good idea to create a different student folder or subfolder for each decision period so that you have a backup of all of the firm's plan files and reports files for each period.

- Master files path. Instructor reports, summary files, and files used to save simulation results from past periods are stored in this folder. (Note that when you first start the game, the Master files folder will be empty.) To change the path currently specified, click the "Change" button to go to the Set Path Window. However, we recommend that you stick with the same Master files folder (and thus Master files path) throughout the game.

- Unencrypted report files path. If you request that student reports be created in encrypted form, unencrypted versions of student reports are stored in this folder for your convenience. This path needs to be set only if you request encryption of student reports on the Simulation Command Center screen. To change the path currently specified, click the "Change" button to go to the Set Path Window. You may find it convenient to create a different unencrypted report files folder (that will have a different path) for each period of the game.

Restriction on Paths Placed on Removable Drives. The unencrypted report files path and the student files path may not share the same removable drive, due to requirements during simulation processing. If you have two removable drives, one path may point to each; otherwise, at least one of these two paths must be on a hard drive.

Selection Buttons, Main Screen. The following selection buttons are available on the Main Screen:

- Type in Marketing Plan(s) button. Click this button if you wish to enter one or more marketing plans for firms. A window will appear asking you to enter the starting industry letter and firm number for plan entry. The Marketing Plan Decisions Screen will then be displayed. Each time you save a plan file, the industry letter and firm number will be automatically adjusted to allow you to enter the next firm's plan. Plan files will be saved in the student files path you specified.

- Open/Modify Existing Plan button. Click this button if you wish to make changes to a firm's plan (including special adjustments such as budget changes, fines, and additional charges). A window will appear asking you to enter the industry letter and firm number of the firm whose plan you wish to modify. This firm's plan file must exist in the student files path you specified.

- Run Simulation button. Click this button to activate the Simulation Command Center Screen in order to run the simulation for a decision period.

- View/Print Report button. Click this button to activate the File Viewer, which allows you to view and print student and instructor reports.

- Help button. Click this button to get help on the Main Screen, or on other aspects of TMGSim.

- Exit button. Click this button to exit the program.

Menus, Main Screen. The following options are available on the Main Screen's menu bar:

- File menu. Select this option on the menu bar to see a drop-down menu of other choices (listed below).

    o Print Setup. Select this menu item to select a Windows-configured printer for use when printing a copy of the file. Note, however, that you can setup a printer whenever you click the print button by selecting the relevant options when the printer dialog opens.

    o Exit. Select this menu item to exit the program.

- Help menu. Select this option on the menu bar to see a drop-down menu with several options for obtaining help on the program. See the Getting Help topic for more information on these menu items.

Set Path Window. This window appears when you ask to change one of the file paths used by TMGSim to locate and store the files it uses. The window allows you to set a drive and folder for the path, and to see a list of files in the folder you have selected. This helps you to verify that your selection is correct.

- Drive/Folder List Box. At the top of the box, you will see the current setting for the folder. You can change this value using the following elements of the box:

- Drive. To change the drive on which the folder is located, click the arrow in the box. A drop-down list of available drives will appear. Scroll through to select the desired drive. If you select a floppy drive, it's a good idea to put the floppy in that drive first.

- Folder. To change the folder, scroll through the list of folders on the selected drive. Click on the folder you wish to select.

- List of files. The box at the bottom of the panel will show you the files in the folder currently selected. You can browse this list to make sure you have selected the correct folder.

- OK button. Click this button when you have finished selecting a folder. If you have made a change, TMGSim will ask you if you want the change saved to your setup environment file. If you answer "yes," the change will be saved for the next time you run TMGSim. If you answer "no," the change is only good until you exit TMGSim. The next time you run TMGSim, the folder setting will revert to its prior value.

- Cancel button. Click this button to cancel folder selection and retain the previous setting.

- Help button. Click this button to get help on the Set Path Window or on other aspects of TMGSim.

Create New Setup Screen

The Create New Setup Screen is the first of two screens used to establish a setup environment for *The Marketing Game!*. On this screen, you provide the setup information for the first industry (or click the default values button beside the entry fields to just use the default values). The setup values for the first industry are then used as a "template" that is automatically duplicated for other industries. (Then, on the Setup Values Screen, you can view the setup values for all industries at the same time, and modify any individual values as needed.)

Note that at the Create New Setup Screen you can duplicate all of the setup values for the first industry, or with the radio button selections at the bottom of the screen you can select specific setup values to be duplicated, leaving the other values uninitialized until you go to the Setup Values Screen.

You can also set the file paths required by TMGSim on the Create New Setup Screen.

- **Creating a Setup Values Template**

By entering setup values for Industry A, you create a template of values that can then be duplicated for other industries. This automates and simplifies creation of a setup environment.

- **Number of Industries**

Enter the number of industries (4 firms each) you wish to set up for the game. You must have at least one industry, with a maximum of 26. Note that 26 industries accommodate 104 firms. However, if you want to use TMG with more than 104 firms, simply think in terms of setting up different "economies." That way, the decisions, files, etc. for the different economies are then kept in separate folders.

- **Reset Defaults Button**

Click this button if you wish to revert to default values for the Industry A setup template. Default values are:

Setup Option	Default value
Level	1
Discretionary budget	200,000
Economic index	100
Economies of scale	No
Accelerated life cycle	No

- **Setup Values**

There are five setup values for each industry. They are briefly reviewed below, but discussed in more detail in Chapter 4.

Level. The level (1-3) at which the game will be run for this industry. See the TMG Instructor's Manual for a more complete discussion of the different levels and for ideas about when to use which level. In general, it's often best to start at Level 1 (even if for just a few periods) so that students get accustomed to the competition, etc. However, it can also work fine to start at Level 2 or Level 3.

You can change the game level at any point in the competition. Usually, that means increasing the level (i.e., making the game more challenging) over time. So, for example, if you want to have students move from Level 1 to Level 2 for the third decision period, you should tell students to develop a Level 2 plan (and read Chapter 5 in the text) after you have run period 2 decisions. Then, before you run the period 3 plan files, change the setup for all industries to Level 2.

Different industries can be run at different levels. However, it's usually simplest and best to just have all firms move to a different level at the same time. Another reason for keeping all firms at the same level is that it preserves equal opportunity among firms. They all start with exactly the same circumstance and along the way have the same opportunities for growth.

Discretionary Budget. The discretionary budget is an amount available to be spent in addition to the allocated marketing budget. You decide the dollar amount of discretionary funds you wish to make available to each firm in the industry. Unlike the marketing budget, unused discretionary funds carry forward from one period to the next; thus, allocation of discretionary funds gives firms added flexibility. It also adds a financial dimension to the decisions (i.e., do we invest in marketing spending now or save the money so it will be available later if we need it?). If a firm exceeds its regular budget in a given period, the simulation checks to see if that firm has money left in its discretionary budget. If it does, the extra spending is allowed and it is charged to the discretionary budget. The simulation software keeps track of the total and reports how much discretionary budget is left.

You may want to increase the discretionary budget during the game. An increase in discretionary funds can be helpful to cover extraordinary expenses (for example, development costs for the second product, if you are moving to Level 3). Keep in mind that if you want to increase the discretionary budget, you enter the new total amount--not the change from before. The simulation software keeps track of how much each firm has spent from its discretionary budget. So, if during the game you increase the value of the discretionary, the simulation will update its accounting to reflect the amount of unspent money that remains in the discretionary budget.

Economic Index. A normal economic environment has an economic index of 100. We recommend that you stick with that value, at least the first time you run the game. However, you can alter the Economic Index for one or all industries to boost demand or decrease it. Think of the deviation about the normal index (100) as the percentage change in demand. Thus, an economic index of 110 will create an economic environment that is about 10 percent higher (in a given period) than it would be if it were 100. Similarly, an index of 85 would be about 85 percent of normal demand.

Some instructors like to inject economic changes into the simulation. However, we recommend careful consideration of the pedagogical issues when doing this. For example, you might want to "signal" students that the economy is changing before it actually happens. The game tends to reinforce good decisions with good results, which motivates learning. However, improved decision-making might still produce worse results if the economy is going down hill! So, it's good to balance the pedagogical issues with the "realism" of having to cope with uncertainty when changing the Economic Index.

Economies of Scale. Click the check box to implement economies of scale, or leave it unchecked to stick with the default—which is to not include economies of scale. With introductory students, leaving the Economies of Scale option unchecked keeps the focus more on the marketing plan decisions because it does not introduce a more complex cost structure.

This option has the effect of decreasing the cost of goods sold somewhat over time as the firm's cumulative sales increases. Basically, when economies of scale is checked production costs are reduced by about 3 percent for each additional 100,000 units the firm produces up until about 1 million units in cumulative production, then the incremental cost savings taper off to 1% per 100,000 and above 2,000,000 units costs are level again. The possibility of the firm achieving economies of scale is discussed in Chapter 3 of the student text, and it says that the president will make an announcement if this is something for the marketing managers to consider. If you check this option, you should probably tell students that there are economies of scale in production so that in their financial planning they will know to adjust their cost estimates.

Selecting economies of scale has two basic effects. First, it tends to favor firms that are going after target markets that may be larger but more price sensitive. However, it does not do this to the extreme that it fundamentally alters the options available. Where it has the most effect is in situations where the game is run for a larger number of periods and the instructor wants to simulate the nature of more mature markets where growth has subsided and the balance between unit volume and profit margins involves sensitive trade-offs. Second, introducing economies of scale requires students to pay more attention in creating a pro forma or estimates of costs associated with a plan; the pro forma produced by the TMGPlan software does NOT take economies of scale into consideration.

Accelerated Life Cycle. Click the check box to activate the accelerated product life cycle. It is usually best to leave this option unchecked, especially the first time you use the game.

The Accelerated Life Cycle option should be selected at the beginning of the game and used throughout the competition, or alternatively not be used. Changing this option during the competition is not prohibited by the software, but is not recommended because it can quite significantly alter the decision environment from one period to the next.

However, the Accelerated Life Cycle option provides the instructor flexibility and it may be helpful in different situations. For example, if the instructor wants to emphasize high growth marketing situations it is useful. Similarly, if the instructor wants to start in a high growth environment and continue into a more mature market environment, this option allows this progression in about half the number of decision periods that would otherwise be required. For example, under normal circumstances the market for product 1 moves to maturity after about 10 decisions. With the Accelerated Life Cycle Option, the market moves to maturity after about 5 decision periods—because growth in the early periods is greater.

- **Duplicating the Setup Template for All Industries**

After you have entered setup values for Industry A, you can control the way in which these values are used as a template for other industries. The radio buttons and check boxes in the panel in the middle of the screen control this duplication process. Note that the choices you make here are simply for convenience in filling in initial values for other industries. It does not in any way limit adjustments that can be made at the Setup Values Screen.

"All industries to have all the same setup values" radio button.
Click this radio button if you want each industry to take on the setup values you specified for Industry A. Note that you can select this option, and then modify some setup values on the Setup Values screen. In other words, selecting this option does not permanently force all values to be identical for each industry.

"Values checked below will be the same for all industries" radio button.
Click this radio button if you want to pick and choose among the Industry A setup values that will be duplicated for all industries. You then specify the specific setup values you want duplicated by checking the appropriate check boxes.

- **Selection Buttons, Create New Setup Screen**

The following selection buttons are available on the Create New Setup Screen.

Help button. Click this button to get help on the Create New Setup Screen or other aspects of TMGSim.

Fill in Values button. Click this button after you have entered the desired values for the template and are ready to have the values duplicated for all industries. TMGSim will display the Setup Values Screen, allowing you to customize your setup environment as required.

Cancel button. Click this button to cancel the changes and revert to your prior setup environment. The previous screen will then be displayed.

Exit button. Click this button to exit TMGSim.

Setup Values Screen

This screen is used for two purposes. It is the second of two screens (after the Create New Setup Screen) used to create a new setup environment. In addition, it is used to view or modify an existing setup environment. You may modify setup values as often as you like; in fact, if necessary, each decision period could be run with a different group of setup values.

The screen displays one row per industry (based on the number of industries you specified in the setup environment). For each industry, it displays all game parameters, allowing you to individually adjust them as required.

If you have an existing setup environment and need to change the number of industries, you must create a new setup environment. If you have a large number of industries and need to change a setup value for all industries, it may be easier to create a new setup environment than to modify the value for each industry individually.

- **Selection Buttons, Setup Values Screen**

The following selection buttons are available on the Setup Values Screen.

Save/Go to Main button. Click this button to save the setup environment and return to the Main Screen. *Keep in mind that the setup is **NOT saved automatically**.* Thus, if you modify values on the Setup Values Screen but don't click the Save button the setup file itself is not changed!

Create New Setup button. Click this button to start from scratch, creating a new setup environment. The Create New Setup Screen will be displayed. Select this button also if you want to modify an existing setup file for a new game, say where there are more industries (and, thus, more rows/industries on the Setup Values Screen).

Cancel button. Click this button to discard changes to the setup and return to the Main Screen.

Exit button. Click this button to exit TMGSim.

Simulation Command Center Screen

The Simulation Command Center Screen, as its name suggests, is the "heart" of the simulation software. It allows you to control the running of the marketing simulation for a decision period. Here, you select industries for which the simulation should run (which typically is all of them), specify the decision period to be run (which typically is the same for all industries), select the method to be used in producing reports, and then run the simulation.

In the sections below you will find more information about each of the following topics.
- Industry Selection Panel
- Simulation Period
- TMGSim File Paths
- Selection Buttons
- History Reset Confirmation Window

For an overview, see also the section Quick Reference Guide on Running the Simulation (earlier in this chapter).

- **Industry Selection Panel, Simulation Command Center**

Most of the Simulation Command Center Screen consists of a panel showing the status of all industries configured in your setup environment file. This panel has as many columns as the number of industries specified in your setup file. Each column is labeled with a letter that corresponds to an industry. It is here that you select industries for processing in the simulation, and this panel also provides an overview of the availability of different files used to run the simulation for different industries. Conversely, if a file is missing, the Simulation Command Center helps pinpoint the problem.

Industry check boxes. The top row of the industry selection panel consists of a series of check boxes, where each check box corresponds to one industry configured in your setup environment file. Industry letter codes, starting with A, appear in the row immediately below the check boxes. Clicking on a check box causes a check to be displayed, which means that the corresponding industry is selected for processing by the simulation. If a check already appears in the box, clicking the box clears the check mark and un-selects the industry for processing.

Industry file status displays. The remainder of the column, below the check box and industry letter code, is a color-coded summary of file status information for the associated industry. Each column in the display has the following entries:

Item	Meaning
Letter (A to Z)	Industry letter code
1	Firm 1 plan file status
2	Firm 2 plan file status
3	Firm 3 plan file status
4	Firm 4 plan file status
H	History file(s) status
S	Summary files status
(a number)	Last decision period run

The background color for an item in the list (i.e., type of file) indicates the status of the corresponding file. The color scheme is discussed below. This color-coding is especially helpful because if makes it obvious if you are missing a file (for example, a firm's plan file is not in the folder you have specified). Then you can find the missing file and put it in the folder where it is supposed to be— before its absence becomes a problem! It's important to know that *files are checked and background colors are set when you open the Simulation Command Center.* If other words, when you see in the panel that a file is missing and then do something about it, TMGSim does not automatically recognize that the file is no longer missing. In order to bring the color-coding on the panel up to date, you must first click the Return button (which takes you back to the Main Screen) and then again click the "Run Simulation" button on the Main Screen.

WARNING: The colors described below may be different on your screen if you have customized the color palette for Windows.

Items in the display may be interpreted as follows:
A to Z: The industry letter – a letter from A to Z, depending on the number of industries you specified in the setup file.

1, 2, 3, and 4: Represent the plan files (PLANif.TMG, where "i" is the industry letter and "f" is the firm number) for this industry. TMGSim looks for these files in the Student files folder you specified in your setup environment. Background colors have the following meaning:

- Green: the plan file is present and ready for processing.
- Red: the plan file is missing from the Student files folder. It must be copied there before the simulation can be run for this industry.
- Yellow: the Student files folder is on a removable drive; you will be asked to load the disk containing these files when the simulation is run.

H: Represents the necessary history (HISTORYi.TMG) and history backup (HISTip.BAK) files for this industry. Except when running the simulation in Period 1, the file HISTORYi.TMG (where "i" is the industry letter code) must exist in the Master files folder you specified in your setup environment. If you are attempting to rerun the simulation for a prior period, the file HISTip.BAK (where "p" is the period you are trying to rerun) must also exist in the Master files folder. Background colors have the following meanings:

- Green: the necessary history files are present.
- Red: a required history file is missing from the Master files folder. It must be loaded there before the simulation can be run for this industry.
- Yellow: your Master files folder is on a removable drive; you will be asked to load the disk containing these files when the simulation is run.
- Gray: The decision period you have asked to run is Period 1; thus, history files are not needed.

S: Represents the necessary summary files (SUMMARYi.TMG and INDSUMi.TMG) for this industry. Except when running the simulation in Period 1, these files must be present in the Master files folder you specified in your setup environment. Background colors have the following meanings:

- Green: both files are present.
- Red: at least one of the files is missing from the Master files folder. It must be loaded there before the simulation can be run for this industry.
- Yellow: the Master files folder is on a removable drive; you will be asked to load the disk containing these files when the simulation is run.
- Gray: The decision period you have asked to run is Period 1; thus, summary files are not needed.

N: A digit indicating the last period for which the simulation was run for this industry. A zero indicates either that the simulation has not been run yet, or that the last period run cannot be determined from the available files. If the last period run is displayed on a purple background, the decision period you are asking to run is too far in the future. This is a problem, because it is not possible (and you are not permitted) to "skip" decision periods. For example, if the last period run for Industry A is 4, you cannot skip period 5 and run the simulation for period 6.

- **Simulation Period**

When you enter the Simulation Command Center, TMGSim checks the most recent period for which the simulation has been run for each industry. The Simulation Period box on the screen is set as follows:

- Look at the last period run for *each* industry;
- If the last period run is the same for each industry (which normally it should be), then set the value of Simulation Period to the last period plus 1. This will be the next period that runs assuming that the instructor does not have some special need to "reset" the simulation to rerun an earlier period.
- If the last period run is NOT the same for each industry, the value in the Simulation Period to run is the most frequently observed value for the last period plus 1.

Warning! In the typical case, this method will load into the Simulation Period data entry box the value for the period the instructor is ready to run. However, care is required if the last period run differs from one industry to another, or if you want to rerun a past period for one or more industries. In either of these cases, do NOT select all of the industries to run at the same time. Rather, select only an industry or industries that are to be run for the same period, and set the value of the Simulation Period to the correct number for those specific firms.

If the value in the box is not the one you wish to use, click the up or down arrow button until the box contains the number of the decision period you wish to run.

Rerunning a past period. If you need to rerun the simulation for a past period, click the down arrow button until the box contains the correct decision period number. When you run the simulation, the History Reset Confirmation Window will appear, asking you to confirm that you wish to rerun a past period.

In general, the only reason to rerun a past period is if there has been some sort of instructor error that needs to be corrected. For example, let's assume that the instructor has told students that there will be an increase in the discretionary budget, but then forgets to change it in the setup file before running the decisions. To correct the problem, the instructor would fix the setup program to reflect the new discretionary budget and then rerun the industries at the earlier period. In the same vein, an instructor might rerun an earlier period if there is an error in a plan file. However, as a policy issue most instructors don't rerun earlier periods when it is due to a student error because it is likely to have ripple effects on other firms. Students will be more careful if they know that they live with their decisions, even if they have been careless in making them or entering them into the TMGPlan software.

- **Selection Buttons, Simulation Command Center**

 The following selection buttons are available on the Simulation Command Center Screen:

Select All Industries button. Click this button to automatically select all industries that are ready to run (i.e., with no required files missing) for simulation processing. The check boxes for all ready industries (i.e., those for which there are not known missing files) will be checked.

Deselect All Industries button. Click this button to clear the check boxes for all industries.

Run Selected Industries button. Click this button to run the simulation for all selected (checked) industries for the selected decision period. If the decision period you specified requires that a past period be re-run for one or more industries, the History Reset Confirmation Window will appear, asking you to confirm that you wish to rerun a past period. Note that the actual processing of the files is very fast. If the student and master files are all on a hard drive, processing 26 industries takes less than a minute. As the simulation is run for each industry, the status bar at the bottom of the screen (highlighted in yellow during simulation processing) will be updated to show you the industries that have been processed. When processing is complete, you will receive a confirmation message.

View or Print a Report button. Click this button to activate the File Viewer Screen.

Return button. Click this button to return to the Main Screen.

Exit button. Click this button to exit the program.

- **History Reset Confirmation Window**

This window appears after you activate simulation processing in the Simulation Command Center if the decision period you asked to run has already been run for one or more of the selected industries. You are given four choices:
   1. Reset all remaining industries (i.e., those which have not yet been processed) to the past period
   2. Reset the current industry to the past period
   3. Skip all remaining industries (i.e., those which have not yet been processed)
   4. Skip the current industry

Reset This Industry button. Click this button to reset the current industry to the past period. If other industries must also be reset, you will be prompted again when TMGSim attempts to process these industries.

Reset Remaining Industries button. Click this button to tell TMGSim to reset all industries not yet processed to the past period. By using this button, you can avoid the need to confirm the reset of each industry individually. However, we urge caution in this regard. Once you select this option, the program will reset any effected industries without pausing, even if you later decide that was not your intent!

Skip This Industry button. Click this button to skip processing of the current industry, proceeding to the next industry selected for processing.

Cancel button. Click this button to cancel the remainder of the simulation processing, skipping any selected industries not yet processed.

Help button. Click this button to get help on the History Reset Confirmation Window or on other aspects of TMGSim.

Marketing Plan Decisions Form Screen

- **Industry/Firm/Level Window**

This window is displayed when you click the "Type in Marketing Plans" or "Open/Modify Plan" buttons on the Main Screen. The inputs on this screen are used to select the firm whose plan information will be processed on the Marketing Plan Decisions Screen, and to customize the appearance of that screen for the game level you select.

Industry. Enter the industry letter (A-Z) of the firm whose plan you wish to enter or modify. You must enter a value.

Firm. Enter the firm number (1-4) of the firm whose plan you wish to enter or modify. You must enter a value.

Level. Enter the game level (1-3) at which this plan file should be processed. You must enter a value. If the selected plan was created at a different level than the one indicated, a message will appear on screen.

"OK" button. Click this button when you have entered values for industry, firm, and level. If your inputs are valid, the Marketing Plan Decisions Screen will be displayed.

"Cancel" button. Click this button if you change your mind, and do not wish to enter or modify a plan. You will return to the Main Screen.

- **Creating Marketing Plan Files**

TMGSim is set up to allow you or a helper to easily enter a series of students' marketing plan files, in case your students are submitting written forms with their plan decisions. (When an instructor enters plan decisions, it's usually for more than one firm. So, this works a bit different in the instructor software than it does in the individual student software.)

First, organize the students' written forms in order by firm ID code (i.e., firm A1, then A2, then A3, then A4, then B1, and so on). Then click on "Type in Marketing Plan(s)" on the Main Screen. TMGSim will display the Firm/Industry/Level Window, asking you for the starting industry and firm, and the game level for which the plan should be entered. If you are entering plans for all firms, the starting firm ID would be "A1." Or, if you are just going to enter decisions for one firm, enter its firm ID code.

Next, TMGSim will display a blank decision input form, customized for the marketing game level you just entered. Now, enter the values that you want to use for your marketing decisions. Acceptable ranges of values for most edit boxes are listed on the screen or in the hints displayed in the status bar.

When you are finished entering a firm's plan, click the "Save" button. A window will appear prompting you for a password, used to encrypt the plan file. The file will be saved in the Student files directory you specified on the Main Screen. Unless you save the file, the data you have entered is temporary, and will be lost if you exit the program or return to the Main Screen.

After the file has been saved, TMGSim will automatically display another blank screen, and will increment the firm ID code to the next firm in the sequence (i.e., firm A4 follows A3; firm B1 follows A4). Enter the decision values for this firm and then save the file as before. If you are finished entering marketing plans, click the "Cancel" button to return to the Main Screen. If you need to skip a firm in the sequence because its plan input form is missing, you can modify the Firm and Industry fields that appear on the screen with the other plan values. Note that the student software does NOT have this feature.

- **Modifying an Existing Marketing Plan**

When you click the "Open/modify existing plan" button, a small window will be displayed asking you for the industry and firm whose plan you want to modify, and the marketing game level for which the plan was entered. TMGSim looks in the Student files directory you specified on the Main Screen to find the plan file. You can modify any or all of the values on the screen. You can also click the adjustments button to enter information about a fine or budget adjustment. When you click the "Save" button, a window will appear displaying the file's current password. You can either save the file with a new password or leave it as is. Note: When you open an existing plan file, the software will check to see if it was created at the same level as is specified on the TMGSim Setup and Selection Screen. If it was not, a message box will appear and ask if you want to change the level for the screen to be consistent with the level specified in the file itself. This is convenient if you want to start with a plan that is at one level to create a plan that is at another level. On the other hand, if you get this message unexpectedly give some thought to why the file is at a different level than expected. It is important to select the correct game level—since that level value controls which specific decisions you must provide to complete the marketing plan.

- **Instructor-Only Fields and Selection Buttons, Marketing Plan Decisions Screen**

Industry and Firm. If you are modifying a plan, these fields will be set to the industry letter (A-Z) and the firm number (1-4) for the firm whose plan file you are modifying. These fields (for industry letter and firm number) may not be modified. If you wish to modify a different firm's plan, click the "Cancel" button and again select "Open/Modify a Plan" from the Main Screen.

If you are entering values for a new plan, these fields are initially set to the industry letter code and firm number you specified in the Starting Firm ID Window that was displayed when you clicked the "Type in Marketing Plans" button on the Main Screen. Each time you save a plan, these fields are incremented to point to the next firm in sequence (for example, firm A2 follows firm A1, and firm B1 follows firm A4). If this sequence is not the order in which you wish to enter plan information, you may also modify these fields to reflect the firm whose plan information you are entering.

Adjustments button. Click this button to bring up the Marketing Plan Adjustments Screen, which allows you to assess fines and other charges, and to make changes to a firm's marketing budget.

The Marketing Plan Adjustments Screen allows you to enter special adjustments to a firm's budget or expenses. These adjustments are useful in situations such as making a change to a firm's budget for a period, assessing a fine (for example, failing to submit a decision or submitting it late), charging for special items (for example, extra marketing research reports supplied manually, or consulting services).

The entry fields and buttons on this screen are for the most part straightforward, but for completeness are reviewed below.

- Extra Marketing Research. Enter the dollar amount to be charged to the firm for consulting and additional marketing research. This amount will be reflected in the "Marketing Research" line on the firm's financial summary, and will be charged against the firm's marketing budget.

- Fines. Enter the dollar amount of fines to be assessed against the firm. This amount will be shown in the "Fines" line on the firm's financial summary. Fines are not charged against the firm's marketing budget.

- Budget Change. Enter the dollar amount by which the firm's marketing budget for the period should be increased (positive numbers) or decreased (negative numbers). Note that the *budget change amount is an adjustment applied to the current budget, not a replacement value for the total marketing budget.*

- "OK" button. Click this button after entering desired values. The values will be recorded, and you will return to the Marketing Plan Decisions Screen. *These values, though, will **not** be made permanent until you save the plan file.*

- "Cancel" button. Click this button to discard any values entered and return to the Marketing Plan Decisions Screen.

- "Help" button. Click this button to get help on the Marketing Plan Adjustments Screen, or on other aspects of TMGSim.

File Viewer Screen

The File Viewer Screen can be used to view TMG reports and pro forma files that have previously been saved. In particular, password-protected TMG reports (those with names ending in '.TMG') can be viewed only through the File Viewer Screen. Saved pro forma files and TMG reports which are not password protected (those with names ending in '.TXT' may be viewed either through the File Viewer Screen, or outside of the program, using a text editor or word processor.

When you first enter the screen, a dialog box will appear and it features a drop-down list that allows you to select the report or pro forma file that you want to view. You can press the F1 key while the dialog box is open for more information about how to select a file.

The File Viewer Screen allows you to perform several operations with an open file. You may browse through the file, skip to a specific line number, search for a word or phrase, copy part or all of the file to the Windows clipboard, print the file, or save the file under another name.

- **Opening a File in the File Viewer Screen**

When you click the "Review or Print a File" button on the Setup and Selections Screen, an open dialog box will appear to allow you to select a drive, folder, and file name. This dialog box will also appear if you click the "Open" button on the Viewer screen, or select the File/Open menu item.

Detailed help on using the dialog box can be obtained by clicking on the item for which you want help and pressing the F1 key. Here are some hints:

- The first time you view a file after starting TMG, the open dialog will start at your default directory for TMG files. You can select a different drive or folder by clicking on the box labeled "Look in:", scrolling through the options there, and selecting one. (If a folder has subfolders, they will be displayed in the window; you can double-click one to select it as the current folder).

- When you see the file name you want to use in the window, either double-click on the file name, or single-click the file name and click the "Open" button.
- The "Files of Type" box controls the types of files that will appear in the window. The choices are:
- TMG Encrypted Report File: These are report files that have been password protected. File names are of the form REPORTid.TMG, where "id" is the firm ID code.
- TMG Report File: These are text-formatted report files that have not been password protected. File names are of the form REPORTid.TXT.
- TMG Pro Forma File: These are text-formatted pro forma files. File names are of the form PROFORid.TXT.

- **Saving Text Versions of Password-Protected Reports**

If students wish to create a text-formatted version of the report file which can be read outside TMGPlan, the only way to do so is to open the report file in the viewer, provide the correct password, and then click the Save button or select the File/Save menu option. In both cases, a version of the file will be saved that is not password protected. Students can then read the file with a text editor or word processor.

However, since unencrypted versions of the reports will be placed in the Unencrypted Reports Directory that you (as the instructor) specified in your setup, you do not need to use this feature to obtain unencrypted versions of reports.

Password Entry Window. TMGSim uses password protection and encryption to protect the contents of plan and report files from unauthorized viewing and modification. When you save a plan file, you must supply a password to be used to protect the file. When opening an existing file, students using TMGPlan must supply the same password that was supplied when the file was saved; however, in TMGSim you (the instructor) can open the file without supplying a password.

Whenever you ask to save a plan file (in the Marketing Plan Decisions or Pro Forma Estimates Screens), the Password Entry Window will be displayed. You will be asked to provide a password for the file, and then to re-enter the same password for confirmation. If the two passwords do not match, or if you fail to enter a password in either of the two edit boxes, you will receive an error message.

If you are modifying and re-saving an existing plan file, you may specify a different password from the one you used previously, or you may leave the existing password unchanged.

Using the Password Entry Window. The Password Edit Box(es) allow the password to be up to sixteen characters long. Letters, numbers, and most special characters are permitted. If you are re-saving an existing file, the boxes will display the current password (which you may leave alone, or modify if you wish).

The password is sensitive to differences in upper and lower case characters. In other words, when a student wants to open a file later the password must look exactly as it did when the plan file was entered. A password will not work unless each character is in the case it was in when the password was saved. For example, the 15-character password MyMarketingGame does NOT match variations of the same letters in other cases such as mymarketinggame or myMarketingGame--or anything other than MyMarketingGame.

Selection Buttons. The following selection buttons are available on the Password Entry Window.

- OK button. Click this button when you have finished entering the password and are ready to proceed.

- Cancel button. Click this button to skip providing a password. In this case, the file will not be saved.

- Help button. Click this button to get help on using the Password Entry Window, or other help in using the program.

CORRECTING MISTAKES AFTER THE GAME HAS BEEN RUN

Unfortunately, mistakes do sometimes occur – and if they do they need to be corrected. For example, if students are handing in their decisions forms and you (or an assistant) are entering these decisions into the computer, you may inadvertently mistype an entry – say, in decision period 2 firm A3 wrote down a production quantity of 30,000, but it was entered as 3,000. After the game is run, you notice this firm's low unit sales, review their decision form, and recognize the input error. Fortunately, with *The Marketing Game!* it is quite simple to correct such errors. Two steps are needed:

1. From the TMGSim Main Screen click the Modify a Plan button, correct the Plan file, and save it to the student folder. Then, select the Run Simulation button, which takes you to the Command Center Screen. Click the check box for the firm for which you want to rerun a previous period.

2. Set the Period to Run box back to the number for the period that was run with the error. Then simply click the Run Selected Industries button. The game will recognize that this decision period has already been run, and issue a warning. To continue, you must confirm that you do want to rerun this period. Once confirmed, the simulation will rerun that period (for the specified industry) using the corrected input data file.

The best way to avoid input errors is to carefully check the data as it is entered. That is, review what you have entered on the screen *before* selecting the Save button. However, if an input is entered incorrectly and the simulation run, follow the two steps above to correct the input and rerun the decision period. Normally, you should never need to "go back" further than the most recently run period. Nevertheless, it is possible to rerun any previous period – however, once you "go back" in time, the only way to go forward again is one period at a time. For example, if you go back to period 4, then the game will take that as the current period, and move forward to year 5 next. Although it is possible to "go back" in time, it is *not* possible to jump forward. If you try to jump forward, the simulation will advise you that it cannot be done.

TROUBLESHOOTING PRINTER PROBLEMS

If no default printer is configured on the computer when the TMG programs start, the print features of the program are disabled. To enable the printer features, you must exit the program, install a Windows printer, and then restart the program. See the general Windows help file for information about how to install and configure a default printer.

When the print dialog opens you can set the properties of the default printer or select another printer (if there is another printer installed on the computer). If you have a printer problem and there is more than one printer installed on the computer, first switch your printer selection away from the one causing the problem. Then, test your new printer selection to determine if it is operating correctly.

If a printer is installed on the computer and you have trouble printing from a TMG program, print a test page from a program that you regularly use with the printer (for example, a word processing program) and confirm that the printer is working. Ideally, your test should use a graphics page rather than a standard text page. One easy way to do this to insert or paste clip art on the page before printing it. If you have a problem printing a standard graphic from a program that otherwise has been working with the printer, it is likely that the properties of the printer are not set correctly for graphics. In that case, the best bet is to check the help file or manual that came with the printer. However, a few general suggestions are provided below.

The screen forms are printed as graphics images. A form is a relatively large and complicated graphic, so it may take quite a bit of memory to print it. If the printer resolution is set too high and it doesn't have enough RAM to render the entire page, you may get garbled or missing output, depending on the printer and/or driver. One way to check if this is the problem is to lower the printer's resolution through its properties and then try again to print the form.

In addition, if the page comes out blank when you print a form, or if the form prints in an incomplete way, first close all other Windows programs that are open before reclicking the Print Form button.

Some printers require that the graphics properties be set in a precise way before they will print a large graphics file such as the one that is involved in printing the configuration file form. For example, several newer models in the Hewlett Packard (HP) LaserJet printer series need to be setup for LaserJet 3 compatibility to print the form properly. To get to this option (when the printer dialog opens): first select the Setup button and then the Properties button for the printer that is having problems.

You may also need to check the page protect option in the printer driver properties and/or set the DPI (dots per inch) property to 300 or a lower value. There have been reports of problems with the HP LaserJet 4 and LaserJet 5 model printers. With these printers in particular you should make sure that you are using the current driver from HP's website (www.hp.com). However, regardless of which model printer you are using, checking for an updated driver is probably a sensible step.

INTRODUCTION TO THE TMGFTP PROGRAM

What Does the TMGftp Program Do?

The Marketing Game! TMGftp program makes it easy for a student to use a Windows computer to submit Plan files to the instructor and/or retrieve encrypted Report files over the Internet or a school's network/intranet. TMGftp uses the Internet's TCP/IP and FTP (file transfer protocol) communication tools. It simplifies the process of uploading files to or downloading files from a remote "host" computer—an FTP server. Most schools have an FTP server that is setup to provide this host computer capability.

Of course, the TMGftp program requires that the computer used by the student have Internet access (perhaps via dial-up networking and a modem) or a networked connection to the FTP server. The program may be setup on an individual student's computer or in a campus computer lab. Computers in a computer lab are often on a network, and the network often has direct access to the FTP server.

The TMGftp default configuration works "as is" for a standard FTP setup, and most schools fall into that category. However, the hidden power of the TMGftp program is that it will automatically load configuration files that adapt the program to a very wide set of circumstances. For example, a configuration file makes it possible for the student to start the program, enter Industry and Firm identification information, and then with two button clicks connect to the FTP host computer and upload a Plan file. It's very simple, fast and convenient.

- **TMGftp Provides a Verification Number for Uploads and Downloads**

When a student uses the TMGftp program to upload a Plan file, after a successful upload a message dialog appears and it provides the student with a verification number that the file was uploaded. The program's session report also documents the verification number and "time stamp" for exactly when the file transfer took place. An instructor can ask students to print the report or save it as a file and keep this information until after decision files have been run so that there is an "audit trail" that a file was actually uploaded. Usually this is not necessary, but if there is ever a question about a Plan file having been submitted on time the verification number may be useful.

The help file does not explain how to interpret the verification number because students have access to the help file. However, **there is a direct and simple relationship between the verification number and the time and date when the file was uploaded**. Specifically, the verification number is equal to the sum of the year, number for the month, number of the day in the month, and hour the file was uploaded. So, for example, if the verification report says that the file was successfully transferred on 4/14/01 at 12:54:33pm, the verification number would be 2001+4+14+12 = 2031. This is perhaps a simplistic "code", but on the other hand with nothing more than a little mental instructor can figure out from the confirmation number if the file was actually submitted when a student says it was submitted (and if it was by the deadline). The verification number provides no other role, so an instructor can ignore the verification numbers (and tell students to ignore them) if he or she so pleases.

- **There Are Limitations**

Although the TMGftp program is a very powerful and flexible program, some schools have networking standards or security restrictions that prohibit use of this sort of program. For example, sometimes a network administrator will setup a "firewall" on a FTP server to only allow *certain types of files* to be uploaded or downloaded. If these rules do not allow transfers of files with the *.TMG filename extension, for example, TMGftp will not work on that system. While it's usually easy to change the rules programmed for the firewall, a network administrator may not be willing to do that.

It is also difficult to create a file transfer program that is "bullet proof" across all FTP situations. For example, some host computers do not accept FTP instructions to change directories. Constraints such as these may create some limits on use of this program. However, the program makes it easy to interactively specify the details of an FTP connection, test them to make sure that everything works well, save the configuration file, and then give it to students.

A final issue concerns error checking by the program. The program has a variety of built-in diagnostics and error-checking routines that produce a message dialog box when a problem is detected. However, there are some types of errors that can't be detected by the program. For example, the program has no way to know in advance if the name of an upload directory is correct or even exists on the host computer; further, with some FTP servers the messages provided when there is a problem are not very complete or clear. So, in such a situation diagnostics from the TMGftp program may not be as complete as would be desired. Of course, this also means that it is important for the user to be careful when entering information in fields.

- **System Requirements**

This program requires a computer that runs Windows 95, 98, Me, 2000, or NT. The computer must have a way to access the Internet (for example, a dial-up networking connection to an Internet service provider) or a network connection to the FTP host computer that will be used for file transfers. In general, if the computer can use a web browser like Internet Explorer to view websites on the World Wide Web or if it can get and send email it has an Internet connection. **TMGftp also requires a 32-bit TCP/IP stack, WSOCK32.DLL, that is normally included with versions of Windows after Windows 95.** However, it may not have been installed when Windows was installed on the computer. In that case, TMGftp won't work until it is installed.

Custom Configuration Files, with Security Features

TMGftp uses information in a configuration file to automate some or all of what needs to be done to connect to a (remote) FTP host computer and upload a Plan file, download a Report file, or both. It also has options to specify what capabilities of the program will work for a particular FTP server. Depending on what features are activated, it may also alter the appearance of the screen that the user sees when the program is running.

- **Configuration File Is Encrypted**

First, this is not a standard text file and it cannot be viewed with any editor or word processing program. Second, it is in an encrypted format. Therefore, students can't view the contents of the file when it is loaded to configure the TMGftp program.

- **Automatic Loading of a Configuration File**

When the TMGftp program starts, it looks for an automatic configuration file named TMGftp1.CFG. The program looks for this file only in the directory on the user's computer where the program file (TMGftp.EXE) is itself stored. If the file is found and it is verified to be in the correct format, it is loaded. The values in the file are then used to set up the appearance/features of the user screen and the specifications to be used for an FTP connection to a host computer.

- **When No Automatic Configuration File Is Found**

If the automatic configuration file is not found in the same directory as the program, the program uses a default configuration. This default configuration sets the FTP port value to 21, and provides edit fields for the user to specify other needed information such as the user log-on name and password, name of the FTP host computer, and names for the upload and download directories on the host computer.

- **Folder for Automatic Configuration File**

Note that when the TMGftp software is initially installed there is NO automatic configuration file. If the instructor provides students with an automatic configuration file, it can be copied (with the Windows Explorer program or some other standard file manager) to the program directly so that it will be loaded automatically when the program starts. In the standard installation, this program resides on the primary hard drive in a subdirectory of the Windows Program File directory with the specific folder name
C:\Program Files\TMG\TMGftp\

- **Browse Folders and Load a Configuration File**

Alternatively, a user can click the Load Configuration File button to browse drives and folders on the local computer to select a specific configuration file that has been provided by the instructor.

Step-by-Step Overview: Student Uploading and Downloading

The appearance of the TMGftp screen depends on (1) the configuration file that is used and also (2) what features are activated at a given point in the FTP process. Basically, however, the whole process is simple and typically takes less than a minute.

1. Connect to the Internet (if the computer isn't already online). For example, this may mean activating a dial-up networking connection to an Internet service provider.
2. Click on Start>Programs>TMG>TMGftp. It may take a few seconds before a flash screen appears and then the program loads.
3. The initial screen will appear almost empty, except for edit boxes for the TMG industry letter and firm number. Fill in these and then click the Ok button beside them. This is a required first step and other items will not appear on the screen until this is done.
4. If the "FTP Remote Log-on Specification for Upload or Download" panel is visible, fill in the edit fields as per instructions from your instructor.

5. Check the Internet Connection Status Panel and indicator light at the bottom of the screen to confirm your Internet connection. If the program can detect an online connection to the Internet/Intranet, the light will be green; otherwise, it will be red. If you believe you are connected to the Internet but the indicator light is not green, you may continue to the next step to determine if a connection can be established.
6. Click the "Connect to FTP host computer" button. It may take a few seconds to establish the connection.
7. When a connection is established, the indicator light next to the button turns green. If no connection can be established (or if a connection is lost because of network problems), it is red.
8. When a connection is established, the Download button, Upload button, or both will appear. Click the desired button, and when the file dialog opens select the directory on your local computer from which the PLANid.TMG file will be uploaded or to which the REPORTid.TMG file will be downloaded.
9. Click the Ok button when the file transfer confirmation message appears.
10. Check the Session Report window to confirm that the transfer was completed successfully, and print the report or save it as a text file.
11. That's it. It takes longer to read about the nine steps above than to do them. Don't worry about doing something in the wrong sequence because the program is structured to prevent you from doing that.

OVERVIEW: TMGFTP CONFIGURATION FILE CREATOR

The TMGftp program makes it easy for the instructor to create custom configuration files unique to a particular set of FTP specifications or instructor preferences.

TMGftp creates and saves configuration files using advanced 128-bit encryption technology and a configuration file password. Thus, if a configuration file includes proprietary information (for example, includes a network user log-on name and password), the information is secure. It cannot be viewed by anyone who isn't authorized to view it.

Why Create and Use a Configuration File?

- **Think about the Teaching/Learning Model, not Technology**

The basic reason to create a configuration file (and have your students use the TMGftp program) is that it will make it even faster to run *The Marketing Game!* in your course. It will save you time. The more students you have, the more time you will save.

It will also make it easier for your students and save them time. From a pedagogical standpoint, it also makes it easy for you to provide students with very fast feedback. In fact, feedback can be almost instantaneous. When they've submitted decisions you're minutes away from having feedback ready for them, and they can get the feedback at their convenience.

The traditional model in education has assumed that course assignments are completed by students (individually or in groups), but that it then falls on the instructor to gather their work, evaluate it, and then distribute it back to them. *The Marketing Game!* can work that way if you wish. But this new edition enables a powerful new model. The instructor doesn't gather, the students submit. The instructor doesn't have the main responsibility for individual evaluation, the software does. The instructor also doesn't distribute individual feedback, the students retrieve it. This may sound like semantics at first, but in practice it is a very different approach and a very effective one. Let's think through it in more detail.

When students complete their assignments (i.e., analysis and development of marketing plans), they individually take responsibility to submit their work (with the TMGftp program). At that point, all of the individual work is organized, together, and ready to be evaluated. Then, the instructor runs the TMG simulation software. It is designed to do the primary evaluation. Moreover, it does that evaluation in just a few minutes, even if there are a very large number of students. After all, their work is already organized and together. The simulation also produces individual feedback, in the form of digital reports. All of the reports are also together in the same place. The instructor simply copies them all at once to a place where individual students can retrieve their own feedback. They retrieve them easily and in about a minute, with a few clicks of buttons on the TMGftp program screen. Thus, once the deadline passes for students to submit their Plans, feedback is available to them in 15 minutes or less.

Does this mean that the instructor doesn't play a role? Of course not. But it does mean that the instructor saves time by not having to deal with the mechanics of "the old model." The instructor can use that time for value-added teaching, either on other aspects of the course or perhaps in providing more evaluation and feedback and diagnosis on student progress (although TMG also helps here by providing diagnostic indices for the instructor's use).

- **Some of the Other Benefits**

We've been talking in the abstract, but let's switch gears and talk about some of the specific benefits. And the benefits of creating a configuration file and using it with the TMGftp program are really just the flip side of some of the obstacles that you might run into if you try to use state-of-the-art technology.

- **Confirm How Simple It Is for Students**

First, let's look at things from the student side. If you want to use technology to have students submit and retrieve files, it really needs to be straightforward, fast, and easy. By easy we mean it also has to be "bullet-proof"...so students don't make mistakes and the instructor isn't left trying to unravel the problems. When TMGftp is used with a configuration file there is almost nothing that requires time or effort on the part of the student. It's easier than checking email and doesn't require the front-end investment of learning email software.

Specifically, the configuration file handles all of the details of the technology, and the software is set up so that it takes the student through the process. You can see this for yourself in the TMGftp tutorial, which is a demo of the upload and download process. But, here's an overview of what's typical. When the student clicks on the program icon the program starts and automatically loads the configuration file. The opening screen is empty except for two edit fields, and all the student has to do is enter his or her TMG industry letter and firm number. When those are correctly entered, a Connect to the FTP Host Computer button appears on the screen. The student clicks the button and an indicator light turns green to show that the FTP connection is established. At the same time the Upload and Download buttons are activated on the screen. The student selects the one that's relevant. A standard Windows dialog opens and the student clicks on the relevant folder and file (only the correct type of files are shown, so there's no getting the wrong type of file). And then a message appears that the file transfer has taken place. Before the student exits the program he or she clicks the Print Session Report button to get a copy of the session report. It includes a verification number (that the file was uploaded) and also the exact time it was saved on the host computer. There's no question about whether the file was delivered, or whether the deadline for submitting a decision was met.

It takes longer to read the above paragraph than it takes the student to do the whole process. What's more, if the student has a personal computer with Internet access (and most do), he can upload files or download files at any time. Students who are spread out (even in different parts of the world, in distributed educational settings) can do it with equal ease. If a student doesn't have a personal computer, almost every school has a computer lab and increasingly there are computers with Internet access in libraries, dorms, cafeterias, and everywhere else. Unlike most Windows software, the TMGftp program can run from a floppy disk, so the student can run it on just about any computer without having to bother with installing it.

- **It Is Very Easy for the Instructor**

It is very easy for the instructor to create a configuration file. This warrants some discussion because at first blush it might appear that it is complicated. However, consider the analogy of using a word-processing program. If you just want to type a few lines and save a file, there's not much to learn to use the program.

On the other hand, word processors offer hundreds of features that someone somewhere might want to use. If you want to know about and use all of them, it's a lot more complicated. The TMGftp configuration file creator only does one thing. Usually it's a very simple thing and a few instructions take care of it. On the other hand, it has a lot more flexibility and options for those people who want them (say, because they're at a school that has made things complicated). For the instructors who don't know about this stuff (and probably don't want to!) and for those who do know about it but are at schools where it's hard to get help, there's an even easier solution.

You can use the McGraw-Hill FTP server to host *The Marketing Game!* uploads and downloads for your course. All you have to do is apply for an account when you adopt *The Marketing Game!* McGraw-Hill will send you the account information by email. The help file shows you exactly what to do with the account information to create your own TMGftp configuration file in about 5 minutes. Because you'll be using a "standard" computer that we've already tested and had experience with, there's absolutely nothing to it. We provide a configuration file template for that server. You load it in the configuration file creator, enter a few information items (like the title for your course, the account number) and that's it. We also provide a standard website template at that site if you want to use it. So you get a high tech, convenient package without the hassles and with all of the benefits.

- **There Are Computer System Security Benefits**

There are a number of computer system security benefits of the TMGftp program. Often instructors don't need to concern themselves with these matters. On the other hand, a school's network staff does. And their job may require that a number of restrictions be placed on how the network can be used. That might limit an instructor's access, or make it complicated. However, because the TMGftp program anticipates and addresses most of the site-specific issues that might arise, it makes it possible to live with the security restrictions and still accomplish the objectives of the course.

- **It Helps Protect against Viruses**

In a university setting, there are lots of ways that computer viruses can be spread. Almost any virus can be an inconvenience, but many of them are really destructive. However, when the TMGftp program is used with a configuration file these risks are reduced or eliminated. The TMG files are virus resistant. Since the TMGftp program will only transfer TMG files, other files that might host a virus or hidden virus files on someone's floppy disk won't get near the host server or the instructor's computer.

- **Eliminate File Handling**

When students use the TMGftp program to upload Plans, all of the student Plan files are placed together in the same computer folder. That makes it very fast and easy to process them all at once ... without handling floppy disks. In the same vein, all that needs to be done to distribute the encrypted reports is to copy them to the host computer's download directory.

ACCESS TO THE TMGFTP CONFIGURATION CREATOR

To use the TMGftp Configuration Creator, start the program and then enter an industry letter and firm number (say, for example A and 1) and then click the Ok button. Next, click the FTP item on the menu bar. Then, on the drop down menu list that appears, click Create Custom Configuration. The Instructor Access Password Screen will open.

Instructor Access Password Screen

The correct Instructor Access Password must be entered to gain entry to the section of the TMGftp program that is used by instructors to create configuration files. The Instructor Access Password is: IAMTHEINSTRUCTOR

It should be entered exactly this way in the access keyword entry field. Note that the password is the easy-to-remember phrase I AM THE INSTRUCTOR but without the spaces between the words.

[Note: TMGftp also uses another type of password, the Configuration File Password. When a configuration file is created and saved, it can be protected with a configuration file password. A password-protected configuration file can't be viewed except by a person who has that specific password, even if the person is an instructor and has the Instructor Access Password].

- **Access Password Entry Field**

Enter the Instructor Access Password given above and then click the Ok button.
  - If the Ok button is clicked and the correct Access Password has been entered, the Configuration File Creator Screen opens.
  - If a configuration file is loaded in the main section of the program and it is not encrypted with its own unique password, the values from the configuration file will be displayed on the screen.
  - If the file is password protected, a Configuration File Password Screen will also open. If the configuration file password is correctly entered the values from the configuration will be displayed on the screen.
  - If the password is not known and the user clicks the Cancel button, the values of a default configuration will appear on the screen.

- If the Ok button is clicked and the Access Password is not correct, a message dialog opens and allows the user to try again. However, for security reasons, the number of tries is limited. After several incorrect tries the program will display a message and then terminate.

- **Help Button (Access Password Screen)**

The Help button on this screen simply displays the section of the help file related to creating a configuration file.

- **Cancel Button (Access Password Screen)**

If the user presses the Cancel button while the Instructor Access Password Screen is open, access to the configuration file creator section of TMGftp is cancelled and the Main Screen reopens. This occurs regardless of whether the correct Access Password has been entered in the entry field.

WHERE TO START IN CREATING A CONFIGURATION FILE

Introduction

Even if you don't know what FTP services your school offers, most schools do have FTP services and if you don't already have access it's usually easy to get "rights" (that is, an account). The best way to start is to read the section *A Simple Step-by-Step Process for Creating a Configuration File*. You will probably have to make a phone call or two to find out what you need to know, but in most cases there's not much to it.

- **Factors to Consider in Deciding to Use FTP**

There are several factors to consider. However, most of them relate to the type of computer network access and technical support that is available to you. Having your computer hooked to a school network can make it more convenient to copy and paste groups of files between your computer and the server. Usually this is simply a matter of using the familiar Windows Explorer file manager. If your school is networked and/or has Internet access, there's probably a help desk or someone who can quickly answer any questions you might have about setting up a configuration file. If you don't have a network at school, or if it's difficult to get information about how to do anything, it might be fastest and easiest to just distribute files from a computer in a computer lab or one of the other approaches discussed in Chapter 4.

Most faculty don't know much about FTP. But if you're one of those that do, there's another way to start. Just take a look at the Configuration File Creator Screen and see if you already know the information that it collects, or where best to get it (for example, your local computer lab help desk). If it looks straightforward to you, it will be. Just give it a try. You can get online help while you're filling out the form. And if you have any questions just refer back to the next section (remember, these materials are also in the help file for the TMGftp program).

A Simple Step-by-Step Process for Creating a Configuration File

Below is a set of steps you can follow to create a custom configuration file that is specific to your school's network system.

1. Make a copy of the Configuration File Creator Form on the next page. This is just a screen image from TMGftp (you can also print it by selecting the Print Form button at TMGftp Configuration File Creator Screen).
2. Review and/or copy the next section in this manual, which includes a "script" with what to ask of a computer/IT support person.
3. If your school has a computer help desk, computer lab, or standard approach for getting information about computer matters, contact them. If you don't know what support you have at your school, check in the school directory to see if there is a general number for a computer, network, or information technology office. Often this information is available on the web if a school has a detailed website.
4. Use the script to talk through what you want to do with the person you contact. If you school has a standard FTP arrangement, you'll be able to get the information to fill in the form over the phone in a few minutes.
5. If your school has a complicated situation, it might be efficient to send or fax the form to the support person or arrange a meeting.
6. Start the TMGftp program, enter any industry code and firm number, and then click the FTP menu bar, and then click the Create Configuration selection in the drop-down menu. After entering the Instructor Access Password:

IAMTHEINSTRUCTOR

you'll be at the Configuration File Creator Screen. (Note that this is the easy to remember phrase "I AM THE INSTRUCTOR" but without the spaces between the words).

7. Type in the information you've been given, double-check it for possible typos, and then save it. Print a copy of the completed form for your records.
8. Click the Apply/Check Config button and you should be ready to connect to the FTP server. For more detail see the next section on *Testing a Configuration File*.
9. After the file is prepared, distribute it to students in your class using one of the methods suggested in the section below.

- **TMGftp Configuration Creator Form**

The Marketing Game! -- TMGftp Configuration File Creator

Descriptive label for this configuration file

1 Number to identify this custom configuration file

Name of person creating configuration

Upload/download capabilities you want user to have

○ Both upload and download   ○ Only upload a plan   ○ Only download a report

Config file password (optional)

If you assign a password, you'll need to know it to view the configuration again!

FTP log-on specs to be based on student input (edit field) on main screen
□ 1. User log-on name   □ 3. FTP host name   □ 5. FTP upload directory
□ 2. User log-on password   □ 4. FTP port number   □ 6. FTP download directory

The Marketing Game!
by Mason and Perreault

FTP logon specifications to be based on configuration file (leave blank if checked above)
User name (log-on id)   User log-on password

FTP host computer name or IP address

Name of upload directory on host computer

Name of download directory on host computer

0 Port with which to connect   0   Response timeout (in milliseconds) [Note: 0 = never]

Auto_detect ▼   Auto detect vendor (of remote host) or select from list   False ▼ Passive FTP connection type

Firewall specifications for host ftp site to be used for all logins

Firewall method   Authenticate   Firewall user id
User ▼   ○ Yes
                  ● No   Firewall user password

Proxy server specifications to be used by all logins
Name or IP address of proxy server if one is used (blank otherwise)

0 Proxy port with which to connect

Enter value for any fields needed to logon to the FTP host (that won't be entered by students per check boxes above)

Testing a Configuration File

Testing a configuration file really just means using the TMGftp program, after creating and/or loading a configuration file. However, the idea is to be certain that the specs in the configuration file work for your host server and that it automates the uploading and downloading process.

- **Start by Saving the Test Version of the Configuration File**

If you are preparing to test a newly created configuration, make certain that you have first saved the configuration file from the Configuration File Creator Screen. You do that by selecting the Save Config button. One reason for doing this is that it does some preliminary checking/testing of the specs in the configuration. If there is some obvious problem a message box appears. Read the message and follow up as necessary. Another reason for starting with a saved file is that it will be a starting point if you have to make any modifications. The program protects against as many different types of errors as possible, but a configuration value that is really off base might cause the program to terminate when you connect to an FTP server (usually with a diagnostic message). If that occurs, you can start the program again, reopen the "draft" configuration file, and modify it before testing it again.

Testing the program involves confirming that it connects to the FTP server, and that it can upload, download, or both (depending on what options have been selected for the configuration file). Thus, you want to be prepared to upload and/or download the relevant file.

1. Create a sample Plan file using the instructions in the student software. Or, simply copy one from the folder named Samples where the instructor software was installed. To test a download, you first need to copy an encrypted TMG Report file to the download directory on the server. Be certain that the industry letter and firm number identification is the same for both files. For example, if you are testing a Plan file for Firm A1 (PlanA1.TMG), the Report file should be for the same firm (ReportA1.TMG). Note that *the TMGftp program is designed to download encrypted Report files*, not text versions of the Report files. This is a security precaution to prevent someone from getting access to a file that is not his or hers.
2. Next, load the configuration file from the main screen of the program, or if you have been creating it at the Configuration File Creator Screen click the Apply/Check Config button.
3. At the main screen, enter the industry letter and firm number that corresponds to the Plan file and/or Report file you are testing.
4. If you have specified via the configuration file options that edit boxes are to appear on the main screen (for example, for a user name and/or password), fill in the edit boxes with information for an active account.

5. Click the Connect to FTP Host Computer button. If the indicator light turns green, the connection is good. If it does not turn green, check the FTP Session report for diagnostic information and/or pay close attention to error message dialogs that may appear.

6. If a connection could not be established, click the Return to Create button, make the suggested changes in the configuration form, save it again, and then repeat the apply/check process.

7. After you have a good FTP connection (i.e., the indicator light is green), try the Upload and/or Download buttons. A confirmation dialog will appear to confirm that a file has been properly transferred. There will also be information in the session report, including the verification number and time stamp.

8. If the confirmation dialog does not appear, pay attention to any error message that does appear and check the session report for diagnostic information. Revise the configuration file to correct the problem identified, and try again.

9. When you have completed a successful connection to an FTP server, and uploaded/downloaded a configuration file, you're ready to distribute the configuration file to your students.

Distributing a Configuration File to Students

After a configuration file is created and tested, you'll want to make it available to students. There are a variety of simple ways to do this. Below is a list of ideas. You can also check with others at your school who use computer materials in their courses and see if they have come up with an approach that's particularly well suited to your situation and students.

- If your school has a computer lab, put the configuration file on a computer in the lab (or on a network drive) and have students copy the file to their own floppy. In fact, the program can be run from a floppy, too.

- If you use email to send your students messages, and especially if you already have an established email distribution list, just attach the file to an email and send it to students that way. The configuration file is a very small file (smaller than most standard email messages) and can be sent as an email attachment very easily.

- One simple approach is to copy the configuration file to a floppy disk and leave it at a computer lab, reserve desk in a library, secretary's desk, or some similar place where students can check it out and copy it.

- If you are using a website for your course, put the configuration file on the website for download. The website template that we provide for *The Marketing Game!* already has a link set up to download the file; all you need to do is copy the configuration file into the web folder along with the web materials. For more info, see the Instructor's Manual section of the TMG website.

- Have students bring a floppy to class (with a name label) and then ask a secretary, helper, or student from the class to copy the file onto the disks.

Sometimes computer lab monitors are not very busy and will do this if they are given a little lead time.

Asking for Help from IT Support Staff

Here's some advice about asking for help, including a "script" you can read over the telephone that concisely explains what you want to do and what you need to find out.

The language of networks can be complicated, but if your department/school/college/university has a network it probably has an FTP server and there is probably someone who provides user support related to it. It's probably the person who assigns user accounts on the computer system. So, whether you call a help desk or ask a general computer support person (or just look in the phone directory listing) the first step is to get to a person who can help you. So, start with a brief explanation of what you want and to whom you want to talk. The "script" below may help.

> "I am teaching a course that involves a computer simulation and I want to have students submit the very small files that are required to a folder on the network, probably by using FTP client software that comes with the simulation. Can you answer a few questions for me about network folders and FTP here, or if not can you tell me who provides user network support and accounts?"

If that draws a blank, ask for the name of the network administrator or the person in charge. When you're talking to the right person, the script below should be useful:

> "I want to be able to upload and download some small files from a PC to a folder on a network or preferably an FTP host server. [I do not know a lot about FTP, but] the simulation I want to use in my course comes with software that is easy to set up for different FTP systems. Ideally, I'd like to have a password-protected directory/folder with two subdirectories, one for uploads and one for downloads. I'd like to have read and write privileges in that directory. If it is not possible to get my own private folder or directory, a directory where there is public access would be okay. (This often means that a user can upload or download a file by using the username 'Anonymous' and the user's email address as the password; thus, it is sometimes called an anonymous FTP directory rather than public. Because the configuration file is encrypted, students will not know where the files are stored, even if it is a "public" folder).

If the computer support person says that there is an FTP server and that you can access it, ask:

"Could you please tell me what I should use as a username and password to access the server... (and if it takes time for one to be assigned, how long)?"

"I'll also need the IP address or name of the FTP host computer, and the name of the upload and download directory. (If it doesn't matter, then ask that a directory named uploads and one called downloads be created; if there are not separate folders available that is okay. Uploads and downloads can go to the same directory.)"

"Could you please tell me if the Port for FTP services on the server is Port 21? If not, what is it?"

In the majority of cases that's all the information you need. You just fill that information in at the Configuration File Creator Screen, save it as a password-protected configuration file, and test it.

However, before hanging up or leaving it's best to ask:
"Is there anything special I need to know, such as information about use of a proxy server or firewall restrictions?"

If the answer is yes, ask the support person if he or she would be willing to just look at the Config File Form (there's a copy in the Instructor's Manual, or you can print a copy from the software) and help you fill it out, or alternatively just read the information on the form and ask the support person to help you answer the questions.

If a computer support person wants more information, everything they need should be in this help file and/or in this Instructor's Manual. There is also technical information that may be useful. Keep in mind that the help file can be sent as an email attachment, so a support person can quickly look through it even without working with the actual software.

One final note in closing: what you are asking for is all standard stuff at most schools. Some schools don't have it, but most do. The issue is that there are people who use these facilities all of the time. Those who don't use these facilities are unaware they even exist (because they've never had any contact with them). If your school has these facilities and can provide a little help in getting started, you'll find this a very convenient way to use *The Marketing Game!*, and you may also see possibilities and benefits for other aspects of your class as well.

Technical Details for People Who Want to Know Them

This section provides some technical information for those who want to know more. That may include some instructors, but it may also include computer support people who have concerns idiosyncratic to the local computer system.

- **Issues Related to Computer System Security**

The TMGftp program was developed with security in mind. Every aspect of the information related to the FTP connection and configuration used by TMGftp can be maintained as completely confidential. The configuration file has options to setup the user screen so that the log-on user name, password, FTP server IP address, port, and upload and download directories are not known to the user. The configuration file is encrypted and password protected; if necessary, password access to view FTP configuration values can be limited only to network staff.

If the network system is set up for individual students to have their own log-on user names and passwords and read/write privileges, they can be used with TMGftp. The configuration file has options to enable user input fields for these log-on parameters. On the other hand, it is sufficient and perfectly acceptable for the system to operate based on only one user log-on name and password. The program not only makes this information secure but also very strictly limits what FTP functions the user can activate. Beyond connecting, the program only allows the user to upload, download, and abort file transfers. It does not give the user a means to activate any other functions. For example, the user cannot list files in a directory, manually change directories, add or delete directories. Even the connect, upload, download, and abort functions are limited.

The program uses the configuration file to connect to the FTP server. It can upload one type of file and download one type of file. It cannot be configured to upload or download other files. Further, properties of the files selected for upload or download are checked to confirm that they are not something different than they are supposed to be. A file selected to be uploaded is saved on the server with the same name. The program uploads with an upload unique method, so if a file with that name already exists on the server in the upload directory, the new file will be renamed (if the server has enabled the upload unique method; if it has not, the existing file will be overwritten). As discussed in more detail below, the files are small and resistant to viruses.

- **Storage Requirements and Server Load Are Minimal**

The files that the TMGftp program will upload or download are small. They will not create a load on the server (or the student machine). In fact, a Plan file is only about 1k. A Report file usually takes about 8k, and at a max it can be about 16k. Thus, even if the competition in the game involved a large number of industries, the total space required for Plans and Reports would be less than a megabyte. In a typical situation it would be much less than that. For example, a class with 64 students would involve a maximum of 16 industries if each student managed his or her own firm. In that situation all of the Plan files would take about 64k. If students worked in teams of four students per firm, there would be only four industries and 16 Plan files. (Another advantage of the small file size is that students connected to the server via a dial-up connection get very fast downloads and uploads).

- **File Structure and Viruses**

The Plan files are binary files with a packed record structure. These files are not hospitable to viruses. The Report files are encrypted text files. They do not include any macros or provide other handles to which a virus can attach.

- **Consistent Naming Conventions**

The file selection dialog that is triggered when the user selects the Upload button operates with a filter and will only allow the user to select a file of the correct name. That name must have certain properties that are correct to verify that the name matches the type of file expected. Plan files to be uploaded always have a name in the form PLANid.TMG, where id is replaced by a letter (A-Z) and a number between 1 and 4. For example PLANA1.TMG is a valid name and so is PLANZ4.TMG.

The files that will be downloaded from the server use the name REPORTid.TMG, where id is replaced by a letter (A-Z) and a number between 1 and 4. For example, REPORTA2.TMG is a valid file name for purposes of downloading. If more technical information is required about the file structure or other related matters, please contact the authors.

DETAILS OF THE CONFIGURATION FILE CREATOR SCREEN

This screen is basically an "electronic form" with edit (input) fields for the instructor (or a helper) to type in specifications that are used by the school's FTP server/host computer and/or options to setup what FTP capabilities students will have access to. Once the information about the FTP system has been entered, the program reformats it and saves it in an encrypted, digital format—that is, as a configuration file.

When the student section of the TMGftp program reads a configuration file, it provides instructions about how the program should connect to the FTP server and if uploads, downloads, or both will be enabled. It also determines the appearance of the main screen. For example, the screen may or may not include edit fields for students to enter individual user names, passwords, and other information.

It is NOT necessary that an instructor know about the technical details of FTP to be able to fill out the form and use the software. That's the beauty of it. On the other hand, you do have to find out what information to enter. While some faculty may be familiar with what it takes to log-on to an FTP server at their schools, most will not be. Yet, as a practical matter, even a person who is expert on general aspects of FTP and a school's local network would probably need to have a conversation with someone who works at a user help desk or in network support to obtain some of the information about the particulars of the local FTP system. Similarly, it may be necessary for the system administrator to create folders in which to save the uploaded Plans and the downloaded Reports. So, it will be normal to ask for information and/or help from your school's tech support people (see the earlier section *Asking for Help from IT Support Staff*).

Keep in mind that you can print the configuration creator form (or copy it from this manual) and ask your school's computer help desk or a network support person to look at it and give you some help in setting up the configuration file. In most cases only four or five of the fields need to be completed. A person who works with these things daily can do this in a few minutes. It is not a big deal.

Configuration File Specs

The configuration file consists of information that controls the appearance of the Main Screen of the TMGftp program when the student runs it, what the program is enabled to do, and also what specifications will be used in establishing FTP connections. There is quite a bit of flexibility to handle different FTP situations and instructor preferences. All of the configuration file options are discussed below.

- **Descriptive Label for the Configuration File**

This is simply text that provides a descriptive label for the configuration file. It appears at the bottom of the student screen when the configuration file is loaded. If a file is opened after it has been saved, the label also provides a reminder of when or why that configuration file was used. For example, if a configuration file has been created for your Introductory Marketing class the label might be Introductory Marketing: Professor Smith, Section 3.

The descriptive label does not effect the FTP session in any functional way. It can be left blank if you prefer not to have a label. On the other hand, it is a simple way to customize the student screen to show the instructor's name.

- **Number to Identify the Configuration File**

When a configuration file is saved it has a file name in the form: TMGftp#.CFG, where # is replaced with a number value to identify the configuration file.

The default value for this number is 1, which results in a configuration file with the name TMGftp1.CFG. When the program starts, a configuration file with the name TMGftp1.CFG will be automatically loaded by the TMGftp program if it is in the same folder as the program. (The installation procedure puts the TMGftp1 program in the default folder C:\program files\tmg\tmgftp. Thus, this is a simple way to use the configuration file to automatically configure the student's software. However, the student is given the option to change that folder during the install procedure.)

There may be times when it is useful to work with more than one configuration file. For example, an instructor who has an MBA section using TMG at Level 3 and an undergraduate section using it at Level 1 might want to have two different configuration files (with specifications for two different upload and download directories). The configuration file number makes it easy to do this and keep the different files straight.

Note that the student can select the Load Config File button to browse through folders and load a configuration file that was not automatically loaded when the program started.

- **Name of Person Creating Configuration**

The name of the person who creates the configuration file is included in the file for reference purposes and it has no other effect. For example, this might be useful if a network support person helped fill out the form and the instructor wants to contact that person again to make a change. This field can be left blank.

- **Upload/Download Capabilities You Want User to Have**

This allows the instructor to configure TMGftp so that it will upload and download files, only upload, or only download. It also determines what buttons and menu bar items appear on the screen when the student runs the program.

Both Upload and Download. The default is for the student to be able to both upload Plan files and download encrypted Report files. When this option is selected (checked) both download and upload buttons (and the corresponding menu bar selections) appear when the student uses the TMGftp software. However, there may be good reasons to restrict the program so that it does only uploads or only downloads. For example, it is sometimes more convenient for the instructor to have students upload Plan files with the TMGftp program but for them to retrieve their Report files by downloading them from a website.

Only Upload a Plan. If Only Upload a Plan is checked, the Upload button and corresponding menu bar selection appear on the TMGftp screen when the student runs the program, but the Download button and corresponding menu bar selection are not there. Thus, uploading a Plan file is enabled but there is not a capability to download Report files. This is useful when the instructor wants to distribute Reports in a different way (for example, via email).

Only Download a Report. If Only Download a Report is checked, the Download button and corresponding menu bar selection appear on the TMGftp screen when the student runs the program, but the Upload button and corresponding menu bar selection are not there. Thus, downloading Report files is possible but uploading Plan files is not. This is useful when the instructor wants to have students submit Plans in a different way (for example, via email).

- **Config File Password (Optional)**

The Config File Password provides a way to prevent anyone who does not have the password from viewing the values in the encrypted configuration file. If a config file uses the instructor's personal log-on name or password, it's a good idea to specify a password. That way, even if another individual has the general access password (which allows access to the section of the program used for creating configuration files) the information is secure.

If the password field is left blank, a config file can be opened from the Create Configuration File Screen and the values can be viewed.

Whether a config file is password protected or not, students will not be able to view the information in the file at the Main Screen of the program—and they should not be able to reach the Create Configuration File Screen (because they do not have the Instructor Access Password). Further, students do NOT need to know the password to load the configuration file so that it can control their FTP session.

- **Fields You Want to Appear on Student Screen**

The specifications selected in this panel determine the appearance of the Main Screen for students. Specifically, if an item is checked an edit field will appear on the student screen. The student will need to fill in that edit field to be able to connect to the FTP server. When edit fields appear on the screen, it is the information in them (and not what may be in the configuration file) that determines the specs for the FTP session.

If the configuration file includes proprietary information for a particular field (for example, the instructor will use his or her own user name and password for students to log-on), it is important to NOT check the corresponding field. If it is not checked the information will be secure and there is no way students will have access to it for some other purpose.

In general, if the information for a particular field would be the same for all students who are using the program, it is better NOT to have the field appear on the screen and instead for the information to be provided by the corresponding field from the configuration file. For example, many FTP systems allow what is called Anonymous Log-on. In that case, Anonymous is the user name and the system expects the user's email address to be used as the password. In such a situation, it would make sense to check the password field and not check the user name field.

When the student attempts to connect to the FTP server, whatever information is entered in the fields on the student's screen will override the value in the configuration file. So, if the information for a particular field doesn't need to change depending on the individual student, it is best to put it in the configuration file and NOT check the field name.

Note that there is a relationship between which fields are checked and what information will need to be provided by the configuration file. For example, if the field for the name of the FTP host computer is not checked, it will not be possible for students to enter that information when they use the program. Thus, it will be necessary to include the name of the FTP host computer on the form used to create the configuration file.

There are six different fields that the instructor can select to appear on the main (student) screen—i.e., to be completed by students before they connect to the FTP server. These fields are discussed below.

User Log-on Name Field. If this specification is checked, the student screen will show a User Log-on Name field. The student will need to fill in that information before connecting to the FTP server.

In the default configuration, this field is checked. However, if students will not be using their own individual log-on name it is better for this to be unchecked and instead to provide a log-on name in the (encrypted) configuration file itself.

WARNING: If this is checked AND in addition the configuration file is created with information in the User Name (Log-on ID) field, the information from the configuration file will be displayed in the field on the student's screen when the program starts (or the configuration file is loaded). Usually this is not desirable.

In general, when information is provided in the configuration file the corresponding field on the student screen should be unchecked. If a field appears on the student screen, whatever is entered in the field when the student attempts to connect to the FTP server will override the original value in the configuration file. So, if the log-on name information doesn't need to change depending on the individual student it is best to put it in the configuration file and NOT check the field name.

User Log-on Password Field. If this specification is checked, the student screen will show a User Log-on Password field. The student will need to fill in that information before connecting to the FTP server.

WARNING: If this is checked AND in addition the configuration file is created with information in the User Log-on Password field, the information from the configuration file will be displayed in the field on the student's screen when the program starts (or the configuration file is loaded).

In general, when information is provided in the configuration file the corresponding field on the student screen should be unchecked. If a field appears on the student screen, whatever is entered in the field when the student attempts to connect to the FTP server will override the original value in the configuration file. So, if the log-on password information doesn't need to change depending on the individual student it is best to put it in the configuration file and NOT check the field name.

FTP Host Name Field. If this specification is checked, the student screen will show a FTP Host Name field. The student will need to fill in that information before connecting to the FTP server.

WARNING: If this is checked AND in addition the configuration file is created with information in the FTP Host Name field, the information from the configuration file will be displayed in the field on the student's screen when the program starts (or the configuration file is loaded).

In general, when information is provided in the configuration file the corresponding field on the student screen should be unchecked. This also provides security because the student will not see the name of the FTP host computer. If a field appears on the student screen, whatever is entered in the field when the student attempts to connect to the FTP server will override the original value in the configuration file. So, if the log-on host name information doesn't need to change depending on the individual student it is best to put it in the configuration file and NOT check the field name.

FTP Port Number Field. Normally this field should not be checked. If this specification is checked, the student screen will show a FTP Port Number field. The student will need to fill in that information before connecting to the FTP server. Usually, however the Port Number would be the same across all users of the FTP system. Moreover, in the vast majority of cases FTP uses Port Number 21, which is the default value for this field and the configuration file.

WARNING: If this is checked AND in addition the configuration file is created with information in the FTP Port Number field, the information from the configuration file will be displayed in the field on the student's screen when the program starts (or the configuration file is loaded).   This may not be desirable from a security standpoint.

If an FTP Port Number field appears on the student screen, whatever is entered in the field when the student attempts to connect to the FTP server will override the original value in the configuration file. Since the FTP port number information isn't likely to change depending on the individual student, it is usually best to specify the port number in the configuration file and NOT check the field name.

FTP Upload Directory Field. If this specification is checked, the student screen will show a FTP Upload Directory field. The student will need to fill in that information before connecting to the FTP server.

WARNING: If this is checked AND in addition the configuration file is created with information in the FTP Upload Directory field, the information from the configuration file will be displayed in the field on the student's screen when the program starts (or the configuration file is loaded).

In general, when information is provided in the configuration file the corresponding field on the student screen should be unchecked. This also provides security because the student will not see the name of the FTP upload directory. If an upload directory field appears on the student screen, whatever is entered in the field when the student attempts to connect to the FTP server will override the original value in the configuration file. So, if the log-on upload directory information doesn't need to change depending on the individual student it is best to put it in the configuration file and NOT check the field name.

FTP Download Directory Field. If this specification is checked, the student screen will show a FTP Download Directory field. The student will need to fill in that information before connecting to the FTP server.

WARNING: If this is checked AND in addition the configuration file is created with information in the FTP Download Directory field, the information from the configuration file will be displayed in the field on the student's screen when the program starts (or the configuration file is loaded).

In general, when information is provided in the configuration file the corresponding field on the student screen should be unchecked. This also provides security because the student will not see the name of the FTP download directory. If a download directory field appears on the student screen, whatever is entered in the field when the student attempts to connect to the FTP server will override the original value in the configuration file. So, if the log-on download directory information doesn't need to change depending on the individual student it is best to put it in the configuration file and NOT check the field name.

FTP Log-on Specifications Based on Config File

The FTP log-on specifications panel provides a way for the configuration file created by the instructor to control (automate) 9 different aspects of the FTP log-on and directories. An alternative approach is to specify that edit fields should appear on the screen so that the student can provide the information when running the program.

The specifications listed below can be controlled by the config file. For more detail, search for individual items from the list below in the online help file.
- User name (log-on id)
- User log-on password
- FTP host computer name or IP address

- Name of upload directory on host computer
- Name of download directory on host computer
- Host computer port to connect to
- Response timeout interval
- Vendor of FTP host computer
- Passive FTP connection type

• User Name (Log-On ID)

The User Name (Log-on ID) must be a name for a valid account on the FTP server to which you want to connect.

Many servers will accept Anonymous as a user ID and the user's email address as a password for FTP access. When this applies, it may make sense to fill in the User Name field with Anonymous and then specify that the user name field not be displayed. In turn, the User Log-on Password field would be left blank and the user password field would be displayed on the main student screen.

• User Log-On Password

This is simply the password used to log in to the remote FTP host. The password supplied must be the password for the User Name (Log-on ID) specified in the configuration file or provided by the student at run time.

On most systems the password IS CASE SENSITIVE, so it's important to pay attention to whether letters are upper case or lower case. If an invalid password is provided the log-on will fail.

• FTP Host Computer Name or IP Address

The FTP Host Name is the name or dotted IP address of the remote host to which you want to connect.

• Name of Upload Directory on Host Computer

This specification is the name of the directory or folder on the host computer to which Plan files will be uploaded.

Students will not be able to upload to this directory with the TMGftp program unless they have "privileges" or rights to write (save data) to that directory. At some schools a directory for uploading files has already been established and it is simply a matter of learning the name of that directory; many FTP locations follow the convention of naming the public upload folder "\incoming". Regardless of whether a public upload directory/folder already exists, it is usually a simple matter for the network administrator to create a special folder for TMG upload files and to give you and/or your students the right to access that folder and save files to it. So, you may need to ask for write privileges.

It may be useful to you (or to a technical support person helping you) to know how this field is used. As part of the FTP protocol there is a command that transfers (uploads) a file from the client computer to the remote FTP. In a general sense, the transfer takes place to the currently connected folder on the FTP server. So, before that transfer is called, the TMGftp program issues a command to change to the directory specified in the upload field.

If the field is blank, the program does not issue a command to change directory. Instead, it simply uploads the file to the directory to which the original connection was made based on the name of the FTP host computer.

Also, if a TMG PLANid.TMG file already exists on the server with the same name as the name of the file the student is trying to upload, that file may be overwritten or alternatively the FTP server may assign the file with the duplicate name a new file name; usually this is done by appending another number that reflects the sequence of the uploads. It is useful to know how this works on your school's server. When the TMG program attempts to upload a Plan file it uses an FTP command that requests that the uploaded file be given a unique file name if another file with the same name already exists. If that capability is not implemented on the FTP server the file that is already there will be overwritten.

- **Name of Download Directory on Host Computer**

This is the specification of the folder (directory) on the FTP host computer from which Report files will be downloaded.

The Report file that the TMGftp program looks for to download (based on the Industry and Firm information the student has entered) must be in the download directory on the FTP host computer for the transfer to take place.

Students will not be able to download from this directory with the TMGftp program unless they have "privileges" or rights to do so. At some schools a directory for downloading files has already been established and it is simply a matter of learning the name of that directory; many FTP locations follow the convention of naming the download folder "\pub", which is short for public. Regardless of whether a public download directory/folder already exists, it is usually a simple matter for the network administrator to create a special folder for TMG download files and to give you and/or your students the right to access that folder and save files to it. This has advantages because it limits access to the folder and means that the only files in the folder will be the ones you need. So, even if a public download folder exists it may be advantageous to ask for privileges to have your own download folder established.

It may be useful to you (or to a technical support person helping you) to know how this field is used. As part of the FTP protocol there is a command that transfers (downloads) a file from the remote FTP host computer to the local PC.

In a general sense, the transfer takes place from the currently connected folder on the FTP server. So, before that download transfer is called, the TMGftp program issues a command to change to the directory specified in the download field.

If the field is blank, the program does not issue a command to change directory. Instead, it simply downloads the file from the directory to which the original connection was made based on the name of the FTP host computer.

If a file with the same name exists on the local drive, a dialog informs the user and asks if it is okay to overwrite the file with the one being downloaded. If the user doesn't okay the overwrite, the download is cancelled.

- **Host Computer Port to Connect to**

Default value for this specification: 21

The FTP Port number is the number of the port on the remote host computer to which FTP connections should be made.

- **Response Timeout**

Default value for this specification: 0

The Response TimeOut specification concerns the amount of time (in milliseconds) to wait for a response from the socket before an error message (i.e., an "exception") is raised and the current operation is aborted.
The default value of TimeOut, 0, means that an exception is never raised, and operations never time out. (A reason to put a larger time period in here would be that the server may be down or not responding. In such a case, the never timeout option means that users would wait too long before realizing that nothing is going to happen.)

- **Auto Detect Vendor of Remote Host**

Default value for this specification: Auto_detect

This specification concerns the identification of the vendor of the FTP host to which a connection is to be made. Knowing the vendor allows the program to correctly interpret directory information sent from the host. The default value (Auto_detect) should automatically determine the vendor for you. However, if there is a problem it may be necessary to select the vendor from the list of alternatives given.

The alternatives include:
UNIX, WINDOWS, VM, BULL, MAC, TOPS20, VMS, OS2, MVS_IBM, MVS_INTERLINK, NT, OTHER, TANDEM, AS400, OS9, NETWARE

- **Passive FTP Connection Type**

Default value for this specification: false.

This specification determines how a File Transfer Protocol connection is made. If passive is set to false, the program listens for a data connection which is established by the server and the program then tells the server where to connect. If passive is set to true, the program issues a command and the server tells the program where to establish the data connection. The program then connects to the server where the server indicated. This method is sometimes used with a proxy configuration. However, some FTP servers do not support this approach, and some proxy configurations require the other type of transfer (i.e. Passive=false).

- **Firewall Specifications for Host FTP Site**

Firewall Method. There are three different firewall methods. Click the arrow for the drop-down menu and then select the method used by the Firewall at the FTP host site.

Authenticate. The default specification is No. This specifies the type of authentication required for the Socks proxy being used for the client connection. No means that no authentication is required.

When there is no authentication the Firewall User ID and Firewall User Password fields should be left blank.

Yes means that there will be authentication using the values provided in the configuration file fields for the Firewall User ID (user name) and Firewall User Password.

Note that the TMGftp program does NOT provide for a screen setup in which each individual student provides a unique Firewall User ID and Firewall User Password prior to log-on. However, in many situations it will be possible to use a common Firewall User ID and Password (for example, one provided specifically to the instructor or for the class) in the configuration file, regardless of whether students provide individual user names and passwords for the general FTP log-on.

Firewall User ID. When there is no Firewall authentication the Firewall User ID field should be left blank.

Note that the TMGftp program does NOT provide for a screen setup in which each individual student provides a unique Firewall User ID (and Firewall User Password) prior to log-on. However, in many situations it will be possible to use a common Firewall User ID (for example, one provided specifically to the instructor or for the class) in the configuration file, regardless of whether students provide individual user names and passwords for the general FTP log-on.

Firewall User Password. When there is no authentication the Firewall User Password field should be left blank.

Note that the TMGftp program does NOT provide for a screen setup in which each individual student provides a unique Firewall User Password (and Firewall User ID) prior to log-on. However, in many situations it will be possible to use a common Firewall User Password (for example, one provided specifically to the instructor or for the class) in the configuration file, regardless of whether students provide individual user names and passwords for the general FTP log-on.

- **Proxy Server Specifications**

 Name or IP Address of Proxy Server if One Is Used. The default specification: {leave blank, i.e., proxy server isn't being used}.

This specification determines the name or IP Address of a Proxy Server, if one is used. If a proxy server isn't being used, this must be left blank.

Proxy Port to Connect to. Default specification: 0 {a proxy server is not being used}. The Proxy Port to Connect to specifies the port of a Proxy Server to Connect to, if one is used.

If a proxy server is not being used, this property should be left at 0.
If a proxy server is to be used, this port must be set to the proper port of the proxy server.

Configuration File Screen Buttons

The Configuration File Creator Screen features several buttons that activate different program functions. The menu bar selections at the top of the screen provide an alternative way to do the same thing. The purpose of each button is briefly described below.

- **Restore Defaults Button.**

Clears any values already in the edit fields on the screen and reinitializes all of the FTP specifications to a set of default values.

- **Open a Config File Button.**

Activates an open file dialog from which the instructor can select a configuration file to view and if desired modify.

- **Save a Config File Button.**

Activates a save file dialog and saves all of the values currently displayed on the screen as a configuration file.

- **Print Form Button.**

Activates a printer selection dialog (if there is a printer hooked to the system) and prints a copy of the form as it appears on the screen. This requires a graphics printer.

- **Apply/Check Config Button.**

Gathers the values on the screen (without first saving them to a file) and opens the Main Screen so that the configuration can be tested (as if it were read in from a file). It also enables a new Return to Create Config button on the Main Screen.

- **Exit Button.**

Opens a confirmation dialog and, if the user agrees, disconnects any active FTP session and exits the program.

Configuration File Password Screen

When a configuration file is created and saved, it can be protected with a configuration file password. A password-protected configuration file can't be viewed except by a person who has that specific password. However, any valid configuration file can be loaded from the Main (Student) Screen without a password. Although the file is loaded for use behind the scenes, it can't be viewed on screen.

The Configuration File Password Screen appears when an instructor clicks the Open Config File button and selects a config file to load that is password protected. The password must be entered exactly as it was typed when the file was saved. After the password has been typed in the entry field, click Ok.

If a file is not password protected, this screen does not appear. Instead, the file is opened and its values are immediately displayed on the screen.

Note: TMGftp uses another password called the Instructor Access Password. It is used to gain access to the section of the program that creates configuration files.

RUNNING TMGFTP FROM A FLOPPY DISK

Most Windows software does not "behave" well if you try to run it from a floppy disk … and Windows programs are usually too large to fit on a disk anyway. However, we've worked to keep the TMGftp program small so that it will run from a floppy disk. The benefit of this is that a student who does not have a computer with Internet access, or who is going to be away from it at times when a Plan file needs to be submitted, can run the program from just about any available computer with Internet access. While many labs do not allow students to install software on lab machines or a network, most allow students to run a program that they bring on their own disks.

To run the program on a floppy, the first step is to copy the program, its help file, and the configuration file that will be used to the root directory of the disk. This is simply a matter of using the Windows Explorer program to select those files from the hard drive folder where they have been installed and copy/paste or drag them to the floppy. The files to be copied are TMGftp.exe, TMGftp.help, and TMGftp1.cfg. Of course, the Plan file also needs to be saved to the disk so it's available when it's time to upload!

To start the program, simply click on the TMGftp file on the floppy.

There are two cautions if you run the program from a floppy disk. First, it will take longer for the software to load when it is initially started. Once it has started it will operate about as quickly as it does from a hard drive. You can upload Plans from the floppy and download a Report file to the disk. (An encrypted Report file can only be read by the TMGPlan or TMGSim software, but it can be opened directly from the floppy by selecting the A: drive in the file selection dialog for the file viewer).

Second, when the program is run from a floppy disk it may not automatically load the configuration file. The panel at the bottom of the screen will give the name of the configuration file if it has loaded properly. However, to be certain that the config file loaded properly, it's best to load it yourself. To do that, start the program and enter the Industry letter and Firm number as usual. Then, click the Ok button in the normal way. The Load Configuration button will appear. Select the Load Configuration button and, when the open file selection dialog activates, change to the A: drive and click the config file and then the Ok button. Now the program should be ready to connect to the FTP server and upload or download files.

6. *The Starting Position*

This chapter summarizes the firms' starting positions at the beginning of the game and provides an instructor's report for the starting period. In addition, the similarities and differences between the students' reports and the instructor's reports are described. (For complete sample copies of the students' reports, see Chapters 4 and 5 of the Student Manual).

FIRMS' STARTING POSITIONS

Each firm starts in exactly the same position. Furthermore, the same starting position is used for all three levels of the game. The decisions areas that firms are responsible for vary with the different game levels and there are some differences in the format and content of the reports they receive for the different levels, but all firms at all levels start in the same place.

At the start of the game, each firm has one product—a voice recognition device—with the same (relatively low) levels on each of the three design features. The number of special commands can range from 5 to 20; it is initially set at 8. Both the error protection and the ease of learning ratings, which have the potential to vary from 1 to 10, are initially set at 3.

In the channels of distribution, the firms begin with retail distribution intensity (% of dealers) of 30% in each channel. That is, each firm's sales reps are expected to call on 30% of the possible outlets within each channel. The possible range for distribution intensity is from 0%—if a channel is not used at all—to 100%—the most intensive distribution. Each firm initially has 20 sales reps and they are evenly divided between the two channels. The initial sales commission rate is 5%, and all sales reps spend 10% of their time on non-selling, or support, activities.

Recent advertising expenditures were $250,000. The type of advertising was unspecified. Thus, for game levels 2 and 3, firms will have to decide the type of advertising based on the descriptions in the Student Manual (but without having prior decisions).

The previous expenditure to support the customer service function was $92,500 per firm.

In levels 2 and 3, firms may spend some of their budget on sales promotion. Previously, sales promotion spending was $0 in each channel.

Wholesale prices in the previous period were $95 in both channels of distribution.

The requested Production Order Quantity was 25,000. Actual production was 25,151.

Finally, in the previous period, firms purchased market research reports 1, 2, 4, and 5. These are the Market Share by Segment Report, the Market Share by Channel Report, the Marketing Effectiveness Study, and the Detailed Sales Analysis. Total spending on market research totaled $67,000. (Students get copies of these reports in their text.)

Each firm's initial budget is $984,000. Note that this appears on the reports in the student manual. If students say that they don't know what their budget is, be aware that they have not studied the report!

In the previous period, each firm spent $809,500 on budget items. Thus, a firm can maintain past levels of spending in advertising, sales force salaries and market research, and still have $174,500 left to spend on R&D for product modifications, sales promotion, or increased levels of advertising, customer service, sales force, or market research.

THE INSTRUCTOR'S REPORT

Exhibit 6A—which starts on page 129 —contains the instructor's report for the beginning of the game. (When you run the game, it will create a report like this for each industry, and save it in the master folder as a file called REPORTA.TXT—where the A is the letter for the industry involved.)

Summary of Plan Decisions

The first page of the Instructor's Report summarizes the input decisions made by each firm. It also provides the passwords and the summary of the folders from the setup file.

In addition to providing a side-by-side listing of input decisions, this summary can be used (as a fail-safe backup) if it is ever necessary to rerun the simulation from scratch and the original input forms have been lost. Following the summary of inputs is a listing of the different setup options currently specified.

Financial Summary and Production Summary for Each Firm

The next four pages of the report—one page for each firm—provides the Financial Summary and Production Summary for each firm. These reports are identical to the reports that the firms receive.

Marketing Research Reports

Next are three market research reports that provide general industry information. These reports are the Industry Sales Report, the Product Features & Prices Report, and the Marketing Activity Report. Each firm also automatically receives copies of these reports for each period at no charge. Please note all reports contain information for the game period which just ended—that is, the most recent period.

The next two reports are more detailed market share reports—Market Share by Segment and Market Share by Channel. **The instructor automatically receives these reports**, but firms must purchase them as market research reports 1 and 2 respectively.

The next report is the Average Customer Preferences Report. This is identical to market research report 3 which the firms may purchase. The numbers in the Average Customer Preferences Report will vary slightly from firm to firm to reflect normal sampling error typical of survey research

Instructor-Only Reports

The next two reports are provided *only for the instructor and include information that is not available to the firms*.

- **Unit Sales by Segment and Channel Report**

First is the Unit Sales by Segment and Channel report. This gives the most detailed breakdown of actual sales. Although this entire report is not available to firms, a firm can purchase a similar report containing actual unit sales by segment and channel for their brand(s) only. This is the Detailed Sales Analysis, or market research report 4.

- **The True Customer Preferences Report**

The second "instructor-only" report is the TRUE Customer Preferences Report. These numbers are reported *without error* and are useful for checking how well different brands are targeting the different market segments.

One reason for including both the Average Customer Preferences Report and the TRUE Customer Preferences Report is that the instructor may choose to let firms purchase market research reports after the results for one period are handed back, but before the next period's decisions are due. That way, if a firm realizes after the fact that they should have purchased a report but didn't, they still have the chance to get the information without waiting a full game period. Typically, a premium of 50% or more over the normal report price should be charged and entered as Extra Market Research (Select the Modify a Plan button on the Main Screen, open the firm's plan file, click the Adjustments button on the Plan Decisions Form Screen, add the amount for the extra market research, and resave the Plan file.)

Next is the Product Positioning Report, which is identical to market research report 7 which firms may purchase. For each product, this report prints a table of how far each brand is from each segment's ideal point. Lower numbers indicate that a brand is "close" to the segment's ideal point. By looking at the numbers in the column for any segment, you can quickly see which brands are close and which are far from that segment's ideal. The numbers in this table incorporate the importance weights (see Chapter 14–The Model Structure for the actual importance weights) for each segment and product attribute. Thus, although two brands may each be "off" by one in meeting a segment's ideal, the brand that is off on the less important attribute will be "closer" to the ideal.

- **Diagnostic Index Summary**

The final report for the instructor is the **Diagnostic Index Summary**. This gives the values of the various sales force, customer service and advertising indices for each firm. This diagnostic report is provided for the *instructor only* and is very helpful in quickly pinpointing a firm's strengths and weaknesses. However, you should never show this report to a firm! (See Chapter 7–Diagnosing a Firm's Position for hints and suggestions for assessing a firm's competitive position.) In addition to firm-level indices, the Diagnostic Index Summary also reports several overall industry-level indices. These reflect the combined effects of the firms' decisions in customer service, advertising, and product design.

- **Summary**

In summary, the instructor's report contains the same information as the firms' reports, plus additional reports just for the instructor. These extra reports are the TRUE Customer Preference Report, the Unit Sales by Segment and Channel Report, and the Diagnostic Index Summary.

The specific format of the output reports varies somewhat depending on the game level. At the more difficult levels, the reports have additional items not given in the more basic levels. For example, at level 2, the Marketing Activity Report includes information about advertising type and sales promotion that is not relevant for level 1. For level 3, the reports can be considerably longer as new products are introduced. To accommodate the extra length, the order of the reports in level 3 differs somewhat from the order described above and shown in Exhibit 6A.

- ## Exhibit 6A - Instructor's Report for the Previous Period

```
INDUSTRY B  FIRM 1  Period 0 Results
*************** Financial Summary ***************

FIRM 1                   Channel 1      Channel 2         Total
------
Units Sold                  14074          11077           25151
Wholesale Price            $95.00         $95.00
Unit Cost                  $47.00         $47.00

Gross Sales            $1,337,030     $1,052,315      $2,389,345
Cost of Goods Sold       $661,478       $520,619      $1,182,097
Transfer Charges                                             $0
Gross Margin                                         $1,207,248

Expenses
Advertising                                            $250,000
Sales Force-Salary       $200,000       $200,000        $400,000
          -Firing Costs                                      $0
          -Commission      $66,852        $52,616        $119,468
Customer Service                                         $92,500
Sales Promotion                $0             $0              $0
R&D for Product Modifications                                $0
Marketing Research                                      $67,000
Total Expenses                                         $928,968

Net Contribution (Loss)                                $278,280

Budget for Next Period:     $984,000    ( 25% of Industry Total)
```

```
*************** Production Summary ***************

          Requested    Actual      Units    Inventory        Unit
  Brand   Production   Production   Sold     Transferred      Cost
  -----   ----------   ----------   -----    -----------      ----

  FIRM 1     25000       25151      25151          0          47.00
```

```
INDUSTRY B  FIRM 2  Period 0 Results
**************** Financial Summary ****************
```

FIRM 2	Channel 1	Channel 2	Total
Units Sold	14074	11077	25151
Wholesale Price	$95.00	$95.00	
Unit Cost	$47.00	$47.00	
Gross Sales	$1,337,030	$1,052,315	$2,389,345
Cost of Goods Sold	$661,478	$520,619	$1,182,097
Transfer Charges			$0
Gross Margin			$1,207,248
Expenses			
Advertising			$250,000
Sales Force-Salary	$200,000	$200,000	$400,000
-Firing Costs			$0
-Commission	$66,852	$52,616	$119,468
Customer Service			$92,500
Sales Promotion	$0	$0	$0
R&D for Product Modifications			$0
Marketing Research			$67,000
Total Expenses			$928,968
Net Contribution (Loss)			$278,280

```
Budget for Next Period:    $984,000    ( 25% of Industry Total)
```

```
*************** Production Summary ***************
```

Brand	Requested Production	Actual Production	Units Sold	Inventory Transferred	Unit Cost
FIRM 2	25000	25151	25151	0	$47.00

```
INDUSTRY B  FIRM 3  Period 0 Results
*************** Financial Summary ****************
```

FIRM 3	Channel 1	Channel 2	Total
Units Sold	14074	11077	25151
Wholesale Price	$95.00	$95.00	
Unit Cost	$47.00	$47.00	
Gross Sales	$1,337,030	$1,052,315	$2,389,345
Cost of Goods Sold	$661,478	$520,619	$1,182,097
Transfer Charges			$0
Gross Margin			$1,207,248
Expenses			
Advertising			$250,000
Sales Force-Salary	$200,000	$200,000	$400,000
-Firing Costs			$0
-Commission	$66,852	$52,616	$119,468
Customer Service			$92,500
Sales Promotion	$0	$0	$0
R&D for Product Modifications			$0
Marketing Research			$67,000
Total Expenses			$928,968
Net Contribution (Loss)			$278,280

```
Budget for Next Period:   $984,000   ( 25% of Industry Total)
```

```
*************** Production Summary ****************
```

Brand	Requested Production	Actual Production	Units Sold	Inventory Transferred	Unit Cost
FIRM 3	25000	25151	25151	0	$47.00

```
INDUSTRY B   FIRM 4   Period 0 Results
*************** Financial Summary ****************

FIRM 4                  Channel 1      Channel 2          Total
------
Units Sold                  14074          11077          25151
Wholesale Price            $95.00         $95.00
Unit Cost                  $47.00         $47.00

Gross Sales            $1,337,030     $1,052,315     $2,389,345
Cost of Goods Sold       $661,478       $520,619     $1,182,097
Transfer Charges                                             $0
Gross Margin                                         $1,207,248

Expenses
Advertising                                            $250,000
Sales Force-Salary       $200,000       $200,000       $400,000
           -Firing Costs                                     $0
           -Commission    $66,852        $52,616       $119,468
Customer Service                                        $92,500
Sales Promotion                $0             $0             $0
Product Modifications                                        $0
Marketing Research                                      $67,000
Total Expenses                                         $928,968

Net Contribution (Loss)                                $278,280

Budget for Next Period:    $984,000     ( 25% of Industry Total)
```

```
************** Production Summary ****************

         Requested    Actual      Units    Inventory       Unit
Brand    Production   Production  Sold     Transferred      Cost
_____    _____   _____  _____    _____      ____

FIRM 4     25000       25151      25151          0        $47.00
```

```
*************** Industry Sales Report ***************
```

VRD Brand	Unit Sales	Market Share (Units)	$ Sales (Retail)	Market Share ($ Sales)
FIRM 1	25,151	0.250	$4,292,964	0.250
FIRM 2	25,151	0.250	$4,292,964	0.250
FIRM 3	25,151	0.250	$4,292,964	0.250
FIRM 4	25,151	0.250	$4,292,964	0.250
Total	100,604		$17,171,854	

Channel	Unit Sales	$ Sales
1	56,296	$10,696,240
2	44,308	$6,475,614

```
********** Product Features & Prices Report ***********
```

VRD Brand	Special Commands	Error Protection	Ease of Learning	Average Retail Price Channel 1	Average Retail Price Channel 2
FIRM 1	8	3	3	$190.00	$146.15
FIRM 2	8	3	3	$190.00	$146.15
FIRM 3	8	3	3	$190.00	$146.15
FIRM 4	8	3	3	$190.00	$146.15

```
*************** Marketing Activity Report ***************
          (Data Reported Is from Period 0)
```

	Firm 1	Firm 2	Firm 3	Firm 4
Advertising Dollars	$250,000	$250,000	$250,000	250,000
Advertising Type				
Sales Promotion				
Channel 1	$0	$0	$0	$0
Channel 2	$0	$0	$0	$0
Number of Sales Reps				
Channel 1	10	10	10	10
Channel 2	10	10	10	10
Commission	5%	5%	5%	5%
Customer Service	$92,500	$92,500	$92,500	$92,500

```
********* Report 1: Market Share By Segment *********
```

Brand	Students	Home	Assistants	Creators	Managers	Parents
FIRM 1	0.250	0.250	0.250	0.250	0.250	0.250
FIRM 2	0.250	0.250	0.250	0.250	0.250	0.250
FIRM 3	0.250	0.250	0.250	0.250	0.250	0.250
FIRM 4	0.250	0.250	0.250	0.250	0.250	0.250
Total Sales (in Units)	20,028	15,084	25,104	10,240	22,056	8,092

```
********** Report 2: Market Share By Channel *********
```

Brand	Channel 1	Channel 2
FIRM 1	0.250	0.250
FIRM 2	0.250	0.250
FIRM 3	0.250	0.250
FIRM 4	0.250	0.250
Total Sales (in Units)	56,296	44,308

```
******** Report 3: Average Customer Preferences *********
```

Segment	Special Commands	Error Protection	Ease of Learning	Approximate Price Range
Students	11.4	3.0	2.2	$125.00 - $155.00
Home	8.5	3.1	7.1	$140.00 - $177.50
Assistant	13.0	6.3	7.1	$210.00 - $270.00
Creators	15.3	2.7	4.5	$220.00 - $280.00
Managers	17.0	5.9	3.4	$250.00 - $325.00
Parents	6.1	3.5	8.4	$151.43 - $194.29

```
*************** Unit Sales By Segment and Channel***************
```

Brand	Students	Home	Assistants	Creators	Managers	Parents
Channel 1						
FIRM 1	708	936	5,080	1,578	4,752	1,020
FIRM 2	708	936	5,080	1,578	4,752	1,020
FIRM 3	708	936	5,080	1,578	4,752	1,020
FIRM 4	708	936	5,080	1,578	4,752	1,020
Channel 2						
FIRM 1	4,299	2,835	1,196	982	762	1,003
FIRM 2	4,299	2,835	1,196	982	762	1,003
FIRM 3	4,299	2,835	1,196	982	762	1,003
FIRM 4	4,299	2,835	1,196	982	762	1,003
Total Sales (in Units)	20,028	15,084	25,104	10,240	22,056	8,092

```
*************** TRUE Customer Preferences ***************
```

Segment	Special Commands	Error Protection	Ease of Learning	Reference Price
Students	11.0	3.0	3.0	$145.00
Home	9.0	4.0	8.0	$165.00
Assistants	12.0	7.0	8.0	$250.00
Creators	14.0	2.0	4.0	$260.00
Managers	16.0	6.0	3.0	$300.00
Parents	6.0	3.0	9.0	$180.00

```
*************** Diagnostic Index Summary ***************
```

Index	Firm 1	Firm 2	Firm 3	Firm 4
Customer Service:				
Individual Firm Rating	100%	100%	100%	100%
Competitive Impact	1.000	1.000	1.000	1.000
Sales Rep Effort	1.000	1.000	1.000	1.000
Channel 1:				
Trade Promotion	1.000	1.000	1.000	1.000
Distribution Index	1.000	1.000	1.000	1.000
Call Effectiveness	1.000	1.000	1.000	1.000
Composite Salesforce Index	1.000	1.000	1.000	1.000
SalesRep Workload	100%	100%	100%	100%
Channel Push	0.500	0.500	0.500	0.500
Channel 2:				
Trade Promotion	1.000	1.000	1.000	1.000
Distribution Index	1.000	1.000	1.000	1.000
Call Effectiveness	1.000	1.000	1.000	1.000
Composite Salesforce Index	1.000	1.000	1.000	1.000
SalesRep Workload	100%	100%	100%	100%
Channel Push	0.500	0.500	0.500	0.500
VRD Product:				
Ad Effectiveness	1.000	1.000	1.000	1.000
Brand Awareness	0.550	0.550	0.550	0.550

Industry-wide Indices

	VRD
Industry Advertising	1.000
Customer Service	1.000
Product Appeal:	
Students	.980
Home	.937
Assistants	.926
Artists	.941
Managers	.930
Parents	.932

For an explanation of indices, see Chapter 7 (and for more detail see Chapter 14) of the *Instructor's Manual*.

7. *Diagnosing a Firm's Position*

INTRODUCTION

This chapter provides some hints and suggestions to help diagnose a firm's competitive position and to pinpoint its strengths and weaknesses. These can aid in following a firm's progress throughout the game and also in providing criticism, advice or "therapy" if a student comes looking for help. *The Marketing Game!* includes several diagnostic reports for the instructor's use. Four of these reports—the TRUE Customer Preferences Report, the Product Positioning Report, and the Unit Sales by Segment and Channel, and the Diagnostic Index Summary—are automatically included in the instructor's report generated each period of the game. Another report—the Industry Summary Report—summarizes key decisions and results for each firm in the industry from the beginning of the game up through the current game period. **The Industry Summary Report is automatically generated each time the simulation is run.**

In addition, instructors who would like to do supplementary analysis, graphing, and evaluation using other popular software packages will find the TMGtoXLS program helpful. It is installed by the Instructor CD-Rom along with the the other instructor software. TMGtoXLS provides a way to export data about each firm, industry and decision period to one consolidated database in standard spreadsheet format. Specifically, **TMGtoXLS creates a file named Summary.XLS in Microsoft Excel™ (version 5) format.** This file format can be read by later versions of Excel and can also be imported by most other programs that do graphing, statistical analysis, database management, and the like. More information about the TMGtoXLS program, and more detail about the organization and contents of the Summary.XLS file, is provided in Appendix H of this manual and in the TMGtoXLS help file.

Hints and suggestions for using the special instructor's diagnostic reports, as well as the remaining reports which both the instructor and firms receive, are given below.

TRUE CUSTOMER PREFERENCES

This report lists the levels of the design features that are most preferred by each market segment. This can be used to provide a quick check on how well a particular brand is satisfying the different market segments on each feature.

PRODUCT POSITIONING REPORT

How "far" a brand is from a market segment's ideal product depends both on how much the brand's features deviate from the ideal and also on how important those features are to that specific market segment. For example, ease of learning is the most important attribute for the assistants segment, whereas the number of special commands is most important for the managers. Being "off" by one on a feature considered to be important is worse than being "off" by one on a relatively unimportant attribute. Although the ideal points gradually evolve throughout the game, the importance weights do not. These weights are given in Exhibit 14F.

The Product Positioning Report (available to students as market research report 7) incorporates the information on the segments' ideal products as well as the importance weights for the three design features (i.e., excluding price) of each product. This report gives the (weighted) "distance" between each firm's product and each segment's ideal.

UNIT SALES BY SEGMENT AND CHANNEL

This report can be used to identify firms that have high sales volumes in a particular combination of distribution channel and market segment. Students sometimes think and say that they are targeting specific segments when in fact they are not. This report shows at a glance the source of a firm's sales.

DIAGNOSTIC INDEX SUMMARY

The Diagnostic Index Summary reports the values of many of the indices used in the simulation model. These indices provide information on how well each firm is managing its decision variables, and also how a firm stands relative to competitors. The specific indices reported will vary with the game level and are summarized below along with the range of values they can assume. In all cases, *a higher level indicates a stronger competitive position*. The following indices are reported for each firm:

Firm-Specific Indices

- ### Customer Service - Individual Firm Rating

range: 0 - no upper limit
measures: the ratio of actual spending to the "expected" spending based on the firm's active customer base
interpretation: values less than 100% indicate under spending relative to what consumers' expect
affected by: the firm's customer service spending and last year's total unit sales
applies in: all levels

- ### Customer Service - Competitive Impact

range: 0.90 - 1.10
measures: the effectiveness of the firm's customer service relative to other firms in the industry
interpretation: values less than 1.0 indicate a weak position relative to other firms in the industry, values greater than 1.0 indicate relative strength
affected by: customer service spending of all firms
applies in: all levels

- ### Sales Rep Effort Index:

range: 0.50 - 1.50
measures: the motivation of the firm's sales reps and how much effort they put into their jobs.
interpretation: values less than 1.00 indicate that the sales reps receive a low commission rate – either relative to other firms and/or compared to their starting commission
affected by: sales commission rates
applies in: levels 2 and 3

- ### Trade Promotion Index (for Each Channel):

range: 0.85 - 1.15 in Channel 1,
0.95 - 1.05 in Channel 2
measures: the amount of promotion impact on dealers in a channel
interpretation: values greater than 1.00 indicate strength relative to competing firms, values less than 1.00 indicate relative weakness
affected by: sales promotion spending
applies in: levels 2 and 3

- ### Distribution Index (for Each Channel):

range: 0.50 - 1.10
measures: how effectively a firm is managing its distribution intensity, given the number of sales reps and their available time to call on dealers
interpretation: values less than 1.0 indicate that a firm has too few sales reps to adequately cover the % of dealers specified by the channel's distribution intensity, values greater than 1.00 may indicate that the firm has more sales reps than needed in that channel

affected by: number of sales reps, exposure goal, % non-selling time
applies in: levels 1, 2, and 3

- **Call Effectiveness Index (for Each Channel):**

range: 0.60 - 1.40 in Channel 1,
0.90 - 1.10 in Channel 2
measures: how satisfied dealers are with the amount of support they receive from a firm's sales reps.
interpretation: values less than 1.00 indicate that the firm's reps are spending relatively less time on supporting activities than reps from competing firms, whereas values greater than 1.00 indicate the opposite
affected by: percent non-selling time
applies in: Levels 2 and 3

- **Composite Sales Force Index (for Each Channel):**

range: 0.13 - 2.66 in Channel 1,
0.21 - 1.91 in Channel 2
measures: the overall effectiveness of the sales force in a channel. This index is a composite of the effort, goodwill, retail penetration and call effectiveness indices.
interpretation: values less than 1.00 indicate that the firm is in a relatively weak position on at least one component of this index
applies in: Levels 1, 2, and 3

- **Channel Push (for Each Channel)**

range: 0.0 - 1.00
measures: the overall strength or "push" that a firm has in a channel
interpretation: high values indicate "strength" in the channel, although values greater than 0.80 are rare; low values are only a concern if the firm is intending to emphasize that channel
affected by: Sales Force Index, the size of the sales force, and the number of products a firm has.
applies in: levels 1, 2, and 3

- **Ad Effectiveness Index (for Each Product):**

range: 0.0 - 1.40
measures: the immediate effectiveness of a firm's advertising in the current period
interpretation: values less than 1.0 typically indicate that a firm is using reminder advertising although brand familiarity is low; values greater than 1.0 indicate that the firm is stressing competitive advertising
affected by: advertising type
applies in: levels 2 and 3

- ## Brand Awareness (for Each Product):

range: 0.0 - 0.90
measures: the percentage of customers who are aware of a firm's brand
interpretation: high numbers indicate high brand awareness
affected by: advertising spending, Ad Effectiveness Index
applies in: levels 1, 2, and 3

Industry Wide Indices

- ## Industry Advertising (for Each Product)

range: 0.80 - 1.20
effect: total demand for the product is multiplied by the value of this index
affected by: total industry advertising level compared to "threshold" value for the industry sales volume
applies in: all levels

- ## Customer Service

range: 0.95 - 1.05
effect: total demand (across all segments and all products) is multiplied by the value of this index
affected by: the total industry spending on customer service relative to the "expected" amount given the current customer base
applies in: all levels

- ## Product Appeal (for Each Product and Segment)

range: 0.90 - 1.10
effect: segment demand for that product is multiplied by the value of this index
affected by: the features of the available products, the segment ideal points, and the importance weights
applies in: all levels

Using the Diagnostic Index Summary

When using the Diagnostic Index Summary, it is helpful to look for index values that are either high or low relative to competitors. High values indicate a strong position, whereas low values indicate a weak position. However, low values are not always undesirable. For example, a firm may choose to focus on only one channel of distribution. In such a situation, that firm would hope to have a high Channel Push Index in the channel being emphasized, and a low value in the other channel.

Exhibit 7A contains a sample Diagnostic Index Summary report. Following the summary report are some comments that highlight some of the strengths and weaknesses that are evident from this report.

• Exhibit 7A - Sample Diagnostic Index Summary Report

```
***INSTRUCTOR COPY***

*********** Diagnostic Index Summary ***********
```

Index	Firm 1	Firm 2	Firm 3	Firm 4
Customer Service:				
Individual Firm Rating	73%	83%	77%	70%
Competitive Impact	0.997	1.009	1.001	0.992
Sales Rep Effort	0.965	1.056	1.130	0.965
Channel 1:				
Trade Promotion	1.080	1.098	0.850	0.850
Distribution Index	0.962	0.813	0.890	1.100
Call Effectiveness	0.953	0.953	0.953	1.112
Composite Salesforce Index	0.956	0.898	0.815	1.003
SalesRep Workload	108%	148%	125%	53%
Channel Push	0.422	0.474	0.319	0.409
Channel 2:				
Trade Promotion	0.950	1.044	0.950	0.950
Distribution Index	0.916	0.901	0.948	0.786
Call Effectiveness	1.003	1.003	1.025	0.959
Composite Salesforce Index	0.842	0.996	1.043	0.691
SalesRep Workload	119%	122%	111%	158%
Channel Push	0.403	0.414	0.499	0.261
VRD Product:				
Ad Effectiveness	1.200	1.200	1.200	1.200
Brand Awareness	57.7%	61.2%	66.9%	66.9%

```
        Industry-wide Indices
        ---------------------
```

	VRD

Industry Advertising	1.042
Customer Service	.966
Product Appeal	
Students	0.965
Home	0.938
Assistants	0.938
Creators	0.947
Managers	0.955
Parents	0.939

- **Comments and Observations on Sample Diagnostic Index Report**

1. Looking at customer service: In an absolute sense, all four firms are under spending relative to what is "expected" by customers. Compared to other firms in the industry, firm 2 is the leader, and firm 4 is the poorest.

2. No one firm has very strong "push" in channel 1, although firm 2 is the leader despite having overworked sales reps (i.e. they are working at 148% of normal capacity). From the low workload index, it is clear that firm 4 should either increase its distribution intensity or reduce the number of sales reps in channel 1 – currently firm 4 is not making effective use of its sales reps' time.

3. Firm 3 has the strongest position in Channel 2 – although its position is far from dominant. Firm 4 is the weakest in this channel – although its strategy may be to focus on channel 1.

4. The Sales Rep Effort Index shows that firm 3's sales reps are the most motivated as a result of receiving a higher commission rate than the other three firms' sales reps.

5. The Trade Promotion indices are determined by sales promotion spending and show the effects of spending by firms 2 and 3 in Channel 1, and firm 2 in channel 2.

6. Firm 1 is lagging in brand awareness – which is the result of both current advertising spending as well as expenditures in previous years.

7. The under spending on customer service by all four firms leads to an industry-wide customer service index of .966 – meaning that some of the latent demand was not realized due to the relatively poor reputation for customer service.

8. Healthy spending on advertising across the industry resulted in an advertising index of 1.042 – meaning that the relatively large investment in advertising has stimulated category demand for the VRD product.

9. The fact that the product appeal indices for all six segments are below 1.00 indicates that none of the four firms has done a particularly good job of targeting its product's attributes to match any of the consumer segments.

MARKET SHARE BY SEGMENT

This report is useful for identifying firms that have a dominant position (based on market share in units) in one or more market segments. A market share in excess of 0.500 would indicate a strong position, and a market share greater than 0.700 indicates a very strong position.

In addition to looking for leaders in each segment (i.e. looking down each column), it is useful to scan this report across each row. This may point out firms with no clear target market. For example, a firm whose share is less than 0.250 in every segment is not successfully targeting any segment.

MARKET SHARE BY CHANNEL

This report is useful for determining a firm's channel strategy. A market share of 0.400 or more indicates a very strong position in that channel.

INDUSTRY SALES REPORT

This report can help identify firms with unusually high or low margins. If a firm's market share in units is significantly higher than its dollar market share, then it has a low price-high volume strategy. Conversely, a firm with a high dollar share and substantially lower unit share would appear to have a high price-low volume strategy.

INDUSTRY SUMMARY REPORT

This report is particularly useful for following a firm's strategy over time. Key decisions and results for each firm in the industry are highlighted. Exhibit 7B contains parts of a sample Industry Summary Report – the summary for one firm is given, followed by the overall industry summary. Following the report are some comments based on the information in the summary report. Each row in the report summarizes key decisions, indices, and outcomes for a firm or the industry over time. The abbreviated format of this report is intentional. It makes it possible to summarize data for ten decision periods on a single page. Additional decision periods will continue on a new page. Brief explanations of the abbreviations used are given below:

1. 'Net. Contr.' is Net Contribution.
2. 'Budget' is the firm's budget available for the following period.
3. 'MR Report' includes the numbers corresponding to the market research reports which were purchased.
4. 'AD Dollars' is advertising dollars.
5. 'Ad Type' is the type of advertising. If blank, then no type was specified, or that option was not in effect for that game period.
6. Dollar amounts for Net. Contr., Budget, AD Dollars, and Sales Promotion are given in thousands of dollars.

- ## Exhibit 7B - Sample Industry Summary Report

```
INDUSTRY:  B FIRM: 1
```

Period	1	2	3	4	5	6
Net Contr.	192	581	655	1214	207	-73
Budget	838	940	955	1048	843	1000
# Sales Reps						
Channel 1	12	12	14	14	15	16
Channel 2	10	10	7	7	8	10
% Distribution Intensity						
Channel 1						
Channel 2						
Commission	5	5	5	5	5	7
BRAND: WORDSPLUS						
MR Report	3	6		4		
AD Dollars	320	334	370	420	490	215
Ad Type		P	I	I	D	D
Sales Promotion						
Channel 1	0	0	0	0	2	75
Channel 2	0	0	0	0	0	75
Product Features						
Feature 1	10	11	12	14	16	11
Feature 2	3	6	7	7	8	6
Feature 3	5	6	6	6	6	6
Wholesale Price						
Channel 1	97	115	123	148	141	113
Channel 2	97	115	123	148	148	86
Gross Margin/Unit						
Channel 1	38	41	42	59	41	39
Channel 2	38	41	42	59	48	12
INDICES						
Aware - P1	0.599	0.575	0.566	0.582	0.615	0.479
Service						
Push - C1	0.430	0.369	0.379	0.460	0.417	0.451
Push - C2	0.518	0.417	0.204	0.349	0.276	0.456

```
OVERALL INDUSTRY B SUMMARY
```

Period	1	2	3	4	5	6
Tot.Contr.	1764	1320	3325	6621	7752	9125
# Sales Reps						
Channel 1	32	50	61	70	64	65
Channel 2	53	37	47	56	57	60
Commission	5.25	5.25	5.25	5.25	5.25	5.50
VRD						
Unit Sales	139801	188925	221108	253855	270472	331309
$ Sales	24638	38217	45129	54128	62967	77719
Tot. Adv.$	1395	1820	1550	1500	1104	1259
Sales Promotion						
Channel 1	80	80	20	0	250	250
Channel 2	170	75	100	50	100	150
Average Gross Margin/Unit						
Channel 1	50.67	45.41	44.69	54.73	80.52	95.26
Channel 2	39.50	32.24	44.10	31.14	39.83	45.32

- **Comments and Observations on Sample Summary Report**

1. This firm's profitability has really fallen off in years 5 and 6. This can be largely attributed to the drop in gross margin per unit. In year 4, the gross margin per unit was $59 in both channels. In year 6, it was $39 in Channel 1 and $12 in Channel 2!

2. This firm has purchased very little market research. In year 1, report 3 was bought. In year 2, report 6 was purchased. Finally, in year 4, report 4 was purchased. With so little market research, the firm cannot know which segments are buying its brand, how it stands relative to competitors, etc.

3. Spending on advertising steadily increased until year 6 when it appears that some of the advertising spending was diverted to sales promotion.

4. The firm has continuously modified its product features. This may indicate that the firm is unable to decide on a target market, or is trying a trial-and-error approach. The lack of marketing research seems to indicate the latter.

5. The indices for Channel Push suggest no clear channel focus. The indices over time for Channel 2 in particular have been quite volatile. This may be in part the result of changes in distribution intensity.

6. At the overall industry level, sales and profits continue to grow. Spending on advertising has dropped some, whereas spending on sales promotion is increasing. Sales commissions were steady throughout the first 5 years, with a slight increase in year 6. Gross margins – especially in channel 1 – have increased in the past two years.

PART THREE

Teaching and Learning Tools

Part Three of this manual provides a variety of teaching and learning tools that can be used in conjunction with *The Marketing Game!*

8. *The Student Software*

INTRODUCTION

The TMGPlan, TMGTutor, TMGftp and the associated help files and video files for the tutorials comprise the student software for *The Marketing Game!* The software comes on a CD-Rom that is packaged with each copy of the Student Manual, and is also included on the Instructor Software disk. The CD-Rom features a program that automatically starts when the CD is inserted in a drive and one click of a button installs the software.

Support Available from Tutorials, Help Files, and the Appendix to Student Text

Complete instructions for using the TMGPlan program are included in Appendix A of *The Marketing Game!* Student Manual and in the TMGPlan.hlp online help system. TMGTutor and TMGftp also feature context-sensitive help systems. Furthermore, TMGTutor provides step-by-step tutorials (narrated, full-motion video clips) on using both TMGPlan and TMGftp. Students should find the software easy to install and use.

Comments on Use of the TMGPlan Program

- **Only Way for Students to View Password-Protected Report Files**

The TMGPlan program is the only way for students to view, print, or save a password-protected report file. However, if the instructor elects to distribute reports in standard text format they can be opened with a standard text editor or word processing programming.

- **Use of TMGPlan Is Optional, but Recommended**

Thus, use of the student software is optional. The simulation does not require that students use the programs—but it is recommended. Using this student

software can offer advantages for both the instructor and the students. The TMGPLAN program:
1. allows students to enter their marketing game decisions and save them as a password-protected file,
2. computes a pro forma financial summary that allows students to easily evaluate the marketing and financial implications of alternative marketing plans,
3. provides a simple way to view and print reports, and
4. is the only way for students to view password-protected reports.

- **Advantages**

Having students turn in their plan decisions as a file (on a disk or via other digital approaches) can save time for the instructor – especially with large classes. Furthermore, the responsibility for input errors rests with the students. For example, if a team fails to check its work and turns in a plan that calls for $40,000 in advertising expenditures -- rather than the $400,000 that was intended – they have no one to blame but themselves.

A second advantage of using the TMGPlan software is the pro forma analysis. Once students have entered their plan decisions, the TMGPlan program makes it easy to compute a pro forma financial summary, including the expected contribution to profit and the total spending against budget. If desired, students can then modify their marketing plan decisions. When they are done, the final pro forma can be printed and/or saved as a file.

System Requirements

The Marketing Game! student software is designed for a computer with a CD-Rom drive that runs with Windows 95 or later. The software requires about 3 megabytes of memory beyond what is required for the operating system. The software requires about 4 megabytes of available space on a hard drive. The TMGTutor program requires a multimedia PC with a sound card and speakers (or headphone).

Virus Considerations

An unfortunate reality is that computer "viruses" are widespread, and can wreak havoc. In light of this, we have designed the TMG Plan and report files so that it is nearly impossible to attach a virus to these files.

However, if a Plan file is submitted on a disk that includes other files (including hidden files or system files), a virus may attach to these other files and be transferred to the instructor's computer. So, when students submit their plans on disks, we recommend that they be instructed to put ONLY the Plan file on the disk, and to use a disk that is formatted without system files.

Even with these precautions, it is wise for instructors to have up-to-date virus checking software installed on their computers. Students should also be encouraged to take responsibility for virus checking before turning in a disk. Ask your computer support personnel to make virus-checking software available in your computer labs –*and remind students to use it!*

Compatibility with Earlier Editions

The student software for this edition of *The Marketing Game!* creates plan files that have a different naming convention (for example, for firm A1 the file is now called PlanA1.TMG rather than INPUTSA1.DAT) and different structure than the files created with earlier editions, among other reasons because the new files are password-protected. There are also differences that result from the upgrade to 32-bit Windows operating system.

These changes are irrelevant to students because it will only be in a rare case that a student will have used the earlier software. On the other hand, it may be useful for the instructor to know that a file created by the earlier edition of the software can be read by the TMGSim program, but only if the file is first renamed to adhere to the new filename convention.

This is likely to be relevant only in two situations. The first is the situation where the instructor would like to rerun "familiar" decisions (that is, handed in by students in a previous year) with the new software to get a feel for the improvements in the software.

The other situation might arise if students in a course do not have access to a computer that runs on Windows 95 (or later). In that event, it is possible (but not recommended) for a student to use the student software (in DOS format) from the earlier edition to create a file. For that reason, we provide a copy of the student software from the earlier edition on the Instructor CD-Rom. This software will run on most DOS machines and in a "DOS box" on most Windows 3.1 machines. For more information, see the readme.txt file on the Instructor CD-Rom in the folder \DiskOnly\DOSPlan.

We have maintained this "backward compatibility" in the event that it meets the needs of a specific instructor. However, we recommend against using this approach if it can be avoided. And usually it can be avoided by putting the Plan software on a computer or network server in a computer lab so that students who do not have their own computers can still use the software. Note that the tutorials can be run directly from the student's own CD-Rom--without being installed on a lab computer.

9. *PowerPoint Slides and Transparency Masters*

FILES ARE ON THE INSTRUCTOR CD-ROM

The Instructor CD-Rom includes a PowerPoint electronic slide show that can be used to introduce TMG and, later on, to emphasize key points, introduce new features, or tie TMG into other class lectures.

Provided in Various Formats, with a Viewer if It's Needed

The PowerPoint files are provided in various formats (and the PowerPoint Viewer software is also provided) to accommodate faculty who do not have the most recent version of PowerPoint. The PowerPoint Viewer software (with its own setup procedure) is provided for instructors who don't have access to PowerPoint at all. There is a readme.txt file in the \PowerPoint folder on the CD-Rom that explains the differences among the files provided.

The slide show includes a wide variety of full-color slides so that an instructor can pick and choose those that fit his or her needs and the time available. It is easy to create a customized show by using the PowerPoint feature to "hide" the slides that you don't want to use.

Last Slide Is a List that Is Hyperlinked to Each of the Other Slides

Alternatively, at the bottom of each slide there is an information icon, and when it is clicked during a slide show the last slide in the set appears. That slide has a list of all of the slides, and each item in the list is hyperlinked to that specific slide. Thus, if you select which slides you want to show and simply click the hyperlink you go directly to those slides.

Black and White Masters for Producing Overhead Transparencies

Although the CD-Rom includes the files for the full-color slides in electronic formats, this chapter also provides black and white masters for each of the slides in case your preference is to use overhead transparencies. **Note that the pages with the masters are not numbered** (so that there will not be page numbers on the transparencies). However, there is a number on each transparency master that corresponds to the slide number in the PowerPoint file. Even if you plan to use the electronic versions, the printed copies may also be useful to you in planning which slides you want to use. A complete list of the slides is provided below:

List of All PowerPoint Slides (and Transparency Masters)

1. Title slide
2. The Marketing Game: What Is It?
3. A Little Background
4. Special Objectives Served by TMG
5. Role of the Marketing Game
6. Integrative Marketing Strategy Planning Process
7. Overview
8. The Process
9. Industry Environment
10. Six Key Product-Market Segments
11. Past Sales by Market Segment (VRD)
12. Distribution Channels
13. Product Features – Voice Recognition Device
14. Computing Costs of R&D for Product Modifications
15. Product Features – Digital Vocal Communicator
16. Types of Advertising
17. Marketing Decision Responsibilities – Level 1
18. Expanded Marketing Responsibilities – Level 2
19. Expanded Marketing Responsibilities – Level 3
20. Production Economies of Scale
21. Response Functions
22. Budget Items – Level 1
23. Budget Items – Levels 2 and 3
24. Discretionary Budget
25. Computing Prices
26. Retail Prices Charged Final Consumers
27. A "Good" Wholesale Price
28. Competitor Analysis
29. Industry Sales Report
30. Product Features and Prices Report
31. Marketing Activity Report (Sample)
32. Market Research Reports – Level 1
33. Market Research Reports – Level 2

34. Market Research Reports – Level 3
35. TMG Software
36. Submitting Marketing Plans / Policies
37. Overview of Market Research Reports
38. Market Share by Segment
39. Market Share by Channel
40. Average Customer Preferences
41. Marketing Effectiveness Report
42. Detailed Sales Analysis
43. Customer Shopping Habits
44. Product Positioning Report
45. Recommendations
46. Blank slide (end of show)
47. List of all slides (with hyperlinks)

The Marketing Game!

3rd edition

Charlotte H. Mason • William D. Perreault, Jr.

1

The Marketing Game: What is It?

► A *"living"* case, where you learn about a situation, evaluate opportunities, develop a strategy, and make marketing plan decisions.

► In which you get regular *feedback*, in a report that summarizes your marketing outcomes and related financial results, based on both your plan and competitors' decisions.

► Where you *analyze* what you've learned by doing … to figure out answers to what you do not know (and could not know!) at the beginning.

► That challenges you *to improve your strategy* in light of the learning…

A Little Background

▲ Originally developed as the first PC-based marketing strategy simulation in 1985 …

➢ Routinely revised and updated since that time.

▲ Now one of the most widely used teaching simulations in the world.

➢ Used in hundreds of universities, exec programs and companies, international competitions, etc.

▲ We'll be using the third edition

➢ You'll need the student manual and accompanying CD-Rom (which has Windows software):

The Marketing Game!, by Charlotte H. Mason and William D. Perreault, Jr., 3rd edition, published by McGraw-Hill/Irwin, Burr Ridge, Illinois, 2001.

Special Objectives Served by TMG

▲ To develop skills in identifying marketing opportunities. This encompasses knowledge of and the ability to apply key marketing frameworks and tools for analyzing customers, competition, and marketing strengths and weaknesses.

▲ To develop insights about creative selection of target markets and making integrative strategy decisions concerning product, price, promotion, place and the needs of a target market.

▲ To develop skills in marketing analysis.

▲ To provide meaningful, practical experience in translating qualitative and quantitative analysis into conclusions about profitable marketing strategies and programs.

4   The Marketing Game!

The Role of the Marketing Game

The Game offers unique learning advantages, compared to other learning approaches (like reading texts and articles, lectures, guest speakers, case analysis and presentation, projects) because it:

▲ *Is dynamic*, like most business situations.

▲ Brings the *competitive* aspects of marketing to life.

▲ Highlights the need for *integrative planning based on* qualitative and quantitative analysis of the market environment.

The Marketing Game is Integrative ... and Covers All Aspects of the Marketing Strategy Planning Process

Narrowing down to focused strategy with quantitative and qualitative screening criteria

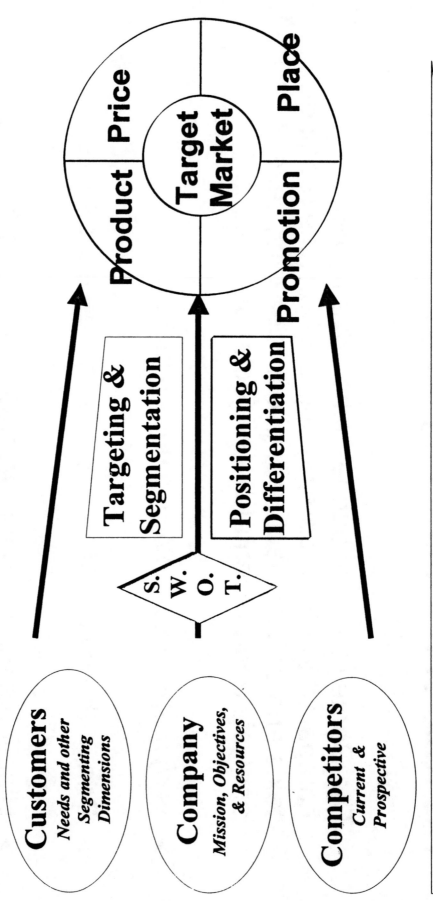

Customers
Needs and other Segmenting Dimensions

Company
Mission, Objectives, & Resources

Competitors
Current & Prospective

Targeting & Segmentation

Positioning & Differentiation

S. W. O. T.

Product Price

Target Market

Place Promotion

External Market Environment
Technology   Political & Legal   Social & Cultural   Economic

The Marketing Game!

6

Overview

▲ You take over marketing management responsibilities for your firm.

   ➢ Must satisfy customers *and* earn profits

▲ Focus is on marketing strategy planning.

▲ Requires integration of all strategy decisions.

▲ Requires attention to competitive environment.

▲ Considers short term and long term perspectives.

▲ Features ongoing, rapid feedback.

The Process

Analysis of market situation/opportunities

⇩

Planning and budgeting

⇩

Make marketing plan DECISIONS!!!

⇩

Submit plan decisions

⇩

The marketing game! simulation

⇩

Company reports returned to firms

Next Decision period

Industry Environment

▲ Market growth

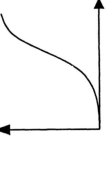

▲ Technological environment

➢ No major innovations expected

➢ Yearly revision cycle

▲ Competitive environment

➢ Type of competition depends on firms' decisions

Six Key Product-Market Segments

High-tech Managers	Modern Students	Concerned Parents
		Professional Creators
Harried Assistants		Home Users

Segments have different needs, preferences, situations, sizes, growth rates.

Past Sales By Market Segment
For Voice Recognition Device

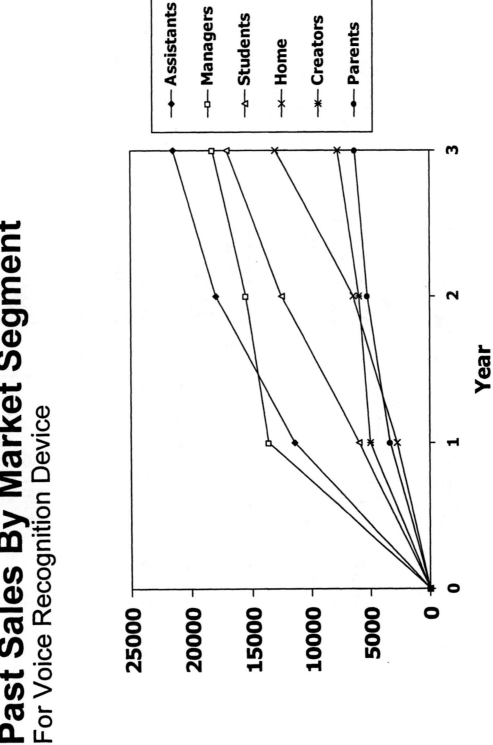

Distribution Channels

Firm 1   Firm 2   Firm 3   Firm 4

Firms reach customers through full-service dealers and Internet/mail-order discount dealers.

Different segments have different shopping preferences.

Channel 1 Traditional Dealers

Channel 2 Discount Dealers

High-tech Managers	Modern Students	Concerned Parents
		Professional Creators
Harried Assistants		Home Users

The Marketing Game!

Product 1: Voice Recognition Device (VRD)

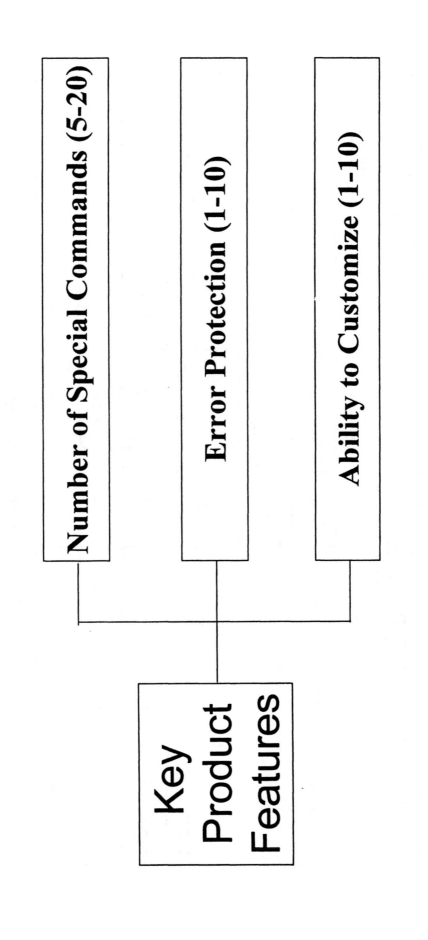

Key Product Features

Number of Special Commands (5-20)

Error Protection (1-10)

Ability to Customize (1-10)

R&D for Product Modifications: Computing Costs

Feature	Cost to Decrease	Cost to Increase
Special Commands (5-20)	$0	$8,000*(change)^2
Error Protection (1-10)	$0	$5,000*(change)^2
Ease of Learning (1-10)	$3,000*change	$3,000*(change)^2

Example

Feature	Last period's product	This period's product	Change	Cost to Change
Special Commands	6	8	+2	$8,000*2*2=$32,000
Error Protection	4	3	-1	$0
Ease of Learning	3	5	+2	$3,000*2*2=$12,000
			Total modification costs:	$44,000

Note: R&D for product changes is more expensive if you have to make big changes in a short period of time...

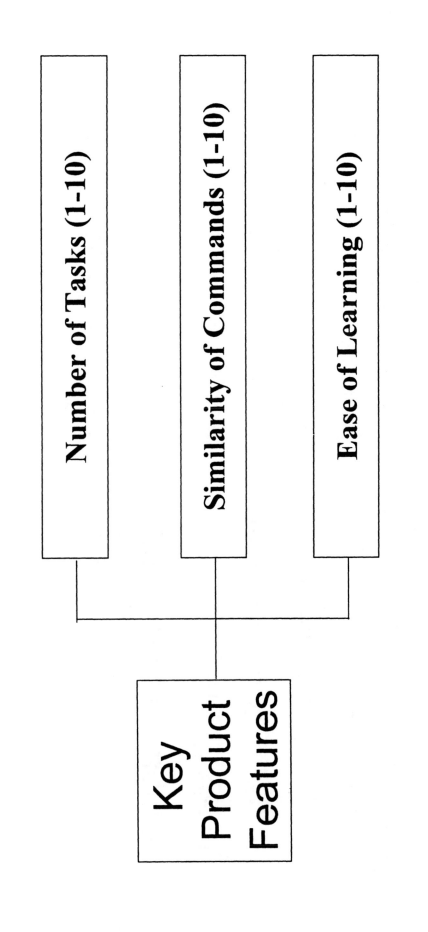

Level 3

Product 2: Digital Vocal Communicator (DVC)

Number of Tasks (1-10)

Similarity of Commands (1-10)

Ease of Learning (1-10)

Key Product Features

Types of Advertising

▲ Pioneering

▲ Direct competitive

▲ Indirect competitive

▲ Reminder

▲ Corporate (Institutional)

Marketing Decision Responsibilities *(Level 1)*

PRODUCT   Features
               (and R&D for product modifications)

PRICE   Wholesale price

PLACE   Distribution intensity in each channel

PROMOTION
-Advertising $ Spending

-Personal selling   Number of sales reps in each channel

CUSTOMER SERVICE $ Spending

MARKET RESEARCH   6 reports may be purchased

Demand forecast/
production order   Number of units

Expanded Marketing Responsibilities *(Level 2)*

PRODUCT Features (and R&D for product modifications)

PRICE Wholesale price in each channel

PLACE Distribution intensity in each channel

PROMOTION
-Advertising $ Spending

Type

-Personal selling Number of sales reps in each channel

Percent non-selling time

Commission rate

-Sales promotion $ Spending per Channel

CUSTOMER SERVICE $ Spending

MARKET RESEARCH 7 Reports May be Purchased

Demand Forecast/ Number of Units
Production order

The
Marketing
18 Game!

Expanded Marketing Responsibilities *(Level 3)*

2 PRODUCTs — Features (and R&D for product modifications)

PRICE — Wholesale price in each channel for each product

PLACE — Distribution intensity by channel, product

PROMOTION

-Advertising — $ Spending for each product
Type for each product

-Personal selling — Number of sales reps in each channel
Percent non-selling time in each channel
Commission rate
$ Spending per channel, product

-Sales promotion — $ Spending

CUSTOMER SERVICE — 7 reports may be purchased

MARKET RESEARCH

Demand forecast/production order — Number of units for each product

19   Marketing Game!

Production Economies of Scale

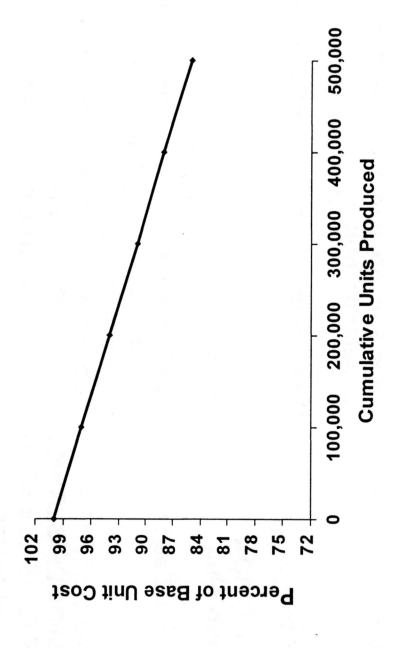

If the president decides to invest in new equipment, unit production costs will decline as cumulative production increases:

Response Functions and Marketing Spending

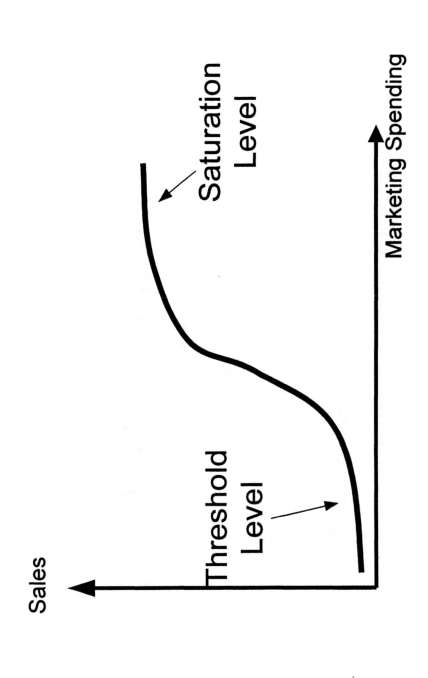

Sales

Threshold Level

Saturation Level

Marketing Spending

Spending too little may have little effect, but spending too much just increases costs and reduces profit.

The Marketing Game!

21

Marketing Budget Items *(Level 1)*

▲ R&D product modification costs

▲ Sales force salaries and severance pay

▲ Advertising expense

▲ Customer service expense

▲ Market research reports expense

BUDGET FOR FIRST PERIOD: $984k

Marketing Budget Items *(Level 2 and 3)*

▶ R&D product modification costs

▶ Sales force salaries and severance pay

▶ Advertising expense

▶ Customer service expense

▶ Sales Promotion Expense

▶ Market research reports expense

BUDGET FOR FIRST PERIOD: $984k

Discretionary Budget

▲ Policy on initial discretionary budget.

▲ Unspent money carries to future periods and earns interest.

▲ "When it's gone, it's gone."

▲ Policy on special budget requests.

Computing Prices

☐ **Computing Retail Prices from Wholesale Prices:**

Expected Retail Price = Wholesale price/(1-% Markup)

Example: Wholesale price = $105
Channel 1 Retail Price = ($105/(1-.50)) = $210

Channel 2 Retail Price = ($105)/(1-.35) = $161.54

▩ **Computing Wholesale Prices from Desired Retail Prices:**

Wholesale Price = Retail Price (1 - % Markup)

Example: Desired Retail Price = $190
Channel 1 Wholesale Price = $190/(1-.50) = $95.00

Channel 2 Wholesale Price = $190/(1-.35) = $123.50

The
Marketing
25   Game!

Retail Prices Charged Final Consumers

The retail price set by a dealer depends on:

▲ The wholesale price in the dealer's channel.

▲ The customary markup used in the channel.

▲ The portion of any sales promotion "deals" that the dealer passes along to consumers as a price reduction.

A "Good" Wholesale Price

▶ Should cover the unit cost of the product (given its features).

▶ Should result in a retail price that will appeal to target consumers.

▶ Should result in a profit margin that will contribute to other expenses and profit.

Competitor Analysis

▶ Estimate competitor's net contribution

▶ Analyze past strategies & likely changes.

▶ Evaluate positioning and target segments.

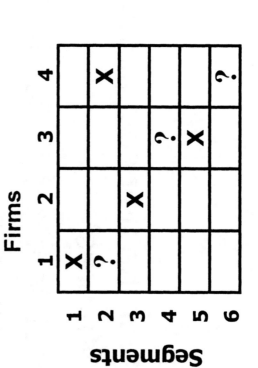

Firms

	1	2	3	4
1	X			
2	?			X
3		X		
4			?	
5			X	
6				?

Segments

Industry Sales Report

Brand	Unit Sales	Share (units)	$ Sales (retail)
Firm 1	25,151	.250	$4,292,964
Firm 2	25,151	.250	$4,292,964
Firm 3	25,151	.250	$4,292,964
Firm 4	25,151	.250	$4,292,964
Total	**100,604**		**$17,171,854**

Channel	Unit Sales	Dollars Sales
1	56,296	$10,696.240
2	44,308	$6,475,614

Product Features and Prices Report

Brand of VRD	Special commands	Error protect- ion	Ease of learning	Retail price channel 1	Retail price channel 2
Firm 1	8	3	3	$190.00	$146.15
Firm 2	8	3	3	$190.00	$146.15
Firm 3	8	3	3	$190.00	$146.15
Firm 4	8	3	3	$190.00	$146.15

The Marketing Game!

Market Activity Report *(Level 2)*

	Firm 1	Firm 2	Firm 3	Firm 4
Adv. Dollars	$250,000	$250,000	$250,000	$250,000
Adv. Type				
Sales Promotion				
Channel 1	$0	$0	$0	$0
Channel 2	$0	$0	$0	$0
No. Sales Reps				
Channel 1	10	10	10	10
Channel 2	10	10	10	10
Commission	5%	5%	5%	5%
Customer Service	$92,500	$92,500	$92,500	$92,500

The Marketing Game!

Market Research Reports *(Level 1)*

► 1. Market share by segment (all brands)

► 2. Market share by channel (all brands)

► 3. Consumer preference study

► 4. Marketing effectiveness report

► 5. Sales by segment by channel (own brand)

► 6. Consumer shopping habits study

Market Research Reports *(Level 2)*

▲ 1. Market share by segment (all brands)

▲ 2. Market share by channel (all brands)

▲ 3. Consumer preference study

▲ 4. Marketing effectiveness report

▲ 5. Sales by segment by channel (own brand)

▲ 6. Consumer shopping habits study

▲ 7. Product positioning report

Market Research Reports *(Level 3)*

▶ 1. Market share by segment (all brands)

▶ 2. Market share by channel (all brands)

▶ 3. Consumer preference study

▶ 4. Marketing effectiveness report

▶ 5. Sales by segment by channel (own brand)

▶ 6. Consumer shopping habits study

▶ 7. Product positioning report

Note: *separate reports are available for each product,*
Except for the consumer shopping habits study

TMGPlan Software

Easy to use for preparing and evaluating plans, managing reports

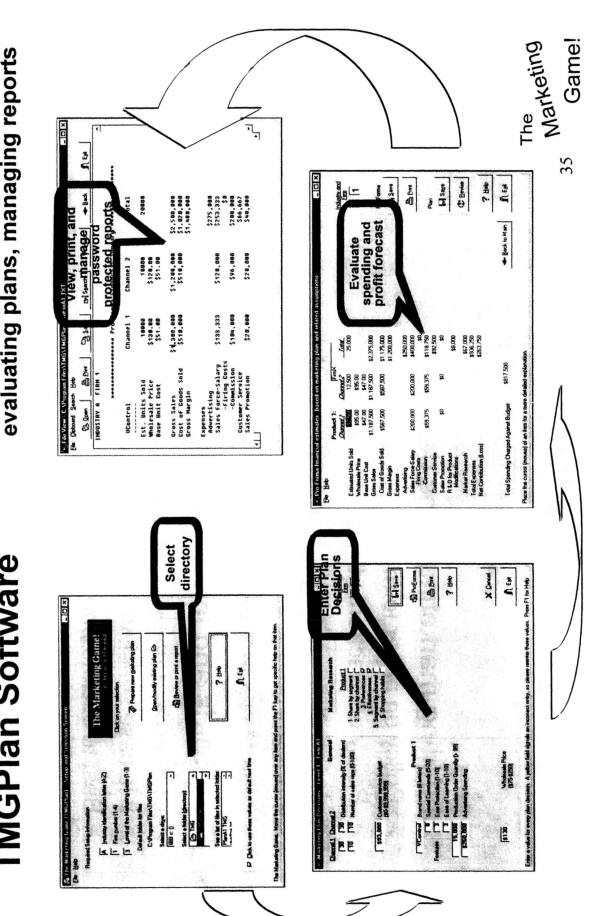

The Marketing Game!

35

Submitting Marketing Plans

▲ Submitting marketing plans decisions
  ➢ Policy on paper form
  ➢ Policy on electronic file

▲ Each firm has a distinct industry and firm identification
  ➢ Need to keep it straight!

▲ Passwords and the TMGPlan software
  ➢ Remember password used to create Plan
  ➢ It is case sensitive (upper and lower case make a difference)
  ➢ Best to stick to one password!

The Marketing Game!

36

Overview of Market Research Reports

▲ Market share by segment (all brands)

▲ Market share by channel (all brands)

▲ Consumer preference study

▲ Marketing effectiveness report

▲ Sales by segment by channel (own brand)

▲ Consumer shopping habits study

▲ Product positioning report (Level 2 & 3)

Market Share by Segment Report

Segment

Brand	1	2	3	4	5	6
Firm 1	0.250	0.250	0.250	0.250	0.250	0.250
Firm 2	0.250	0.250	0.250	0.250	0.250	0.250
Firm 3	0.250	0.250	0.250	0.250	0.250	0.250
Firm 4	0.250	0.250	0.250	0.250	0.250	0.250
Total Sales (units)	20,028	15,084	25,104	10,240	22,056	8,092

Who's selling to whom?
Who's buying what?
What is each firm achieving?
Which segments are buying?

Market Share by Channel Report

Brand	Channel 1	Channel 2
Firm 1	0.250	0.250
Firm 2	0.250	0.250
Firm 3	0.250	0.250
Firm 4	0.250	0.250
Total Sales (units)	56,296	44,308

What's selling where?
Who's buying what?

Consumer Preference Study

Segment	Special Commands	Error Protection	Ease of Learning	Price Range
Students	10-13	2-4	1-3	low
Home Assistants	7-10	2-4	6-8	low
Assistants	10-13	6-8	6-8	high
Creators	12-15	2-4	4-6	high
Managers	13-16	6-8	2-4	high
Parents	5-8	2-4	7-9	low

What kind of product would a segment prefer?
What reference price seems typical for the segment?
How are segments similar and different?

The
Marketing
40   Game!

Marketing Effectiveness Report

	Index	Competitors with lower Index	Competitors with equal or higher Index
Brand Awareness	0.550	0	3
Customer Service			
Consumer Group Rating	100%		
Industry Average Rating	100%		
Channel 1:			
Sales Rep Workload	100%	0	3
Dealer Satisfaction	1.00	0	3
Channel Strength	.500		
("Push")			
Channel 2:			
Sales Rep Workload	100%	0	3
Dealer Satisfaction	1.00	0	3
Channel Strength	.500		
("Push")			

Detailed Sales Analysis

Segment

Firm	<u>1</u>	<u>2</u>	<u>3</u>	<u>4</u>	<u>5</u>	<u>6</u>
Channel 1	896	1,109	5,602	1,808	4,363	1,086
Channel 2	5,269	3,337	1,396	1,196	1,865	1,074

Unit sales by segment and channel
Are you reaching your target?

Customer Shopping Habits

Segment	Percent of Shopping in Channel 1	Percent of Shopping in Channel 2
Students	?	?
Home Assistants	?	?
Creators	?	?
Managers	?	?
Parents	?	?

Who shops where?

How do shopping patterns match distribution focus?

43

Product Positioning Report

Brand	Segment					
	1	2	3	4	5	6
Firm 1	?	?	?	?	?	?
Firm 2	?	?	?	?	?	?
Firm 3	?	?	?	?	?	?
Firm 4	?	?	?	?	?	?

Which brands are closest to which segments?
Which segments have no close brands?

Recommendations

► Analyze the reports as you would analyze a case.

► Make *intentional* changes.

► Find a *balance* in marketing research spending.

► Be *integrative*--think carefully about how each decision impacts each of the others.

► Have some *fun!*

10. *Supplemental Assignments*

This chapter contains some suggestions for additional assignments to supplement *The Marketing Game!* Some of these assignments are broad-based in scope, whereas others focus on a specific topic such as advertising, sales force management, or marketing research. Of course, these are just ideas. Any given assignment might be useful or not—depending on your objectives.

BUDGET PLANNING

To ensure that firms do plan their budgets and evaluate the likely consequences of their decisions, the instructor can require firms to turn in a completed Budget Planning Form along with their Decision Form (or Firm Data Disk). The Budget Planning Form is explained in the Student Manual, and extra copies are provided.

This exercise forces firms to evaluate the likely profitability given their gross margin per unit and expected sales volume. This assignment can also be used selectively for firms who sell more than expected yet still experience poor profitability. Although this can be used with or without the help of the student software, the pro forma capability of the student software makes budget planning quite easy.

STRATEGY SUMMARY

An instructor may require firms to turn in a completed Strategy Summary Form along with the completed Decision Form (or Firm Plan file). This forces firms to articulate their strategy, and provides the instructor with an understanding of firms' strategies without second-guessing them based on firms' decisions. Copies of the Strategy Summary Form are provided in the Student Manual.

MARKETING PLAN

At some intermediate point during the game (perhaps midway), it can be useful to ask firms to submit a written report on their Marketing Plans. By assigning this midway through the game, industries have had the chance to evolve from the starting position, and firms have had the chance to develop and refine their strategies. In their plans, firms can look back and assess past periods, as well as explain their plans for the future. Although each instructor is likely to want to tailor the assignment to fit with his or her course objectives, a possible starting point or 'skeleton' assignment for a Marketing Plan is given below:

"To aid with long-range corporate planning, the president has requested that all divisions submit a Marketing Plan. This plan should explain your marketing strategy and plans for implementation. Topics to include are a discussion of your objectives, analysis of the marketing environment including your competition, the market segment or segments that are your primary target market(s), and your marketing mix. Your top management is eager to see both an analysis of your performance in recent years, as well as your plans for the future.

The text of this Marketing Plan must be typed, double-spaced, and must not exceed 5 pages in length. In addition, to help clarify, illustrate, or support your points, you may include up to 5 pages of graphs, tables, figures, and other exhibits. Be certain that any tables are clearly labeled. However, your reasons for providing such exhibits should be made clear in the text of your report."

REPORT/PRESENTATION TO THE BOARD OF DIRECTORS (OR SHAREHOLDERS)

This assignment may be especially useful at the end of the game as it provides firms a chance to recap and assess their marketing strategies. This can be done either as a written assignment or as a class presentation, or both. However, if done at the conclusion of the game, class presentations give firms an opportunity to listen to their competitors and to question them. More detailed suggestions for final class presentations are given in Chapter 12—Concluding the Game and Grading.

If class presentations are made, then the instructor may want to set up a Board of Directors using outside businesspeople, other faculty members, or more advanced students.

COMPETITOR ANALYSIS

The instructor may ask firms to submit a report analyzing their competitors (or perhaps just the one firm who is considered the "closest" competitor). Suggested topics to include are strengths and weaknesses, estimated profitability, past trends and anticipated future actions.

ADVERTISING PLAN

The instructor may ask each firm to develop an advertising plan for its product(s). This can include such items as the advertising objectives, the type of advertising, selection of media, the ad copy, and suggestions for assessing the effectiveness of the proposed plan.

PERSONAL SELLING/SALES PROMOTION KIT

The instructor may ask firms to develop a sales promotion kit for the sales reps to use. This could include a display for dealers, prepared sales presentations (or outlines) for the different channels, and an approach for identifying new prospects.

MARKET RESEARCH PROPOSAL

The instructor may ask firms to develop a proposal for marketing research that is not currently available to the firms. Such a proposal would define the problem, assess what is currently known, describe the type of primary data to be gathered and how it will be obtained, and how the results could be used.

11. *Test and Discussion Questions*

INTRODUCTION

This chapter provides a variety of objective and essay questions that can be used with *The Marketing Game!*

Available on the CD-Rom with Software to Generate Tests

All of the questions provided here are available on the CD-Rom in two electronic formats. One format is simply a word processing file (in rich text format) that can be read by most word processing programs, including Microsoft Word and Corel WordPerfect. The other format is as a test-generator database that makes it easy to select a subset of questions, and then save them as a formatted word-processing file or print them in a finished test format.

This test generator database and program relies on the Diploma software, which is already familiar to many instructors because it is used with many McGraw-Hill texts. To install this software, including the test question database, simply run the setup procedure that is in the \Tests\Diploma folder on the Instructor CD-Rom. It is easy to install and use and has its own online help.

We **recommend that you not use the random question selection feature of the Diploma software**. This is because some of the questions are simply alternative ways of asking about the same material (in the event that you want to use, for example, alternative versions of tests).   However, questions within sections are ordered the way the corresponding material is ordered in the text, so it is easy to see when there are several questions on the same topic. The answer key at the end of each section also provides a page reference for the corresponding material in the student text.

Comments Concerning Test Questions

- **True-False and Multiple-Choice Questions**

The first portion of this chapter contains a variety of true-false and multiple-choice questions for use with *The Marketing Game!* You may want to select some of the questions to include on a test. Or, you may want to use some of them for a "pop-test" or self-test session (graded or not) before the first decision is due—to see if students have studied the text.

Most of these questions are easy—at least for a student who has read the material carefully and/or been working at making marketing decisions. On the other hand, a student who has blown through the decisions is likely to have little idea on many of the questions...easy or not!

If teams are used, individual student answers to even simple "policing" questions can help give you some idea about which students are working and which ones are "being carried" by the group. Of course, you can also give the students copies of the questions—along with an answer key—for them to use as a "self-check." (The Diploma software can create an answer key for each test you create).

The questions are organized in the order of the reading in the student text. The answer key at the end of the sections for the true-false questions and for the multiple-choice questions provide the correct answer and a reference page in the student text.

- **Discussion Questions**

Following the objective test questions are some possible discussion questions (and answers) related to *The Marketing Game!* Some of these are quite challenging, and others are more basic policing-type questions. Questions might be included on a test, assigned as homework, or used for class discussion. Note that a few of the questions toward the end of the set are only appropriate for students who have been competing at the higher level of the game, or using the student software as a decision aid.

TRUE-FALSE QUESTIONS

1. The basic ability to translate "natural language" into digital commands is the main area where VRD firms are limited in how they can compete because it is an area where they can't differentiate from other firms in the industry.
   A) True
   B) False

2. Some VRD customers just want to learn something new and have some fun--and they don't care so much about the cost.
   A) True
   B) False

3. From the very beginning, the four firms in the voice recognition device market offered different marketing mixes and appealed to different marketing segments.
    A) True
    B) False

4. At the start of *The Marketing Game!*, the voice recognition device (VRD) product-market is in the market introduction stage of the product life cycle.
    A) True
    B) False

5. At the start of *The Marketing Game!*, the voice recognition device (VRD) product-market is in the market growth stage of the product life cycle.
    A) True
    B) False

6. The Conscientious Teachers are one of the six main product-market segments for voice recognition devices.
    A) True
    B) False

7. The broad product-market for voice recognition appears to be in the late part of the growth stage of the product life cycle.
    A) True
    B) False

8. The Concerned Parents segment is the smallest market segment at the point when the previous marketing manager turns over responsibility for marketing in the firm.
    A) True
    B) False

9. The primary aim of advertising is to inform dealers about voice recognition devices (VRD) and to promote features of specific brands.
    A) True
    B) False

10. The segment that has the largest unit sales volume is also always the most profitable target market.
    A) True
    B) False

11. Once a firm has established a marketing strategy that has proven effective over time, it would be foolish to change anything about it.
    A) True
    B) False

12. Advertising that helps to pioneer the market by focusing on building awareness and informing consumers may help other firms as well as the firm that does it.
    A) True
    B) False

13. For voice recognition devices (VRD), the main features--those that customers are most concerned about--are the number and variety of special commands, ease of learning, and protection against user errors.
    A) True
    B) False

14. In *The Marketing Game!*, even though there are differences among customers, all customers prefer a voice recognition device that offers a higher level on the "error protection" feature.
    A) True
    B) False

15. It is possible to have too much "error protection" for some target customers.
    A) True
    B) False

16. All four VRD producers sell their VRDs directly to final consumers from a website and also indirectly through traditional dealers.
    A) True
    B) False

17. Differences in the amount of service and warranty coverage provided by the dealers and differences in the quantities they sell have resulted in a higher customary markup percent in Channel 1 than in Channel 2.
    A) True
    B) False

18. In the voice recognition device product-market, there are three channels of distribution: full-service dealers, discount dealers, and direct dealers.
    A) True
    B) False

19. The Internet/mail-order discount dealers overcome customer concerns about buying a product without seeing it by offering a better warranty than the traditional dealers.
    A) True
    B) False

20. The traditional dealers charge a higher price than the Internet/mail-order dealers but they also offer a better warranty.
    A) True
    B) False

21. The amount of marketing emphasis that a dealer is willing to devote to a brand of voice recognition device increases as the distribution intensity and number of dealers in the channel who handle that device increases.
    A) True
    B) False

22. The amount of service that the dealers in Channel 1 provide to their customers is likely to increase if a VRD producer's sales reps puts more emphasis on training and supporting the dealers' sales efforts.
    A) True
    B) False

23. At the point when the previous marketing manager retired (at the start of *The Marketing Game!*), advertising expenditures by the four VRD producers totaled $4 million, with an average of about $1,000,000 per firm.
    A) True
    B) False

24. Pioneer advertising is especially useful for promoting how the features of a particular brand of VRD differ from other brands.
    A) True
    B) False

25. If some firms in the industry make more aggressive use of trade promotion, dealers will expect it and use it as a bargaining lever with other VRD suppliers, which just increases costs.
    A) True
    B) False

26. Direct competitive advertising is likely to have a more positive long-term effect than is indirect competitive advertising.
    A) True
    B) False

27. Direct competitive advertising helps to build selective demand (and share of market) for a firm's own brand.
    A) True
    B) False

28. At the beginning of *The Marketing Game!*, corporate advertising had been the most commonly used type of advertising in the VRD market.
    A) True
    B) False

29. In the VRD product market, sales promotion is often more effective in prompting short-term responses than in building longer-term brand insistence.
    A) True
    B) False

30. The formula for the markup percent used by dealers in the VRD market is:
    Dealer markup percent + (Retail selling price - Wholesale price) / (Wholesale price)
    A) True
    B) False

31. A sales promotion by a VRD producer in the discount channel is likely to be at least partially passed on to consumers in the form of a lower retail price.
    A) True
    B) False

32. Customers in the VRD product-market want the highest quality product, and that means the product with the highest level on each of the three main features.
    A) True
    B) False

33. Currently, the possible range for the number of special commands for a voice recognition device (VRD) is between 5 and 20.
    A) True
    B) False

34. Currently, the possible range for the number of special commands for a voice recognition device is between 1 and 10.
    A) True
    B) False

35. An increase of one in the number of special commands in your voice recognition device (VRD) will add more to the unit production cost than increasing the ease of learning index by one.
    A) True
    B) False

36. For voice recognition devices (VRDs), increases in the Error Protection Index are the most expensive product modifications.
    A) True
    B) False

37. Product modifications that increase the levels of a product's features can be expensive -- however, any modifications that decrease the levels of product features have no cost.
    A) True
    B) False

38. Special commands can be added to a VRD only if a firm it willing to spend some money on R&D.
    A) True
    B) False

39. The previous marketing manager could figure out what the unit production cost for a voice recognition device (VRD) would be by simply knowing the levels of a product's features.
    A) True
    B) False

40. Each sales representative sells both to traditional dealers and Internet/mail-order discount dealers, but not directly to final customers.
    A) True
    B) False

41. Successfully achieving the objectives of a high level of distribution intensity in a channel requires more sales reps than would be needed for a low distribution intensity.
    A) True
    B) False

42. At the start of *The Marketing Game!*, sales representatives are paid on a straight salary basis.
    A) True
    B) False

43. If a firm changed its distribution intensity from 30% to 50%, that would signal a shift towards more exclusive distribution.
    A) True
    B) False

44. For a salesperson to be effective and achieve a high level of sales, he or she must work with both traditional dealers and with Internet mail-order discount dealers.
    A) True
    B) False

45. In *The Marketing Game!*, the sales representatives for a VRD firm sell either to dealers in channel 1 or dealers in channel 2 but not both.
    A) True
    B) False

46. In *The Marketing Game!*, the sales representatives for a VRD firm sell either to final customers or to dealers.
    A) True
    B) False

47. Transferring sales representatives between channels should be avoided whenever possible because all transferred sales representatives must be retrained for the new channel.
    A) True
    B) False

48. In *The Marketing Game!*, advertising by a firm affects its market share, but has no effect on the absolute amount of total industry unit sales.
    A) True
    B) False

49. Newly hired sales representatives are not as productive as experienced reps since they must spend 20 percent of their first year in training.
    A) True
    B) False

50. When deciding how much to spend on advertising, it is important to remember that very low levels of advertising spending -- below some "threshold level" -- will have little impact.
    A) True
    B) False

51. When forecasting demand in order to set a production order quantity, it is only necessary to be within 20 percent (either plus or minus) of the actual demand to avoid the costs associated with over producing or the lost opportunities of under producing.
    A) True
    B) False

52. It is important not to overproduce since unsold products are kept in inventory -- and inventory costs are very high.
    A) True
    B) False

53. In *The Marketing Game!*, a firm's gross sales in a channel are computed by multiplying the number of units sold in that channel by that channel's retail price.
    A) True
    B) False

54. In *The Marketing Game!*, a firm's gross sales in a channel are computed by multiplying the number of units sold in that channel by that channel's wholesale price.
    A) True
    B) False

Answer Key – True-False Questions

1. A, Page: 13	19. B, Page: 22	37. B, Page: 32
2. A, Page: 14	20. A, Page: 22	38. A, Page: 32
3. B, Page: 14	21. B, Page: 23	39. A, Page: 33
4. B, Page: 17	22. A, Page: 24	40. B, Page: 35
5. A, Page: 17	23. B, Page: 24	41. A, Page: 35
6. B, Page: 17	24. B, Page: 24	42. B, Page: 35
7. B, Page: 17	25. A, Page: 25	43. B, Page: 35
8. A, Page: 17	26. B, Page: 25	44. B, Page: 35
9. B, Page: 18	27. A, Page: 25	45. A, Page: 35
10. B, Page: 18	28. B, Page: 25	46. B, Page: 35
11. B, Page: 18-19	29. A, Page: 25	47. B, Page: 36
12. A, Page: 19	30. B, Page: 26	48. B, Page: 36
13. A, Page: 20	31. A, Page: 27	49. A, Page: 36
14. B, Page: 20	32. B, Page: 27	50. A, Page: 36
15. A, Page: 20	33. A, Page: 31	51. A, Page: 41
16. B, Page: 21	34. B, Page: 31	52. B, Page: 42
17. A, Page: 22	35. A, Page: 32	53. B, Page: 46
18. B, Page: 22	36. B, Page: 32	54. A, Page: 46

MULTIPLE CHOICE QUESTIONS

55. At the start of *The Marketing Game!*, the segment with the largest unit sales volume is the:
    A) modern students
    B) home users
    C) harried assistants
    D) professional creators
    E) high-tech managers

56. Concerning market growth at the beginning of *The Marketing Game!*, it is true that:
    A) the various market segments have been growing at equal rates.
    B) the segments that grew the fastest in the past are not necessarily the best targets for the future.
    C) none of the segments increased in size in the past, but that is because the firms had all been offering basically the same marketing mix.
    D) the smallest segments appear to be growing the fastest, whereas the largest segments have actually decreased in size.

57. At the start of *The Marketing Game!*, the voice recognition device (VRD) product-market is in the stage of the product life cycle which is best characterized as:
    A) market introduction
    B) market penetration
    C) market growth
    D) market maturity
    E) sales decline

58. Which of the following features do customers always want more of?
    A) number of special commands
    B) error protection
    C) ease of learning
    D) both (B) and (C) are true
    E) none of the above

59. Given a wholesale price of $100, the likely retail price (to the nearest dollar) in Channel 1 is:
    A) $135
    B) $150
    C) $154
    D) $200
    E) $270

60. Which of the following statements about the dealers in Channel 2 is NOT true?
    A) They offer more service and a better warranty than Channel 1 dealers.
    B) These dealers are mainly "order takers."
    C) They tend to offer lower prices than Channel 1 dealers.
    D) They have more appeal to price sensitive customers.
    E) They usually operate from an Internet website.

61. At the start of *The Marketing Game!*, sales promotion was
    A) a relatively new tool for the software producers.
    B) more effective in building long-term brand insistence than prompting short-term response.
    C) targeted toward final customers rather than dealers.
    D) all of the above are true.
    E) both (A) and (C) are true -- but NOT (B).

62. Based on what you know about the customary markup percents taken by dealers, and given that you want a "target" retail price for your brand of $180 in Channel 2, what wholesale price should you set?
    A) $90
    B) $117
    C) $120
    D) $133

63. The marketing budget allocated to a firm in *The Marketing Game*:
    A) is within 20 percent of its gross sales for the previous period.
    B) is equal to the firm's profit contribution for the previous period.
    C) is equal to the budget for other firms in each period.
    D) increases as profit contribution increases, but is not equal to the profit contribution.

64. The maximum number of special commands that a voice recognition device (VRD) may have is:
    A) 5
    B) 10
    C) 15
    D) 20
    E) 25

65. Which of the following product modifications will be the most expensive?
    A) increasing the number of special commands by one.
    B) increasing the error protection index by one.
    C) increasing the ease of learning index by one.
    D) all of the above are equally expensive.
    E) it is impossible to say without knowing the current levels of the different features.

66. Which of the following items is not paid for out of your marketing budget?
    A) R & D for product modifications
    B) sales force salaries
    C) marketing research
    D) sales force commissions
    E) advertising expenditures

67. In *The Marketing Game!*, which compensation plan is used to pay sales representatives?
    A) straight salary
    B) straight commission
    C) a combination plan with both salary and commission
    D) the compensation plan depends on the channel to which the sales rep is assigned.
    E) salary plus a bonus if sales volume is 20 percent more than the demand estimate (that is, production order quantity)

68. If a firm increases its distribution intensity in one channel from 30% to 50%, then it should probably also:
    A) increase its distribution intensity in the other channel.
    B) select a new target market.
    C) increase the number of sales reps in that channel.
    D) increase its wholesale selling price in that channel.
    E) none of the above is true.

69. Which of the following statements concerning distribution intensity is NOT true?
    A) A distribution intensity of 50% means that a firm wants its product to be available at more dealers than at a 20% level.
    B) It is possible to either increase or decrease the distribution intensity for a channel.
    C) A distribution intensity of 100% corresponds to the most intensive distribution.
    D) Selective distribution is in between exclusive and intensive distribution.
    E) Distribution intensity applies only to Channel 1 because in Channel 2 each VRD firm sells directly from its own Internet website.

70. Which of the following statements is NOT true?
    A) Advertising by a firm affects its market share.
    B) Advertising by a firm affects the market growth.
    C) The primary aim of advertising is to inform dealers about voice recognition devices and to promote features of specific brands.
    D) Very low levels of advertising spending -- below some "threshold level" -- will have very little impact.
    E) The effectiveness of your firm's advertising depends, in part, on the advertising decisions of your competitors.

71. The Brand Awareness Index on the Marketing Effectiveness Report:
    A) measures the proportion of customers who are more aware of your brand than with any of your competitors' brands.
    B) can range from -1.0 to 1.0.
    C) in often .9 or higher for an established brand.
    D) measures the proportion of customers who are aware of your brand.
    E) is the same for all firms in the industry.

72. If your requested production order quantity was 20,000 and actual production was 23,000, then you know that:
    A) the requested production order quantity was within the desired range -- meaning that you neither overproduced, nor did you "stockout" or run short of product to sell.
    B) you may have been able to sell more units -- is you had produced more.
    C) there must be a mistake, since it is impossible to sell more than your requested production order quantity.
    D) the additional 3,000 units over the requested amount must have come from inventory leftover from a previous period.

73. Excess inventory resulting from overproduction:
    A) is stored (at an inventory carrying cost) for sale in future periods.
    B) is sold to an overseas subsidiary for an amount equal to the unit cost.
    C) is sold to an overseas subsidiary for an amount equal to 85% of unit cost.
    D) is sold to an overseas subsidiary for an amount equal to 85% of the wholesale price.
    E) is sold to dealers in the discount channel, and at a lower price than what is charged to dealers in the traditional channel.

74. Which of the following statements concerning the gross margin is NOT true?
    A) The gross margin is the money that is left after the cost of goods sold is subtracted from gross sales.
    B) The gross margin is used to cover expenses (other than the cost of goods sold) and contribute to profits.
    C) Gross margin will always be greater than zero -- although that is no guarantee that the net contribution will be positive.
    D) All of the above are true.

75. If your budget, as a percent of the industry total, is 29%, then you know that:
    A) the dollar amount of your budget is the highest in the industry.
    B) the dollar amount of your budget is average for the industry.
    C) your firm has a higher budget than at least one other firm.
    D) your firm has a lower budget than at least one other firm.
    E) none of the above are true.

76. When preparing a marketing plan decisions form (either on paper or electronically) for a given period, a marketing manager does NOT explicitly specify :
    A) the level of product features.
    B) which segment(s) the firm is targeting.
    C) how sales reps are to be allocated across distribution channels.
    D) the wholesale price.
    E) which marketing research reports, if any, are to be purchased.

77. Which of the following is NOT a decision that is under the control of the marketing manager in *The Marketing Game*?
    A) the wholesale price.
    B) the salary for sales reps.
    C) the level of the product features.
    D) what marketing research reports to receive.
    E) the spending on customer service.

Answer Key – Multiple Choice Questions

55. C, Page: 13-17	63. D, Page: 30	71. D, Page: 40
56. B, Page: 14	64. D, Page: 32	72. A, Page: 41
57. C, Page: 17	65. A, Page: 32	73. C, Page: 42
58. E, Page: 19-20	66. D, Page: 35	74. C, Page: 46
59. D, Page: 19-20	67. C, Page: 35	75. C, Page: 47
60. A, Page: 22-23	68. C, Page: 35	76. B, Page: 58
61. A, Page: 25	69. E, Page: 35	77. B, Page: 58
62. B, Page: 26	70. C, Page: 36	

DISCUSSION QUESTIONS

78. If a firm decides that the features of its product do not meet the needs of its target market, it can modify the product. Under what conditions might it make sense for the firm to make small changes over several periods rather than making a big change all at once in one decision period?

A firm needs to modify its product when the product features do not seem well suited to the target market, or when it is going after a new target market that has different preferences. But, as is often the case in real business situations, big changes in a product may be quite expensive. In *The Marketing Game!*, big changes in product features— especially increases in the levels of the first two features of a product—are much more expensive per unit of change than small changes. Thus, a firm may decide that it does not have the budget to make big expensive changes all at once, or even if it had the needed budget it might conclude that the likely benefits of a small change, relative to the smaller cost, would out weigh the perhaps greater benefits of a big change that costs significantly more to implement in a single period. Risk is another factor. Even with marketing research information about segment preferences, it is usually not possible to be 100 percent confident how customers will respond to a changed product—especially if the preferences of the target market are changing over time. If the current product is doing reasonably well with the target market, it might be wiser to make smaller, more conservative changes—and evaluate the results to see if additional changes seem necessary—rather than making a big change that might result in an unfavorable reaction.

79. An article in a computer magazine recently quoted a marketing manager for a well known software firm as saying: "Some companies spend too much time worrying about customers' needs and not enough time worrying about competitors." Evaluate this statement. Be specific in relating your answer to the product market situation in *The Marketing Game!*

A firm needs to develop a marketing mix that will meet the needs of a target market to be successful. And in that sense there is no such thing as paying too much attention to customers' needs. But the marketing concept says that a firm should aim to satisfy customer needs at a profit through a total company effort. Thus, focusing on customer needs by itself is not enough. There are some target markets that have needs that the firm cannot satisfy at a profit. Competition can be a key factor here. If another firm already is doing a good job of meeting customers' needs, it may be very difficult to compete—especially if the other firm already has the loyalty of the customers, has a strong position with dealers in the channel that reaches that market, or has lower costs or more money to spend. Thus, it usually doesn't make sense to devote a "whole company" effort to a target market unless the company can do so with some competitive advantage. The size of a marketing opportunity is also affected by the nature of competition—even if a competitor does not have a significant advantage at the outset. If two or more firms are targeting the same market segment(s), and doing a similarly effective job of offering a marketing mix to meet the needs of the segment(s), then the purchases of those customers are likely to be split between the different suppliers. A market that might be quite profitable for one—or even two—direct competitors may be too small to support another competitor trying to do the same old thing. A "me-too" marketing strategy may prove to hurt competitors, but in the end not help the firm to achieve a profitable position in the market.

80. Discuss the concept of "competitive advantage" as it applies in *The Marketing Game!*.

In *The Marketing Game!*, all firms in an industry start out in basically the same "position" and with the same resources and limitations. Thus, at the beginning, no firm has a competitive advantage. Over time, however, a firm can develop an advantage—if it does a good job of analyzing market opportunities and developing a marketing mix that meets the needs of the target market. Part of the process of analyzing market opportunities is evaluating what competitors are doing—or are likely to do in the future. Understanding customers and competitor strengths leads to two different approaches for developing a competitive advantage. One approach is to avoid head-to-head (direct) competition by going after a specific segment with a well-blended marketing mix. A firm that does this early begins to achieve success with a target market, and it may be expensive and less attractive for another firm to try to take away the business. A competitor would need to "come from behind" in developing a product to meet the needs of those customers—and big product changes are much more costly than small changes. Further, a competitor might need to adjust the size of its sales force—which requires time for training—or it might need to put more effort in a different channel. In addition, a firm that is "close" to a market will be able to make more effective use of marketing research information. It can fine-tune its marketing mix with a clearer view of the likely results—whereas a newcomer will need to experiment more to learn about how a particular segment responds to its offering. In addition, success in one period helps to contribute to success in the future. A firm that is making better profits will have more money to spend on its marketing program—so it will have resource flexibility. This too can contribute to a competitive advantage.

It is much more difficult for a firm to develop a competitive advantage by going head-to-head against a competitor. But it is possible. Effective use of marketing research information, and careful control of costs—will be especially important in such a situation. The firm that is facing close competition needs to be especially careful to get the greatest possible return from marketing expenditures. For example, very careful spending on advertising will be required to make certain that there is brand awareness, but that money isn't just being wasted. The right amount of sales effort needs to be devoted to the channel—to make certain that dealers will push the firm's products. And—at higher levels of the game—sales promotion to the trade will need to be adjusted to consider both costs and potential benefits.

In short, it is possible for a firm to develop a competitive advantage over time. But the market is dynamic. So no firm can maintain a competitive advantage unless it continues to refine its offering to meet the challenge of changes in customer preferences and changes in competitive threats.

81. It is often necessary for a firm to modify its target market or its marketing mix—or rethink its whole strategy—at different stages of the product life cycle. Discuss why this is so, illustrating your points based on experiences from *The Marketing Game!*

During the product life cycle, markets and competition change. The profitability of different segments may change as their preferences change and as their size changes. A segment that may be attractive early in the life cycle may not grow as rapidly as another segment—or it may be more costly to serve. For example, a segment that wants more features over time will require a more costly product, but may not be willing to pay more. In fact, margins may be squeezed as price competition comes into play. Changes in competition have other effects, too. The nature of competition changes over time, as well. In *The Marketing Game!*, the number of competitors in the overall product market does not change. But strategy changes by a competitor may pose new threats—or open up new opportunities. Thus, the number of direct or close competitors may vary at different points in time. All of these changes may require adjustments in the marketing mix.

82. It is often argued that a firm must carefully blend all of the elements of the marketing mix—so that the pieces fit together as a whole in meeting customer needs. Drawing on your experience in *The Marketing Game!*, give specific examples of ways in which decisions about product, promotion, place, and price decisions must be blended.

Different segments prefer to buy from different types of dealers in different channels of distribution. A firm must make certain that dealers in the channel that reach its target market know about its product and are willing to put effort behind it. That requires that adequate sales force effort be placed on that channel—and that the right selling tasks be emphasized. Of course, product features must be matched to customers needs, too, and that involves costs. A firm must make certain that the price it charges dealers is high enough to cover these costs—and still leave enough for other expenses and contribution to profit—while at the same time resulting in a retail price that customers will pay after dealers have added their markup. This is a challenge, especially since dealers in different channels add different markups —which means that the final price to customers may vary across channels.

83. In *The Marketing Game!,* a firm sold a larger quantity of its product than it originally planned to produce—but it still lost money. If you were the president, what would you think about the firm's marketing manager? Be specific.

It is not unusual for a firm to lose money if it sells less than it expected to sell given its marketing mix. In that case, the revenue will be lower than expected and there may not be enough money to cover all of the costs. But, if the marketing plan has been analyzed before it is submitted and the expected quantity is in fact sold, the manager should know in advance that it was going to be an unprofitable plan. Thus, the firm's president would logically think that the marketing manager has done sloppy planning. An exception to this might arise if a firm is basically offering a marketing mix that has been well thought out, but is nevertheless sacrificing short-term profits for a better long-run position. For example, a marketing manager might develop a marketing plan that involved big (expensive) product modifications in one period—fully expecting that those changes would result in losses in the current period but that they would put the firm in a much stronger competitive position in the future.

84. Consider the following situation in *The Marketing Game!*: A firm developed and submitted a marketing plan. But, when the president of the firm saw the results for the period, he learned that the firm had run out of money. That is, the plan cost more than was available in the marketing budget. When asked about this, the marketing manager for the firm explained: "We sold more than we thought we would sell, so our costs were higher than expected. That's why we were over our budget." What is your reaction to the explanation offered? Be specific.

The explanation is not valid. All of the items charged to the marketing budget are known in advance—regardless of the quantity produced or sold. Variable costs such as sales commissions and unit production costs are not charged to the marketing budget. Thus, a plan that exceeds the budget has not been carefully considered in advance.

85. In *The Marketing Game!*, what factors need to be considered in setting a wholesale price?

There are four basic factors that need to be considered in setting a wholesale price. Costs are a basic consideration. The wholesale price needs to be high enough that it will cover variable costs (production costs and sales commissions) and leave enough to cover other expenses (R&D for product modification costs, marketing research expense, fixed promotion costs and customer service) and contribute to profit. The likely resulting retail price also needs to be considered. The retail price depends on the markup added by the dealer. That will vary depending on the channel involved. But the resulting retail price must be at a level that target customers will pay— given the rest of the marketing mix. Finally, at higher levels of the game, sales promotion to the trade must also be considered. Some dealers—especially those in channel 2—tend to pass along some of the sales promotion deals offered them by a producer as lower prices to customers. Thus, the amount of promotion also may influence the final retail price in the channel.

86. *For use only with students competing at levels 2 or 3 of the game.* In *The Marketing Game!*, a firm can select different types of advertising—depending on its objectives. The choices available include pioneering advertising, direct competitive advertising, indirect competitive advertising, reminder advertising, and corporate (institutional) advertising. Briefly discuss the conditions in which it would make the most sense for a firm to use each of these different types of advertising.

a. Spending on pioneering advertising will make the most sense early in the life cycle of a product—when there is still an opportunity to stimulate market growth. Further, in *The Marketing Game!*, pioneering advertising will make the most sense for a firm that has a large overall share of the market. That way, it will obtain a greater benefit from any increase in the size of the potential market.

b. Direct competitive advertising will be especially useful for a firm when it is facing immediate—perhaps new—competition for its target market. In this situation, the firm is likely to be concerned about winning market share away from competitors. Of course, direct competitive advertising will in general make more sense when the firm's product is in fact superior to a competitor's product (that is, when it does a better job of meeting target market needs).

c. Indirect competitive advertising is likely to be most useful when a firm faces or anticipates greater competition in the future. It wants to build selective demand for its product—and is perhaps willing to trade off some current advertising effect for future benefits. This also suggests that this type of advertising will be most useful when the firm thinks that there will be substantial future growth in the market.

d. Reminder advertising is only useful once a brand is already familiar to customers. Since it usually takes some time to build up awareness of a brand, it is likely to be more effective once a brand moves toward the mature stage of the product life cycle.

e. Corporate (institutional) advertising focuses on promoting the overall firm rather than a specific product. Thus, a firm that only has a single product is likely to get little additional effect from this type of spending. On the other hand, it can be useful for a firm that has more than one product.

87. For use only with students competing at level 3 of the game. It is possible to obtain "economies of scale" in marketing effort in *The Marketing Game!* when a second product is introduced? Briefly explain your answer giving specific examples from the context of the game.

The main opportunities for economies of scale in marketing effort within *The Marketing Game!* come through the sales force. At first this may seem to be a difficult question, but after some thought most good students will realize this. It is discussed in the student text. And the decision form for level 3 (two products) includes decisions on a single sales force for both products. Another type of economy is subtler, but it too is discussed in the text. Market research information about customer shopping habits applies to both products, so only needs to be purchased once. In addition, the cost of the marketing effectiveness report is $25,000 for one product, but only an additional $5,000 for the second product. Another type of economy is not discussed directly, so it is likely that only the best students will think about it. In particular, a firm that has two products can achieve some economies with corporate-type (institutional) advertising. This is implicit in the decision to use corporate advertising, but even so many students will not have thought about the issue this way.

12. *Concluding the Game and Grading*

FINAL PRESENTATIONS BY STUDENTS

After the last period's results are returned to the firms, the learning experience can be extended by some post-game analysis by both the students and the instructor. The end of the game is an ideal time for firms to recap and assess their marketing strategies. Although this can be done as either a written assignment or a class presentation (possibly both), the latter can offer special benefits. Class presentations give firms an opportunity both to listen to their competitors and to question them. Not only do students like the chance to 'talk' with other firms in their industry, but also knowing they must respond to questions from competitors forces firms to be thorough and honest in their post-game assessments.

Various formats can be used for final class presentations. A time limit of between 15-30 minutes including questioning seems reasonable. The organization and content of presentations may be left to the firms to decide, or the same format can be used by all firms. Topics to consider may include the firm's objectives, their target market(s) and marketing mix, assessment of their competitors, overall industry trends, major turning points, successes and failures, and key learning experiences. Firms can be instructed to address their presentations to their shareholders, their Board of Directors, or the incoming marketing management team who will succeed them. Students in the audience can assume these roles and be prepared to ask questions.

FINAL WRAP-UP BY THE INSTRUCTOR

In addition to reports by individual firms, the instructor may want to summarize firms' performances and/or industry performance. Summarizing the performances of firms within an industry can demonstrate how firms—which all started in the same position—have evolved differently as a direct result of their decisions. And in situations where there are multiple industries, comparisons across industries can illustrate many fundamental marketing concepts. For example, there is likely to be one industry where firms competed intensely for the same target markets and ignored others, leading to slow overall sales growth and marginal profitability. This may be contrasted with a different industry in which firms avoided head-on competition, and achieved higher profitability and industry sales growth. Other contrasts may include two industries with comparable profitability, but seemingly different strategies. In one case profits may have resulted from relatively higher margins and lower unit sales volumes, compared with the second case of lower margins coupled with higher unit sales volumes.

Some simple plots of firm and industry trends can illustrate many points. In fact, student learning can occur from putting this information together. So, some instructors may ask individual firms to compile and present their statistics and/or compare them to other firms in an industry.

Keep in mind that the **TMGtoXLS program exports TMG summary data (for every decision period, firm, and industry) to a standard spreadsheet file (see Appendix H), which makes it very easy to plot whatever variables are of interest.** This is especially useful if you want to do comparisons across different industries.

Some suggestions of summary trends and statistics to plot include:

Within each industry:
1. Annual unit sales for each firm.
2. Annual net contribution for each firm.
3. Beginning (at end of year 1) and ending unit (and/or dollar) sales for each market segment.
4. Beginning (at end of year 1) and ending unit (and/or dollar) sales for each channel.
5. Annual spending by firm on advertising (or customer service).

Across industries:
6. Total annual industry sales by industry.
7. Total annual net contribution by industry.
8. Average wholesale price (or gross margin) within each channel by industry.
9. Total number of sales reps within each channel by industry.

Samples of several of these plots are included in Exhibit 12A.

EVALUATING STUDENT PERFORMANCE IN THE GAME

There are many different ways to evaluate student performance in *The Marketing Game!*—and what is best will depend on your preferences and objectives. Thus, there is no "ideal" approach to grading. However, in this section we provide a few ideas that may help you decide on what approach you want to use. Most instructors consider several factors—and then combine them into an overall grade. This can be done qualitatively, or you can give each component of performance its own grade and then developed an average—perhaps weighting the more important components more heavily.

- **Exhibit 12A - Sample Summary Plots of Firm and Industry Trends**

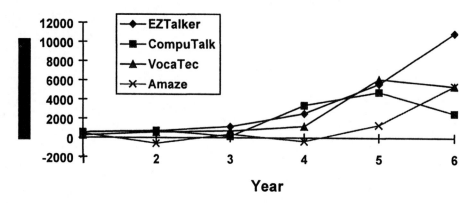

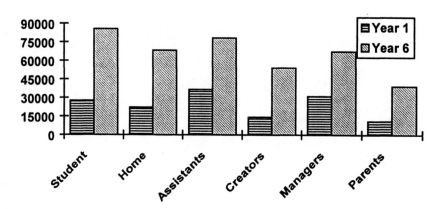

Use Profit Contribution as a Measure

Some instructors like to anchor grades in the game—at least partly—on how much profit a firm has earned over time. There are both advantages and limitations to this approach. From a practical standpoint, a key advantage is that it provides a quantitative summary measure of performance. After all, most businesses point to the "bottom line" as a measure of success. Further, our general experience is that firms that are thoughtfully managed perform well in the game.

On the other hand, simply rank-ordering firms on profit contribution may disregard information—such as how much improvement there has been, how well positioned the firm is at the end of the game to earn future profits, and the like.

If you want to use profit contribution as one element of your grading, you may find it convenient to look at the summary report (or to use the Summary.XLS Excel file created by the TMGtoXLS program) at the end of the game. Either approach gathers the information you need in one place. Then you can focus on the data of concern.

There are, of course, different ways of looking at the profit data. For example, you might want to average profit contribution across periods—or perhaps just for the last three or four periods. Another approach is to remove several of the firms lowest profit contribution periods (and/or highest contribution periods) and focus on the ones that remain—so that you have a clearer picture of profit performance without the extreme values that may have come into play in a few decision periods.

Use Quality of the Strategy as a Measure

Another approach is to assign a grade to the quality of a firm's strategic decisions. Here, the focus is not just on the profit earned but also on the consistency of the strategy and how logical it appeared to be at the time.

A good way to do this is to set up a chart at the beginning of the game—where each firm is a row in the chart and each decision period is a column. Then, you can look at the diagnostic report as you run each period and assign a "subjective" grade. For example, you might grade a firm down if it sets a price that isn't even high enough to cover marginal costs—say nothing about contributing to profit. Or, you might give a student a higher grade if it is clear that the product offered is well suited to a target market, and in addition the student is focusing sales effort on a channel where that target segment likes to shop. In contrast, a firm that seems to have no target and jumps around from one period to the next in what it is trying to do would be graded down.

The process of keeping "score" each period does take some time—but it really can be done quite quickly with the help of the SUMMARY report and the diagnostic reports. The real advantage of keeping track period by period is that this avoids a too heavy reliance on memory—or the bias that may be introduced by a strong performance right at the end.

Of course, even if you score decisions over time you can weight them differently in arriving at a composite grade for this aspect of performance. Here, as with profit measures, you might want to drop the score for the low period—or count the last half of the game more heavily.

Individual vs. Team Grades

If you run the game with student teams—rather than having individual students make decisions for a firm—you will need to decide if you are going to assign all students on the team the same grade. Sometimes this "team grade" approach can work well and promote a cooperative team effort. On the other hand, it can create problems—especially if the instructor makes the assignments to teams. In most classes there will be a few people who have not carried their share of the weight.

One simple—but reasonably effective—way to get at the extent to which individuals have contributed to the group effort is to see if they at least know basic facts about the decisions that you make in the game. For example, you might select some of the test questions from Chapter 11 of this manual and give a short test in class toward the end of the game. Most students will consider these simple "policing" questions easy and get them correct. But, a student who has not participated in the day-to-day process of planning decisions is likely to find some of them hard.

Another approach—one that can be quite effective—is to have students do an evaluation of others on the team. A form is provided on the next page that can be used for this purpose. It asks each student to write a brief evaluation of other students on the team—and then to divide up 100 points among the different team members. If you have not tried this before, you might be surprised how revealing it can be!

If you are going to use this approach, you will want to decide if you are going to tell students in advance that you are going to do it. Telling them in advance may create some pressure toward "equal" shares. But, that is not necessarily a problem. In fact, telling students in advance what you plan to do can have the advantage of keeping a problem from surfacing. In general, you will probably want to assure students that you will keep individual evaluations confidential. You might also want to tell them that it is their responsibility to keep their own evaluations confidential.

Of course, some instructors prefer to have such peer evaluations available to a student. This is not without its problems—but it can work, especially if the students are more mature (say, in an MBA class).

Supplemental Assignments

If you are using supplemental assignments along with the game, they can provide the basis for grades on other components of performance related to the game. For example, you might want to assign grades on budget exercises, a presentation to the "board of directors," a written report on the logic of the firm's marketing plan, etc. Here again, you can assign individual grades or team grades—depending on the nature of the work, whether materials are prepared and submitted by individuals or teams, and of course your own preferences.

Administrative Responsibilities

Some instructors like to treat the administrative responsibilities of the game as a graded aspect of performance. For example, an instructor might give a firm a few bonus points if all assignments and decisions are in on time and in proper order— with all instructions carefully adhered to. By contrast, a few "penalty" points might be subtracted if, say, a firm's decisions are submitted late. Care should be used in adopting this sort of approach—but on a selective basis it can be a good motivator for students to see that they have responsibilities—not just to the instructor but to the whole class—to do what they are supposed to do and when they are supposed to do it.

Explaining the Grading System

Different instructors have different feelings about how much detail they want to provide—either in advance or after the fact—about how performance on the game will be graded. One approach is to outline in general terms (either in class or in the course syllabus) what will "count." That way, there is some flexibility toward the end of the course in using a system that seems the most equitable to all concerned.

On the other hand, some students are upset if they do not know ahead of time how grades will be computed. And others will want some progress report grades along the way. This is a matter that must be decided by the individual instructor. For example, one of the authors always tell students, from the outset, that they are expected to make profitable decisions and that profit contribution will be a major criteria in evaluating performance at the end of the game (in part because it helps to reduce post hoc rationalization by students who have repeatedly turned in decisions that were not well thought out and NOT profitable!) .

Whatever you decide is right for your class and teaching style, having considered it in advance can be very helpful—so that you have a well thought out response ready when a student asks (and almost certainly at least one will ask!).

PART FOUR

Details of the Model

Part Four of this manual contains additional detail about the structure and logic underlying the simulation model used in *The Marketing Game!*

You do not need to study these chapters. On the other hand, they can help you see how student decisions interrelate. Chapter 13 provides a general overview. Chapter 14 is much more detailed, and it reveals the inner workings of the simulation model.

CHAPTER 13, OVERVIEW OF THE EFFECTS OF DECISION VARIABLES

CHAPTER 14, THE MODEL STRUCTURE

13. Overview of the Effects of Decision Variables

The Marketing Game! model is interactive—meaning that a firm's performance depends on its whole set of decisions as well as decisions made by other firms in the industry. As a result, there is no "right" decision in a specific area that will always work. Rather, firms must plan strategies that are consistent across decision areas and that anticipate what competitors are likely to do. Thus, any effort to describe the isolated effects of a specific decision variable risks some oversimplification. On the other hand, it is often useful to have a general overview of the key effects of each decision area.

This chapter offers a concise summary of the major ways in which each of a firm's decisions will affect its results. To keep the discussion focused, this chapter does not delve into the details of the simulation model—or into the specifics of how decision variables interact. That material is provided in the next chapter—which presents a more thorough and detailed explanation of the logic and computational flow of the simulation model. Parts of that chapter are technical in nature.

Either chapter can be read independently and there is some overlap in the discussion. However, you will find that they both offer insights—from somewhat different perspectives—on the market environment of the game.

The Marketing Game! focuses on strategic marketing variables. In each game period, firms make decisions in the following areas (some decisions are marked 'optional' meaning they may not be activated at the less difficult game levels):

Product:	Brand Name (for identification only)
	Product Features
	(optional—second product)
Place:	Distribution intensity (% of dealers) for each channel
Customer Service:	Total firm expenditures

Promotion:
   Advertising: Expenditure level
                         Advertising Type (optional)
                         (optional—second product)

   Personal Selling: Number of sales reps in each distribution channel
                         Percent of non-selling time (optional)
                         Commission rate (optional)

   Sales Promotion: Expenditures in each channel (optional)
                         (optional—by product)

   Price: Wholesale Prices (optional–in each channel)
                         (optional—by product)

   Market Research: Requests for reports
                         (optional—by product)

   Demand Forecasting: Requested production order quantity
                         (optional—by product)

Each of these decision areas is discussed in more detail in the sections that follow.

PRODUCT

Brand Name

The brand name is used for identification purposes only and has no impact on a firm's results. Although there are no restrictions in the computer program that require a firm to keep the same brand name throughout the game, *we strongly recommend that firms not be allowed to change brand names once the game is underway*. Such changes can be confusing to other firms in the industry and serve no useful purpose.

Product Features

Each product type (i.e. voice recognition device and digital vocal communicator) has three design features, which may be modified within the allowable ranges. A brand's features directly affect how attractive that brand is to the different market segments. Other things being equal, a brand with features close to those desired by a segment will have a higher share of sales than brands, which do not match that segment's consumer preferences very well. Thus, product features are one factor which influence a brand's market share of a segment.

Product features have another role in the simulation. In addition to affecting the share of sales that a firm receives, product features also affect demand (and therefore the total unit sales volume). The closer that available brands match the preferences of a segment, the higher the sales volume to that segment will be. In other words, designing brands to satisfy customers increases the market potential.

Product features also affect unit production costs. And changing features results in product modification costs. Larger R&D changes in a single time period are much more expensive than small changes.

PLACE

Distribution Intensity

Firms set the distribution intensity – measured as the percent of dealers in each channel who stock and sell the software. (This is a revision of and replacement for the "market exposure" decision from the previous edition.) Note that the "ideal" level of distribution intensity depends on the rest of the marketing mix. It is especially critical that the firm set the sales force size to match their distribution intensity. The percent of dealers that the firm wants to work with determines how much work sales reps have to do. A distribution intensity that is too high given the number of sales reps leads to a situation where sales reps are overworked and cannot effectively service their accounts. Too low a distribution intensity relative to the sales force size leads to wasted spending on personal selling. Individual firms can keep track of their sales force workload by purchasing the Marketing Effectiveness Report (Report 4).

The distribution intensity also influences the brand's availability to customers – and thus the "push" it gets from dealers in a channel. Other things being equal, the firm with greater distribution intensity will have the greatest channel push.

CUSTOMER SERVICE

In all difficulty levels of the game, firms specify their total annual expenditures on customer service – customer service supports both products if a firm has two products. Spending on customer service affects both market shares and total category demand. For each firm, the "expected" customer service spending depends on the current "installed customer base" as measured by total units sales (of both products) in the previous period. The ratio of actual spending to the "expected" spending results in the individual firm's customer service rating. Furthermore, if a firm's rating is lower than the industry average, sales and market share will drop. Conversely, a higher than average rating will lead to relatively greater sales and market share.

In addition, customer service spending also affects the total industry demand. As the level of total industry customer service expenditures exceed the expected level, category growth is boosted. In contrast, lower than expected spending on customer service can depress industry demand.

PROMOTION

Advertising Expenditures

Each firm decides how much to spend on advertising for each brand. Advertising expenditures have two possible effects: (i) to raise the level of brand awareness among customers and, (ii) to encourage growth of primary demand for the product market. In general, increased advertising spending leads to increased brand awareness. However, expenditures by one firm are compared with the industry average—thus, simultaneous escalation of advertising spending by all firms tends to drown one another out. In addition, there is a saturation point. Outspending competitors beyond the saturation point leads to little additional benefit.

Advertising expenditures also spur the growth of primary market demand. As the level of total industry advertising increases, so does the market potential. In contrast, low levels of industry advertising will reduce the level of market growth. Once again, there is a saturation point beyond which increased total industry spending has little impact.

Advertising Type (Optional)

In levels 2 and 3, firms choose which type of advertising to use for each brand from the following: pioneering, direct competitive, indirect competitive, reminder, and corporate. Each of these types has a different effect on the market:

PIONEERING advertising helps to encourage primary demand for the product market. This can be especially useful early in the game when the total market is relatively small. Pioneering advertising that helps to expand the overall market may be a better choice than competitive advertising that aims to increase a firm's share of the market. Pioneering advertising may also make sense if a firm has a large share of the market— and the firm with the largest share will get the most benefit when the overall market expands.

DIRECT COMPETITIVE advertising increases a firm's advertising effectiveness in the period in which it is used, but has relatively little carryover to future periods. This type of advertising aims to increase a firm's market share in the current period but has little impact on overall market growth.

INDIRECT COMPETITIVE advertising also increases a firm's advertising effectiveness in the period that it is used (although the effect is less than with

Direct Competitive). In addition, compared with direct competitive there is more carryover benefit in future periods.

REMINDER advertising can be useful for a firm that has achieved brand awareness of at least 50 percent. If this is true, then reminder advertising will stretch a firm's advertising dollars. On the other hand, as brand awareness drops below 50 percent, then reminder advertising is increasingly ineffective.

CORPORATE (institutional) advertising is useful for a firm with two products— because institutional advertising for one product has spillover effects to the other product. For a firm with one product, corporate advertising is less effective than the other options.

Number of Sales Reps

Each firm decides the number of sales reps in each distribution channel. The number of sales reps directly affects (i) how well the firm is able to sell to and support the dealers and, (ii) the overall 'push' the dealers give the firm's brand in a channel. The number of dealers that the sales reps must call on is determined by the percent of dealers specified by the distribution intensity decision. Too few sales reps for a given distribution intensity means that the sales reps are stretched too thin, and are unable to give each retail account adequate time and attention. Sales effort in Channel 1 exhibits decreasing returns – that is, it takes increasingly more sales reps to achieve a greater percent of distribution intensity. For example, to increase the percent of dealers from 10% to 20% requires about 3 sales reps selling full-time, whereas an increase from 80% to 90% requires about 4.5 full time sales reps. In contrast, adding sales reps in Channel 2 exhibits constant returns to scale, i.e. is linear.

If a firm has two products, then some increase in the sales force size is needed compared with a single product firm. The number of additional sales reps depends on the relative emphasis the firm places on the two products. If sales of one product are small compared with the other, then not many additional sales reps are needed. On the other hand, if the two products have approximately equal sales volume, then up to 40 percent more sales reps may be needed as compared with a single product firm.

Changes in sales force size from one period to the next also affect a firm's results. When a firm decreases the total number of sales reps, $5,000 in severance pay will be charged for each sales rep fired. When the size of the sales force is increased, the new reps spend 20 percent of their first year in training and are only available for selling 80 percent of their first year (note that the percent non-selling time will reduce their "effective" selling time even further).

Each sales rep gets $20,000 a year in salary. Sales Salary expense is allocated between products when the firm offers two products.

Percent of Non-Selling Time (Optional)

In levels 2 and 3, firms decide how much time the sales reps will devote to non-selling activities. In level 1 the percent of non-selling time is fixed at 10 percent. As described above, one effect of percent non-selling time is to reduce the amount of time a sales rep has for selling. In addition, percent non-selling time determines how satisfied dealers are with the amount of support they receive from a firm's sales reps. In general, increasing the percent non-selling time (relative to competitors) will increase the dealers' satisfaction. This, in turn, leads to a stronger competitive position. The magnitude of the effect of non-selling time varies across the channels. The traditional dealers in Channel 1 are much more responsive to non-selling activities than are the discount dealers in Channel 2.

Commission Rate (Optional)

At levels 2 and 3, firms decide the commission rate for their sales reps. At level 1, the rate is fixed at 5 percent. The commission rate directly affects the motivation of the sales reps and the amount of effort they put into selling. The effect is determined by both the absolute commission rate as well as the commission rate compared with that of competitors. In the absolute sense, 5 percent serves as the anchor point—rates above 5 percent will increase the effort put forth by sales reps, and rates below 5 percent will lead to reduced effort. In a relative sense, the firm with the highest commission percent will have the most aggressive sales force, and the firm with the lowest rate will have the least aggressive sales force.

Sales (Trade) Promotion Expenditures (Optional)

In levels 2 and 3, firms decide on sales promotion spending in each channel and for each brand. Sales promotion expenditures may have two possible effects: (i) reduce the retail price through deals and allowances, and (ii) enhance personal selling effectiveness by building goodwill with dealers. The effects vary across the channels. In Channel 1, the dominant effect of sales promotion is the building of goodwill, whereas in Channel 2 the dominant effect is to reduce the retail price. How much goodwill is prompted through trade promotion spending also depends on the distribution intensity level – the greater the percentage of dealers the firm is trying to serve, the more "diluted" the effort of a given dollar amount of promotion.

It is important to note that sales promotion is a 'relative' issue—if all firms spend equally on sales promotion, the goodwill effect cancels out leaving firms no better off than if they had all spent nothing on sales promotion. (It is only the goodwill effect, and *not* the price reduction through deals, that cancels out.)

WHOLESALE PRICE(S)

In level 1, each firm sets (one) wholesale price for its brand. This one wholesale price is used in both channels of distribution. In levels 2 and 3, firms set the wholesale price separately for each channel. Retail prices are computed from the wholesale prices using a markup on selling price of 50 percent in Channel 1 and 35 percent in Channel 2. These retail prices are then discounted based on the amount of sales promotion expenditures (if any) available for deals and the number of units sold on deal. Different segments have different price sensitivities – so retail price influences the share of a segment's purchases.

MARKET RESEARCH

In each period, firms may purchase any or all of the market research reports listed below. Purchase of market research has no direct effect on a firm's results other than the cost. However, there should be an indirect effect as the information purchased can greatly help a firm to develop and implement an effective strategy.

Report Number	Research Report Title	Cost for Product 1	Cost for Product 2
1	Market Share by Segment	$15,000	$15,000
2	Market Share by Channel	$12,000	$12,000
3	Consumer Preference Study	$30,000	$30,000
4	Marketing Effectiveness Report	$25,000*	$25,000*
5	Unit Sales By Segment and Channel	$15,000	$15,000
6	Customer Shopping Habits	$7,000	N/A
7	Product Positioning Report**	$30,000	$30,000
* Since part of the information in Report 4 is the same for Product 1 and Product 2, the cost to purchase this report is $25,000 for one brand or $30,000 for both brands. ** Report 7 is only available in Levels 2 and 3.			

Reports 1, 2, and 5 contain market share and/or actual sales volume data and will vary with each decision period. Report 4 summarizes the effectiveness of a firm's decisions in the promotion and customer service areas and will also change with each decision period. Report 3 contains average customer preferences. These reported preferences vary from one period to the next due to two factors—some of the variation comes from sampling error and some represents actual changes in preferences. However, these changes are gradual and move in a consistent direction over time. Report 6 provides customer shopping habits. The reported figures vary over time but, unlike report 3, *all* the variation is sampling error and the true shopping habits are constant throughout the simulation. The product positioning numbers in Report 7 depend on the available brands' features (excluding price), the segments' ideal points and importance weights – and will vary from one period to the next.

PRODUCTION ORDER QUANTITY

In each decision period, firms must estimate the demand for their brand(s) in order to decide the amount of production to request. Although the actual production quantity will, in general, differ from the requested amount, the amount requested sets both lower and upper bounds on the actual production. Specifically, actual production is adjusted from the requested amount by up to 20 percent in either direction to meet demand. Thus, if a firm underestimates demand (and hence, the requested production), the actual production will automatically be adjusted upward by as much as 20 percent. Beyond that point however, the firm will lose potential sales due to a product shortage. If this happens and other firms in the industry have not reached their limit on production, then half of the potential lost sales will spillover to competitors and half will simply be lost.

On the other hand, a firm may overestimate demand (and hence, requested production). Once again, actual production will automatically be adjusted downward by as much as 20 percent. Beyond that point however, no further adjustment is possible (since the product is already made and in inventory). If this happens, at the end of the period all excess inventory is automatically transferred to an overseas subsidiary. The revenue received for transferred inventory is equal to only 85% of the product's *unit cost*—the 15% difference (loss) will appear as Transfer Charges on the firm's financial summary. Transfer charges are not charged against the budget.

BUDGET FOR NEXT PERIOD

While not actually a decision variable for firms to decide, the budget amount is a variable in *The Marketing Game!* Initially, all firms start with the same budget of $984,000. However, once the game is underway, a firm's budget will depend on its net contribution. The higher a firm's net profit contribution in the current period, the higher its budget will be for the next period. However, the relationship is nonlinear—as net contribution increases, the budget also increases but at a decreasing rate. And, even if a firm is not profitable, it will still receive a budget for the next period. The minimum budget amount is $800,000 and any firm with a negative net contribution will receive this amount.

Occasionally, firms want to know what happens if they don't spend their entire budget. The answer to this is two-fold. First, whatever isn't spent also isn't an expense. Thus, to the extent that not spending the full budget amount reduces expenses, that will help to increase the net contribution. However, this must be balanced against the expected gains in sales revenues that could have resulted from spending the additional amount. Only if a firm believes that it has reached the point where the gains don't outweigh the extra expenses should a firm try this approach. Second, that portion of their budget that isn't spent cannot be saved for later periods. In each period, the budget for the next period depends solely on net contribution in the current period. For example, assume a firm chooses not to spend its entire budget and winds up with a negative net contribution. Its budget for the next period will be $800,000—the excess does not carry over. (However, any unused residual discretionary reserve funds do carry over to successive periods.)

14. *The Model Structure*

This chapter describes the logic and structure of the simulation model used in *The Marketing Game!* Our objective is to provide a clear, non-technical discussion. For completeness, we sometimes add technical details that may be of interest to some instructors. But, you can skip any of the technical details and still get a complete overview of the "market environment" and how it works. The flow chart in Exhibit 14A presents an overview of the model. Each module in the flowchart is numbered. These numbers are cross-referenced to the sections below.

1. HISTORY FILE

The history file of past decisions and parameters includes the following information:

Game year: starts with 1 and increments with each decision period.

Budget amount: used to verify that a firm's expenditures are within its budget.

Product features in previous period: used to compute product modification costs.

Advertising carryover index: used to compute new brand awareness index.

Brand awareness in previous period: used to compute new brand awareness index.

Sales by segment in previous period: used in computing current period's sales, and also to determine current customer base which needs customer service support.

- **Exhibit 14A – Overview and Structure of** *The Marketing Game!* **Model**

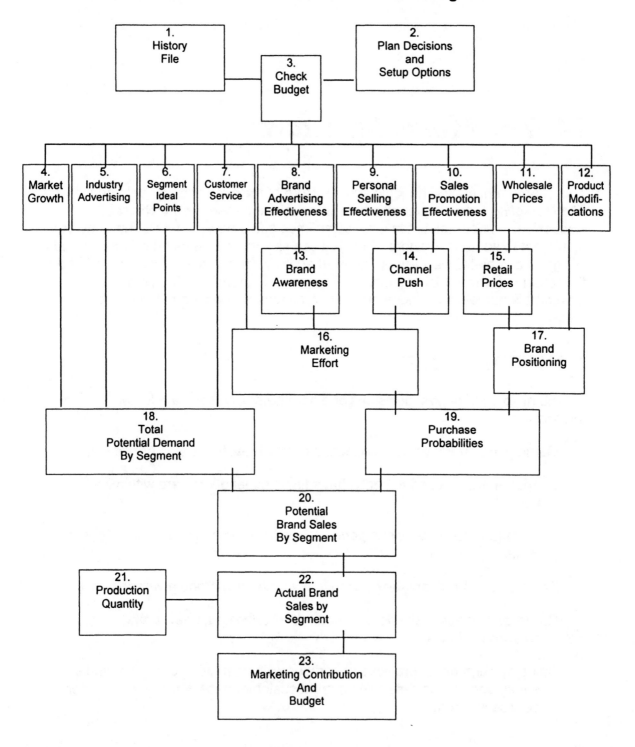

Cumulative spending against discretionary reserve fund (if any): if firms have been granted a discretionary reserve fund, any unspent amount is available against current spending if the budget is not sufficient.

Cumulative production: (if production economies of scale option is used) used to compute unit production cost.

2. INPUT DECISIONS

You may choose from 3 basic configurations of the simulation depending on the desired level of difficulty and number of decision variables (see Chapter 3). The decision variables for each level are summarized in Exhibit 14B. In Level 1, the most basic level, the number of decisions variables has been kept to a minimum while still preserving the essence of marketing strategy planning. Level 2 incorporates a wider range of decision variables by adding depth in the promotion, price and market research decision areas. Finally, Level 3 permits firms to introduce a second product (in a related, but new, category) and encourages the development of a consistent firm-wide marketing program across different target markets, marketing mixes, and marketing strategies.

3. CHECK BUDGET CONSTRAINT

If a firm's spending exceeds their budget plus any available discretionary reserve funds, the amount spent on advertising is automatically reduced until the budget constraint is met (or until advertising is eliminated altogether). If a firm has two products, advertising for each product is reduced in proportion to the product's share of total advertising. For example, if a firm designates two-thirds of the total advertising spending for Product 1 and one-third for Product 2, then two-thirds of the amount over the budget limit will be cut from Product 1's advertising, and one-third from Product 2's advertising.

4. MARKET GROWTH

Both controllable and external (uncontrollable) forces contribute to a growth pattern in market potential for each segment. Market potential for a segment depends on several factors—sales to that segment in the previous year, growth trends, overall industry advertising, overall industry reputation for customer service, and how well the available brands satisfy customer preferences. Actual sales may be less than the market potential if low production order quantities result in product shortages. Overall, the market starts in the middle of the growth stage of the product life cycle, but the various segments exhibit different growth patterns.

Decision Area	Level 1	Level 2	Level 3
Exhibit 14B – Decision Variables for Game Levels 1 through 3			
Product	Product features	Product features	Product features for each product
Price	Wholesale price	Wholesale price in each channel	Wholesale price for each product in each channel
Customer Service	$ Amount	$ Amount	$ Amount
Place	Distribution intensity in each channel	Distribution intensity in each channel	Distribution intensity in each channel
Production Order Quantity (demand est.)	Units	Units	Units for each product
Promotion			
-Advertising	$ Expenditures	$ Expenditures	$ Expenditures for each product
		Advertising type	Advertising type for each product
-Personal selling	# Sales reps in each channel	# Sales reps in each channel	# Sales reps in each channel
		% Non-selling time	% Non-selling time
		Commission rate	Commission rate
-Sales promotion		$ in each channel	$ in each channel*
Marketing research	# Reports (1-6)	# Reports (1-7)	# Reports per product (1 thru 5, 7)
* for each product			

The table in Exhibit 14C gives the percentage growth in market potential and the initial sales volume (in units) for each segment. The initial sales volumes are the units sold to each segment in the period preceding the start of the game. Initial sales volumes are not given for DVC product marketing because the initial sales depend on the sales volume for the VRD product.

If the simulation is continued for more than 10 periods, percentage growth for the VRD product for additional periods is zero. *The growth rates for the DVCs begin with the first period that a DVC brand is introduced.* For example, if the first DVC brand is introduced in period 6, then the growth rate for segment 1 would be 15% in period 6, 15% in period 7, 14% in period 8, etc. (see Exhibit 14C). In such a case, the percentage growth rates for DVCs would be zero for periods beyond period 16. Note however, that the market potential may continue to change depending on industry advertising effects and the fit of products with customer preferences. If the fast product life cycle setup option was activated prior to the first period, it has the effect of increasing the speed at which the market steps through the product life cycle.

		Period									
Product 1:											
Segments:	**Sales**	**1**	**2**	**3**	**4**	**5**	**6**	**7**	**8**	**9**	**10**
Students	20,028	15	15	14	12	10	8	5	3	3	3
Home	15,084	15	15	12	10	10	8	8	5	4	4
Assistants	25,104	10	8	7	4	3	3	3	3	3	3
Creators	10,240	14	12	10	9	8	7	6	6	6	5
Managers	22,056	11	9	6	5	4	4	4	3	3	3
Parents	8,092	5	5	0	5	0	5	0	5	0	5
Product 2:											
Students		15	15	14	12	10	8	5	3	3	3
Home		8	8	8	7	7	7	6	6	5	5
Assistants		14	12	10	9	8	7	6	6	6	5
Creators		5	5	5	5	4	4	4	4	3	2
Managers		11	10	8	6	5	4	4	4	3	3
Parents		5	5	0	5	0	5	0	5	0	5

- **Exhibit 14C - Initial Unit Sales and Percent Growth by Market Segment for Initial 10 Game Periods***

*The growth rates for the second product begin with the first period that the second product is introduced and then continue for ten periods.

5. INDUSTRY ADVERTISING EFFECT

The total potential market demand for VRDs or DVCs (or both) may be increased or decreased somewhat depending on total industry advertising spending. Higher levels of overall advertising will expand the market potential, whereas low levels of industry advertising will shrink the potential. The magnitude of the effect may increase or decrease the market potential by up to 20 percent in early periods of the game. As the market matures in later periods, overall advertising has a diminishing impact on potential market demand.

6. COMPUTE SEGMENT IDEAL POINTS

Each segment has a preference for an "ideal" combination of product features and retail price. Each segment's ideal point evolves slowly over the first ten periods a product is available on the market . (If more than 10 periods of decisions are made, the ideal points will remain fixed after year 10).

The direction and rate of change is the same for each time period—thus, a firm which tracks consumer preferences should be able to predict the future preferences of their target market segment(s). Depending on the segment, the ideal point may shift on one or more of the dimensions which make up the product space.

Exhibit 14D gives both the initial positioning of the ideal points as well as the movement in ideal points over the course of a game.

• **Exhibit 14D - Market Segments' Ideal Points***				
Product-Market: Product 1				
Segment	Number of Special Commands	Error Protection	Ease of Learning	Price
Student	11(-.2)	3 (+.2)	3 (+.2)	$145(+2)
Home	9	4 (+.2)	8	$165
Assistants	12	8	8	$250 (-2)
Creators	14 (+.3)	2	4	$260 (+3)
Managers	16	6	3 (+.3)	$300 (-2)
Parents	6	3 (+.1)	9 (-.1)	$180
Product-Market: Product 2				
Segment	Number of tasks	Similarity of Commands	Ability to customize	Price
Student	2	6	3	$145 (-2)
Home	8	5 (-.1)	5 (+.1)	$210
Assistants	4 (+.2)	7	9	$225 (+2)
Creators	9	3	7(+.1)	$240
Managers	6 (-.1)	8	6	$200
Parents	1	10	1	$175 (-3)
* Numbers without parentheses are initial values for ideal points. Numbers given in parentheses give the direction and magnitude of yearly shift of ideal point values.				

7. CUSTOMER SERVICE

Spending on customer service affects both the potential market demand and market shares among firms. For each firm, the ratio of actual spending on customer service to the "expected" spending level (i.e., what is required to satisfy users) determines their customer service rating. The expected spending level increases as the customer base (defined by last year's total unit sales) increases according to a piecewise linear function shown in the figure below:

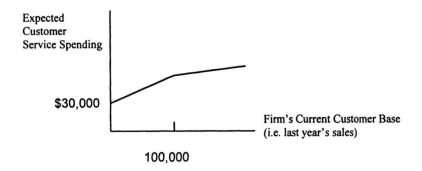

The effect of this function is that there are customer service economies of scale so that, for example, as unit sales double from 50,000 to 100,000 units, the spending required to achieve the expected customer service level does not double. A rating of less than 100% means that the firm is under spending according to consumer group 'norms' (i.e. there is a service gap), whereas a rating greater than 100% indicates the firm's spending and service exceed expectations. A firm's customer service rating, relative to competing firms, will impact its market share.

The potential market demand for a product may be increased or decreased somewhat depending on total industry spending on customer service. Higher than expected levels of overall spending will expand the market potential, whereas low levels of industry spending will shrink the potential. The magnitude of the effect may increase or decrease the market potential by up to 5 percent in each game period.

8. BRAND ADVERTISING EFFECTIVENESS

The effect of a brand's advertising depends on the dollar amount spent on advertising relative to competitors' spending, the type of advertising chosen, and how consistent advertising is with other elements of the marketing plan. The type of advertising chosen will influence one or more of the following:

    (i) the growth of the overall market potential.

    (ii) the Carryover Index which determines how much of a brand's awareness carries over from one period to the next.

    (iii) the brand's Advertising Effectiveness Index which summarizes the effectiveness of a brand's advertising for the current year.

    (iv) the brand's *effective* advertising expenditures which may differ from actual advertising spending if there are spillover effects from corporate advertising.

The specific effects of the various advertising types are described below:

Pioneering. Pioneering advertising develops primary demand and may expand the potential market demand by as much as 20 percent. The amount of the increase is determined by the proportion of total industry advertising that is designated as pioneering. For example, if 100 percent of advertising in the industry is pioneering, then potential market demand will be multiplied by a factor of 1.2 (or 1.00 * 1.2). If 40 percent of industry advertising is pioneering, then the multiplier will be (.40 * 1.20) + (.60 * 1.00) = 1.08.

Direct Competitive has the most impact in the current year and less carryover to future years. The brand's Advertising Effectiveness Index for the current year increases from the default of 1.0 to 1.2, and the Carryover Index decreases from the default of .5 to .4.

Indirect Competitive: has less immediate impact than direct competitive but more carryover effect. The brand's current Advertising Effectiveness Index increases to 1.1 and the Carryover Index increases from .5 to .6.

Reminder: affects the brand's current Advertising Effectiveness Index depending on the level of brand awareness as shown below:

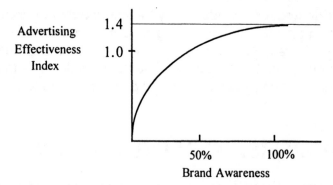

Thus, if brand awareness is greater than 50 percent, then reminder advertising will raise the brand's Advertising Effectiveness Index above the default of 1.0. If awareness is less than 50 percent, reminder advertising will erode the brand's advertising effectiveness.

Corporate or Institutional: is only useful if a firm has two products in the market. Corporate advertising creates a spillover effect from one product to the other. If a firm has two products, Product A and Product B, and uses corporate advertising for Product A, then advertising dollars for Product B are increased by an amount equal to 20 percent of Product A's advertising budget. In effect, Product B gets the full benefit of the advertising budget designated specifically for B, but also receives some benefit from the corporate emphasis of Product A's advertising.

9. PERSONAL SELLING EFFECTIVENESS

The overall effectiveness of the sales force depends on the number of sales representatives that a firm has and on four other factors, each of which is quantified in the simulation by an index. These indices are introduced briefly below and then each is explained in more detail:

1. the **distribution index** indicates how well a firm's specified distribution intensity matches the size of the sales force. Note that it is not necessarily better to have a larger sales force; rather, it is important for a firm to be consistent in matching the size of their sales force to their desired distribution intensity.

2. the **call effectiveness index** depends on the sales representatives' time allocation between selling and supporting activities relative to the time allocation of competitors' sales reps.

3. the **sales rep effort index** depends on both the absolute amount of the commission rate as well as the amount relative to competitors' commission rates.

4. the **trade promotion index** indicates the amount of support or goodwill felt towards the producer by the channel members and depends on the amount of sales (trade) promotion relative to competitors. This is considered in personal selling effectiveness on the basis that the sales reps can't carry the whole promotion effort to dealers. The dealers look at the sales reps in the context of the rest of the marketing mix. Calculation of this index is described in detail below under item 9 (Sales Promotion Effectiveness).

The effective size of the sales force for a given period will be (temporarily) less than the actual number of sales representatives employed if the size of the sales force is increased. Each newly hired sales representative spends 20 percent of his or her first year in training, and only works out in the field for 80 percent of that first year (this does not include transfers between channels).

• **9.1 Distribution Index**

The premise underlying the distribution index is that the appropriate size for the sales force depends on the level of distribution intensity that a firm is trying to achieve and the percent of sales force time devoted to selling. A small sales force may be appropriate if the goal is relatively exclusive distribution. On the other hand, widespread retail distribution requires a larger sales force (and thus more sales expense). Thus, it is necessary to match the sales force size with the firm's specified distribution intensity. 'Too few' sales reps for a given distribution intensity will mean that sales reps are stretched beyond their capacity and are unable to effectively service all their accounts.

For Channel 1, there are decreasing returns to additional sales reps – more and more sales reps are needed to increase distribution intensity as the intensity nears 100%. For example, while 9 sales reps devoting 100% of their time to selling can effectively cover 30% of the Channel 1 dealers, it takes nearly 20 to cover 60%, and more than 32 to cover 90%.

In contrast, Channel 2 exhibits constant returns to scale, requiring the equivalent of 3 "full time selling" sales reps to cover each 10% of Channel 2 dealers. As the number of available sales reps falls below the ideal for the specified distribution intensity, the distribution intensity index falls below 1.0. At the extreme, this index could fall to a low of .5. Conversely, "extra" sales reps beyond what is ideally needed to meet the distribution intensity generate little added value. At the extreme, "extra" sales reps can boost the distribution intensity index to a maximum of 1.1.

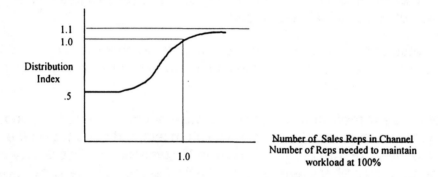

- **9.2 Call Effectiveness Index**

Dealers in the channels expect support from a firm. The Call Effectiveness Index depends on the percent of time a firm's sales reps spend on non-selling (support) time and how that compares to the support provided by other firms. As shown below, the dealers in the two channels put different priorities on support.

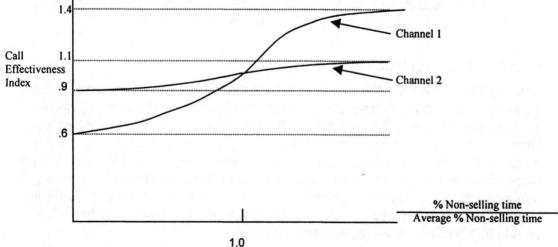

Thus, both channels respond to non-selling or support activities of sales reps, but Channel 1 is considerably more responsive.

- **9.3 Sales Rep Effort Index**

The Sales Rep Effort Index is a surrogate for sales force motivation. The motivation of a firm's sales force is a function of the commission percent—and how it compares to commissions earned by reps in other firms and to the initial commission rate. Thus, a higher commission increases the Sales Rep Effort Index up to a saturation point—but beyond that effort is not improved. Rather, commission costs just increase.

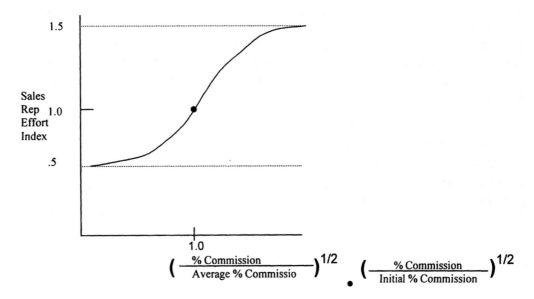

$$\left(\frac{\text{\% Commission}}{\text{Average \% Commissio}} \right)^{1/2} \bullet \left(\frac{\text{\% Commission}}{\text{Initial \% Commission}} \right)^{1/2}$$

10. SALES (TRADE) PROMOTION EFFECTIVENESS

Sales promotion in *The Marketing Game!* is primarily directed toward dealers (the "trade") and has two effects which vary across the two channels. It may:

1. reduce the retail price through deals and allowances passed on to consumers, or
2. enhance personal selling efficiency by building up the 'goodwill' index.

As is explained in more detail below, in Channel 1, the dominant effect of sales promotions is the building of goodwill, whereas in Channel 2, the dominant effect is to reduce the retail price.

- ### 10.1 Retail Price Effect

The amount of the total sales promotion dollars that is used for allowances and price dealing varies by channel as follows:

> 30% of sales promotion budget in Channel 1
> 80% of sales promotion budget in Channel 2

The reduction or discount from the full retail price (i.e. based on the standard markup) depends on both the amount of the budget allocated for allowances and the expected sales volume. For example, a firm that allocates $100,000 for sales promotion and expects to sell (and thus requests production of) 20,000 units would achieve a larger discount from the full retail price than a firm that also spends $100,000 on sales promotion but expects to sell 50,000 units. The maximum discount from the full retail price is 25 percent for Channel 1 and 40 percent for Channel 2.

- ### 10.2 Trade Promotion Index ("Goodwill" Effect)

Relatively high levels of sales promotion can increase a firm's trade promotion index by up to 30 percent in Channel 1 and 10 percent in Channel 2. The exact relationship is shown below.

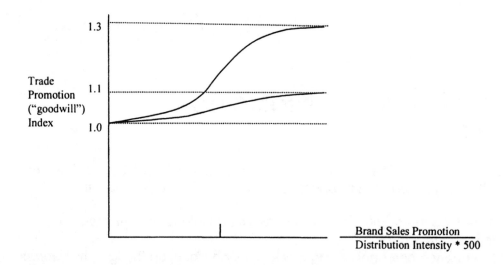

Note that the goodwill effect of sales promotion is a "relative" issue. If everyone is spending equally on sales promotion—the goodwill effect largely washes out!

11. WHOLESALE PRICES

Every firm decides on its own wholesale price(s). Depending on the game level, wholesale prices may or may not be the same in the two channels. Note that, regardless of whether or not wholesale prices are equal in the two channels, retail prices in the two channels may vary because of the different markup percents and the effect of sales promotion.

12. PRODUCT CHARACTERISTICS AND R&D PRODUCT MODIFICATION COSTS

Each brand's base unit production cost is determined by its values on the product's three design features. For Product 1 (the VRD), these are the number of special commands, error protection, and ease of learning. For Product 2 (the DVC product), the design features are the number of tasks, similarity of commands, and the ability to customize. For both products, the three design features may be modified in any decision period and the new brand will be available for sale in the same period. For both the VRD and DVC products, the range of possible product modifications and the R&D product modification costs, and base unit production costs are summarized in Exhibit 14E. Note that bigger changes in a short period significantly increase R&D product modification costs.

Optionally, the instructor can choose to activate the production economies of scale option. Using this feature, a firm's unit production cost decreases as cumulative production increases. Specifically, the unit costs will decrease from the "base" unit cost by 3% for every 100,000 units produced up until about 1 million units in cumulative production, then the incremental cost savings taper off to 1% per 100,000 and above 2,000,000 units costs are level again.

• **Exhibit 14E - Product Modification and Unit Production Costs**			
Product 1 Features	**Range**	**To Decrease Level[a]**	**To Increase Level**
# of Special Commands	5-20	no cost	$8000 x (change)^2
Error Protection	1-10	no cost	$5000 x (change)^2
Ease of Learning	1-10	$3000 x change	$3000 x (change)^2
Product 1 Base Unit cost = $4 x (No. of Special Commands) + $3 x (Error Protection) + $2 x (Ease of Learning)			
Product 2 Features	**Range**	**To Decrease Level[a]**	**To Increase Level**
# of Tasks	1-10	no cost	$8000 x (change)^2
Similarity of Commands	1-10	no cost	$5000 x (change)^2
Ability to Customize	1-10	$3000 x change	$3000 x (change)^2
Product 2 Base Unit cost = $4 x (No. of Tasks) + $3 x (Similarity of Commands) + $2 x (Ability to Customize)			
[a]Note: Although there is no cost to decrease the level of some features, if a firm decreases the level of a feature, and then increases it again in a later period, the full costs for the increase will be incurred.			

13. BRAND AWARENESS

The Brand Awareness Index indicates the proportion of consumers who are familiar with, or aware of, a particular brand. The value of the index for the current year depends on (i) current advertising expenditures, (ii) current advertising type, and (iii) brand awareness in the previous year. The following indices and functions are used to compute current brand awareness:

Advertising Effectiveness Index =	1.2 if direct competitive 1.1 if indirect competitive if reminder:

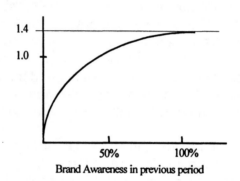

Brand Awareness in previous period

1.0 otherwise

Carryover Index = (from t-1 to t)	.4 if direct competitive .5 otherwise .6 if indirect competitive
Spillover Effect = (if corporate advertising for brand A)	Adjusted Brand B Advertising $ =Actual Brand B Adv. $ + (.20) x (Brand A Adv. $)

Effective Advertising   = <u>Adjusted Brand Adv. $</u> x (Brand Advertising
Expenditures in period t   Avg. Adj. Brand Adv.$ Effectiveness Index)

The value of the Brand Awareness Index has an upper limit of .9, and the lower limit varies with the level of previous awareness and the amount of carryover from one period to the next. The function used to compute brand awareness is portrayed graphically below:

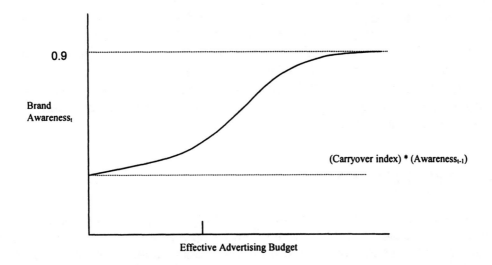

When a firm introduces a second product, the initial level of brand awareness for the new product is 20 percent of the firm's brand awareness for its VRD brand.

14. CHANNEL 'PUSH'

A firm's channel strength or "push" from dealers depends on both the overall effectiveness of the sales force, the firm's distribution intensity relative to competitors, and sales promotion targeted at dealers. The different indices that affect the personal selling effort are combined into a composite Sales Force Index:

Sales Force = Trade Promotion x Distribution x Call Effectiveness x Sales Rep
Index   Index   Index   Index   Effort Index

The range of values that the composite Sales Force Index can assume for Channel 1 is between 0.15 and 3.00 (calculated as: from a minimum of (1.0) * (.5) * (.6) * (.5) to a maximum of (1.30) * (1.1) * (1.4) * (1.5)). For Channel 2 the range is from 0.22 to 2.00 (calculated as: (1.0) * (.5) * (.9) * (.5) to (1.1) * (1.1) * (1.1) * (1.5)). Thus, the overall Sales Force Index can assume a wider range of values in Channel 1, and is likely to be more important than the distribution intensity. In contrast, Channel 2 is less responsive to the Sales Force Index, making distribution intensity somewhat more important.

A firm's "push" in a given channel is summarized by an index ranging between 0.0 and 1.0. The Push Index depends on the overall Sales Force Index, the firm's distribution intensity, and whether sales reps are responsible for 1 or 2 products:

Channel Push = $\dfrac{\text{Distribution Intensity}}{\text{Avg. Distribution Intensity}}$ x (Sales Force x (Adjustment factor
Index) for two products)

The adjustment factor for two products can range between 0.70 and 1.00 and depends on the relative emphasis given to each product. If (unit) sales of one product are small compared with the other, then the adjustment factor will be close to 1.00 and not many additional sales reps are needed. On the other hand, if the two products have approximately equal (unit) sales volumes, then the adjustment factor will be close to 0.70 meaning that approximately 40 percent more sales reps are needed to achieve the same channel push as compared with a single product firm.

15. RETAIL PRICES

Retail prices are computed from the wholesale prices using a markup percentage on selling price of 50 percent for Channel 1 and 35 percent for Channel 2. These retail prices are then discounted based on the amount of sales promotion dollars (if any) available for dealing (see item 10 - Sales Promotion Effectiveness for details on computing the discount).

16. MARKETING EFFORT

The marketing effort of firm F behind a brand B towards segment S in channel C depends on brand familiarity, the channel push, the customer service effect, and the segment's shopping preferences. The segments' shopping preferences or habits are summarized below as the probabilities of shopping in each channel:

Segment	Probability of Shopping in Channel 1	Probability of Shopping in Channel 2
Student	.20	.80
Home	.25	.75
Assistants	.80	.20
Artists	.60	.40
Managers	.70	.30
Parents	.50	.50

Marketing Effort $_{FBSC}$ =
Familiarity $_B$ * Channel Push $_C$ * Customer Service $_F$ * Shopping Habits $_{SC}$

(Note: the multiplicative form implies an interaction effect.)

17. BRAND POSITIONING

The joint space containing the ideal points of the segments and the locations of the brands is defined by four dimensions—the three product design features and the (discounted) retail price. Although each firm has only a *single* brand from a production standpoint—from a positioning perspective there are *two* since there are two channels that provide different services and usually charge different prices. Thus, in an industry of four firms each with a 'single' brand, in effect there are eight brands from the customer's viewpoint.

18. TOTAL POTENTIAL MARKET DEMAND BY SEGMENT

The total potential market demand for each segment depends upon the unit sales volume in the previous period, the (uncontrollable) growth rate for the segment, total industry advertising, industry customer service, and how well the available brands meet the needs of that segment. The segment growth trends, industry advertising and customer service effects have been described earlier (see sections 4, 5, and 7 respectively). In addition, the extent to which the available brands satisfy customer preferences may expand or shrink the potential segment demand. For example, if there are no brands which are close to matching a segment's ideal brand, then demand by that segment will be less than in a situation with one or more brands close to the ideal brand. In other words, some "would-be" buyers may postpone purchases until they find a satisfactory brand. The further away brands are from a segment's ideal, the greater the reduction in the market potential.

19. PURCHASE PROBABILITIES

The purchase probabilities for a brand are computed for each segment and depend on the location of the brand relative to the segment's ideal point and the level of marketing effort behind the brand.

The 'distance' (dissimilarity) between each brand and the segment ideal points are computed using the segment importance weights and an asymmetric functional form. For the design features (those other than price), falling short of what a segment wants is 'worse' than over-designing. Of course, it's best to match the ideal point exactly. For price, it is much worse to price too high than to price too low.

Letting $Distance_{BSC}$ be the 'distance' between the ideal point for segment S and brand B when sold through channel C, the purchase probabilities are computed using the following formula:

$$\text{Purchase Probability }_{BSC} = \frac{\text{Marketing Effort}_{BSC} / \text{Distance}_{BSC}}{\Sigma_b \text{ Marketing Effort}_{bSC} / \text{Distance}_{bSC}}$$

(note: $Distance_{BSC}$ has a minimum value of 0.01 to avoid conceptual as well as zero divide problems.)

Since different segments consider certain features to be more important than others, the weights given in Exhibit 14F are used in computing the distance between a brand and a segment's ideal point.

Product 1	Product Features			
Segment	Number of Special Commands	Error protection	Ease of learning	Price
Students	.7	.6	.5	1.0
Home	.5	.7	.7	.8
Assistants	.7	.8	1.0	.5
Creators	.8	1.0	.8	.5
Managers	1.0	.7	.6	.4
Parents	.9	.7	.9	.7

• Exhibit 14F—Importance Weights

Product 2				
	Number of tasks	Similarity of commands	Ability to customize	Price
Students	.7	.9	.8	.8
Home	.8	.5	.6	.7
Assistants	.8	1.0	1.0	.5
Creators	1.0	.6	.9	.4
Managers	.6	.7	.8	.8
Parents	.9	.6	.7	.9

20. POTENTIAL BRAND SALES BY SEGMENT

The potential sales of a brand to a given segment is computed by multiplying the probability that a segment S will purchase brand B times the total potential market demand for that segment:

Potential Brand Sales = (Purchase Probability$_{BS}$) * (Total Potential Segment Demand$_S$)

21. PRODUCTION QUANTITIES

Actual production quantity for a brand depends on the amount of production requested, the potential sales for that brand, and spillover sales resulting from shortages of competing brands (see section 22). To meet unanticipated demand, production will automatically be increased by up to 20 percent more than requested. Similarly, if demand is less than the requested amount, production will be curtailed by up to 20 percent. Beyond these limits, however, production cannot be adjusted and the firm will lose some sales due to inventory stock outs if it under produces, or will incur inventory transfer charges if it overproduced.

22. ACTUAL BRAND SALES BY SEGMENT

Actual brand sales by segment depend on the availability of products to meet the demand. If potential sales for all brands are each less than or equal to 120 percent of their specified production, then actual sales are equal to potential sales. If one or more brands are not able to meet their demand, then there will be some lost sales and some spillover to other brands. Half of the shortage will become lost sales and the other half will be picked up by competing brands. The spillover amounts are determined for each segment and are allocated to competing brands in proportion to their market shares.

23. MARKETING CONTRIBUTION AND NEXT PERIOD'S BUDGET

The marketing contribution depends on revenues and costs. Costs include:
R&D product modification costs
Advertising expenditures
Sales force expenditures (salaries, firing costs, commissions)
Sales promotion expenditures
Customer service expenditures
Marketing research charges
Transfer charges resulting from overproduction
Cost of goods sold
Fines (at the discretion of the instructor)

Revenues depend on the wholesale prices in each channel and the sales volume. A firm receives a minimum budget of $800,000 even if it is not profitable. On the other hand, the budget increases (at a decreasing rate) as net contribution increases as shown below:

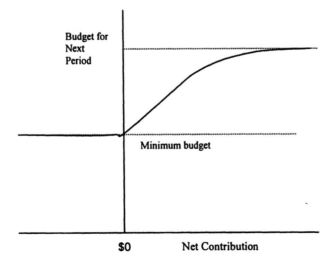

Appendix A. *Instructor CD-Rom Resources*

The Instructor's CD-Rom that accompanies this manual includes all of *The Marketing Game!* software, and a variety of other digital resources that may prove useful to the instructor. Most of these resources are mentioned in the section of this manual that deals with them. For example, the CD-Rom includes the PowerPoint files, the test-generator program and database, the tutorial files, website resources, an electronic version of the Instructor's Manual, files for the sample memos, copies of the form files (in Word document format), and other materials.

A complete overview of the resources on the CD-Rom is provided in a file named Resources.txt that is in the root directory of the CD-Rom. Please check that file. In addition, most of the folders on the CD-Rom also include their own readme.txt files that may provide additional information.

Appendix B. *Website Resources for The Marketing Game!*

INTRODUCTION

This appendix provides information about website resources available to instructors who adopt *The Marketing Game!* These include:

- A complete, ready-to-use *Marketing Game* website (in various configurations to meet the requirements of almost any school's web server).

- A complete website template (similar to the one described above), but available on McGraw-Hill's Page-Out free website hosting service, that makes it easy for an instructor to personalize the website and modify, add, or delete pages and elements of pages.

- The publisher's website (for instructor use) for *The Marketing Game*, which provides information, software updates, and other new information as it becomes available.

Each of these is discussed in more detail below.

PAGES FOR A READY-TO-USE WEBSITE

We have prepared a complete and useful general-purpose website for *The Marketing Game!* that can be used, as is, at most schools. We have prepared this website with Net Objects Fusion, and we provide the source materials in the event that software is available to you. If it is not available, and you want to do your own modifications, you may find the TMG website template (discussed in the next section) more useful.

Different web servers have different requirements concerning various aspects of how a website should be set up. For example, there may be a requirement that the home pages be called home, index, default, or some other name. Similarly, the web server might expect html pages to be labeled with the file extension htm, html, or perhaps shtml. Some web hosts require that the main folder for a website be "flat"—which means that all of the files are in that folder—whereas others expect or require the use of subfolders. To accommodate these differences, on the CD-Rom we provide different folders with website pages configured to match the most common combinations of these different requirements. As a result, one of our configurations should meet your needs (and the specs at your school). Simply do the following: (1) find out what is required at your school, and (2) copy the relevant pages from the CD-Rom to the website folder (or ask the technical support people at your school to help do that).

The readme.txt file in the \website folder on the CD-Rom goes into more detail about the various configurations that are available. The subfolder \website\netobjec holds the Net Objects Fusion source materials from which the various configurations were produced.

The readme.txt file also provides an overview of the structure of the website, what resources it uses, and everything else you need to know.

MCGRAW-HILL'S PAGEOUT WEBSITE HOSTING SERVICE

McGraw-Hill, the firm that publishes and distributes *The Marketing Game!*, offers instructors who adopt *The Marketing Game!* a free website hosting service called Page-Out. We have created a "model"/template website for The Marketing Game and it is available on the Page-Out system so that you can copy the pages for the site into your own folder and then, if you wish, personalize it or modify it as you see fit.

Page-Out provides a variety of online, web-based tools and support that empower instructors to add a variety of digital learning solutions to their courses. This service includes website hosting, website templates, web page design applications, discussion capabilities, online space for an instructor's own files, and much more. It is very well suited for instructors who want to take advantage of a website on the Internet with *The Marketing Game!* To get an overview of the Page-Out system, check out the demonstrations online at http://pageout.net. The Page-Out folder on the Instructor CD also provides a Word format document with instructions on how to use the various Page-Out website development tools.

The first step is to establish your own Page-Out account, and you do that by contacting your McGraw-Hill sales representative. If you don't know how to contact your sales representative, you can use the rep locator at the McGraw-Hill higher education website (www.mhhe.com). You will be asked for the following information:

- Your Complete Name
- Your School Affiliation
- What McGraw-Hill Text You Are Using: *The Marketing Game!*
- Course Enrollment
- Course Dates
- Complete Mailing Address
- Email Address
- Phone/Fax

Then, your Page-Out User ID and Password will be sent to you promptly. After you receive your Page-Out User ID and Password, you'll have what you need to create your own website. A good way to start is to copy the provided website template into your own folder. It comes preconfigured and ready to use, but with the Page-Out tools you can easily personalize with your own name and course information, and with additional pages.

This service also gives you 10 megabytes of space that can be used for your own files. That means that you have a simple way to implement electronic downloads of report files. First, you have to upload the files into the folder where the web pages reside (the web page is already configured to download the file if it is there). The Page-Out service provides a button to upload one file at a time. If you have a large number of industries, it is more efficient to put all of the reports in a zip file and upload them that way. Then, Page-Out has a utility function that will extract the individual report files from the zip file.

Remember that it usually takes a few days to get your Page-Out password, so if you want to establish a website at PageOut it makes sense to get started early enough that you don't find yourself in a time crunch!

MCGRAW-HILL'S WEBSITE FOR THE MARKETING GAME!

It is the current plan for McGraw-Hill to establish a website for *The Marketing Game!* They have not as yet, however, set the address or domain name for the website, so we are not able to provide it at this time. It may be available by the time the final version of the Instructor's Manual goes to press, in which case it will be added. However, we have requested that the web address be:
http: \\www.mhhe.com\TMG
where the mhhe stands for McGraw-Hill Higher Education. It may turn out that the TMG part of the name will need to be entered in lower case. While having the website seems simple and logical to us, we apparently don't understand all of the issues. It seems to require many, many meetings of high-powered people before there can be a final decision on this matter, and of course any "final

decisions" may need to be changed many times. So, if for some reason McGraw-Hill decides not to have a website, we'll set one up on a different server. We'll also take whatever other steps are necessary to find better ways to serve instructors.

Our main purpose for the website is to provide a way to quickly get new information and resources to instructors who use *The Marketing Game!* There may be sections of the website that are designed for student use. Please feel free to email us for the current information on this. Bill Perreault can be reached at Bill_Perreault@UNC.edu and Charlotte Mason can be reached at MasonC@Bschool.UNC.edu.

Appendix C. *Commonly Asked Questions and Answers*

GENERAL QUESTIONS FROM STUDENTS

Q: My firm's net contribution was –$600,000, how can I recover? Can I recover?

A: Yes, you can recover. You are operating in a dynamic, high-tech industry where future performance is not necessarily indicated by past performance. A firm's success depends on how well it is able to meet the current needs of its customers and how well it is able to anticipate and react to competitors. Each period brings new opportunities, new customers and new challenges— so, focus on where you want to be, not where you are. Figure out why your market plan resulted in a poor net contribution, and then fix the problem!

Q: What happens if we spend more than our allotted budget amount?

A: Top management monitors spending by each department. If you exceed your budget, expenses must be cut back somewhere. An exception to this is if firms have been granted a discretionary reserve fund (using the setup option). If firms have a reserve fund, the amount of spending over budget will be drawn from the fund until it is depleted. (Note: you may or may not want to be more explicit about exactly which expenses will be cut. In fact, advertising is cut until the budget is met or until advertising spending is zero, whichever comes first. The rationale for this is that it's not reasonable to alter product modifications, that firing sales reps is more disruptive than cutting advertising, and that market research is often a relatively small expense.)

Q: Do we have to spend our full budget amount? If we don't spend it now, can we reserve it for later?

A: No, it isn't necessary to spend the full budget amount—but you can't save it for later. Whatever you don't spend doesn't appear as an expense. However, you should consider the possible gains from increased sales revenues as a result of spending the full amount. If you believe that the gains do not outweigh the costs, then it is reasonable not to spend your entire budget. However, whatever you don't spend cannot be saved for future periods. Your future budgets will depend on your future performance.

Q: Can we change our brand name?

A: No. Top management doesn't want to risk losing the brand familiarity that is already established or to risk confusing customers by changing brand names. (Note: Although there are no restrictions in the computer programs that require a firm to keep the same brand name throughout the game, *we strongly recommend that firms not be allowed to change brand names once the game is underway.* Such changes can be confusing to other firms in the industry and serve no useful purpose.)

Q: Why do some customers buy brands which are priced considerably higher than the price range indicated on the Customer Preference Report?

A: The range on the Customer Preference Report is a guideline and represents the "average" customer in each market segment. However, even within a segment, there are considerable differences among customers. Some are willing to pay more than others, and may be willing to pay more than indicated in the price range. Of course, it is reasonable to assume that as the price gets higher and higher, there will be fewer and fewer customers willing to buy at that price. (Additionally, you might note that, in general, it is difficult to get good information on the "ideal" price—at best, it is more [usually much more difficult] than getting information on ideal levels of other features.)

Q: Do customers' preferences change from one period to the next?

A: VRDs are still in the growth stage of the product life cycle and each period brings new potential customers and new products. For most relatively new products—and VRDs are included—it's reasonable to assume that customers preferences will change over time as they gain more experience with the product and its uses. (Note: You can be as vague or as explicit as you want when responding to this question. In the game, customer preferences do change over time in a slow, steady progression (see Exhibit 14D for the exact changes). You may tell students this directly. Or you may turn the question around, and ask students what they think the answer to the question is, and why.)

Q: Will our target customers become confused or "penalize" us if we change our price frequently (or substantially)? If we leave our product features the same, but raise (drop) our price will customers think we are taking advantage of them (have cut corners on our product)?

A: In general, it is desirable to avoid erratic and/or frequent price swings. However, since your product is generally a one-time purchase—rather than something purchased regularly—customers may be less aware of price changes from one period to the next. (Note: in the game, there is no penalty for price changes—you may or may not want to be explicit about that. Alternatively, you could note that the advantages of changing price may be clear. For example, if the price was so low as to leave virtually no gross margin, then there really is no alternative but to raise price. Also, in some situations raising the price may make the brand more attractive to some segments—particularly those segments that may be using price as an indicator of quality or status.)

Q: We are already spending much more on advertising than our competitors. How do we know when we've reached the "saturation" point and are simply increasing our expenses without getting a return?

A: That is a very difficult question and one that many companies wrestle with. Because sales revenue depends on your whole marketing mix and competitors' as well, it is very difficult to isolate the effect of advertising. You must use your judgment based on past experience to decide how much is too much. You may want to think about ways to get a better answer—can you "experiment" to get a better understanding about the relationship between advertising and sales?

Q: We are doing much better with our second product than with our first product. Can we discontinue our VRD and focus exclusively on the second product?

A: No. The top management of the company believes that it is important to be in the VRD product-market since that is often the first voice-recognition product purchase that computer owners and users make.

Q: We diversified into a second product and have not been successful. Can we discontinue our second product and return to being a single-product company?

A: Yes. Top management believes that VRD is the main product-market to focus on. The market for the second product is a less-developed, perhaps riskier, market about which less is known. Thus, it is better not to jeopardize your reputation in the VRD product-market and/or your financial position.

Q: Our product is "better" than our competitor's, but they are selling more. Why?

A: There can be many reasons for this. First, your product is only one aspect of your total marketing mix—how do you compare on the other aspects such as personal selling, advertising, etc? Also, how do you conclude that your product is "better"? Better from whose perspective? (Note: some students will assume that "more is better"—for example, that a higher Error Protection Index is always better than a lower one when, in fact, this is not true. You may encourage students to rethink what is "better" and to review the information in Chapter 2 of the student text (which should make it clear that more is not better).

Q: Why doesn't the pro forma displayed by TMGPlan match my calculations?

A: There can be many reasons for discrepancies. As noted on page 47 of the Student Manual, if the difference is only a dollar or two, in your calculations you may have rounded off numbers in a different way than was done by the computer. If the difference is greater than that, you may have entered your plan information incorrectly, or your calculations may have had errors. If the discrepancies are in the area of R&D expenses, you may have entered product feature information incorrectly. On the Inputs for Pro Forma screen of TMGPlan, you are asked to enter the *prior* period's product features. TMGPlan uses these inputs to determine whether or not there were product changes, which impacts the R&D costs for product modifications. If in error you entered the *current* period's features instead, TMGPlan would compute R&D expenses to be zero and the pro forma would not be correct. So, it's always wise to double check that the values you enter are correct.

Q: TMGPlan produces two files, PLANif.TMG and PROFORif.TXT. Which file(s) should I submit?

A: The PLANif file (where "if" is your industry letter and firm number) is the correct file to submit. The PROFORif file is simply a saved copy of the pro forma statement displayed by TMGPlan. It is for your use; it does not contain all of the details of your plan.

Q: TMGPlan overwrites my PLANif.TMG file every time I run it. How can I save this file for future reference?

A: You will always have a copy of your most recent plan file in your default folder, and you should not need to save any version older than that. To attempt to do so generally accomplishes nothing other than to cause confusion. If you want to keep the older files, though, you may do so by copying them into a folder other than the one you select in TMGPlan. For example, you might use Windows Explorer to created a folder for each period, and then save the plan file and report file for that period in the folder.

Q: Our product is identical to one of our competitor's, yet they are selling considerably more than we are? Why?

A: When products are virtually identical, other elements of the marketing mix become more influential in the customer's decision process. For example, when two products are basically the same from the customer's perspective and the customer is more familiar with one (through advertising), the more familiar brand is more likely to be purchased. The dealers can also play a major role—if two products are very similar but one has more support (or 'push') from the dealer, that one is more likely to be bought.

Q: How can I tell how much money is in my discretionary reserve fund?

A: Check your firm's income statement from the most recent period. Towards the bottom of the report, if there is a reserve fund you will see a line labeled, "Remaining Reserve Funds." This amount is the balance in your discretionary reserve fund.

There is one exception to this rule. If the president/instructor decides to increase the discretionary fund for subsequent periods (say, when moving to Level 3 to give students more flexibility about introducing a new product), the change in discretionary funds granted for the next period is **not** reflected in the report for the previous period.

Q: How is the "Interest Income" on my income statement calculated?

A: Any funds in your discretionary reserve fund that are unused at the end of a period earn interest (at 6% per period). This income is added to the firm's net contribution.

Q: We haven't changed our strategy but we're not doing as well as we used to.

A: There are a variety of factors that may cause this. First, some competitors may have changed their strategies and made the competition tougher for you. A competitor may be doing a better job meeting the needs of your target market. Even a "me-too" competitor who follows your lead can cut into your profits. In addition, a strategy that worked in the past may no longer be the best for the current situation. For example, your product may no longer match your target customers' preferences. Finally, if growth is slowing and the product-market is moving into the maturity stage, the competition is likely to become tougher and profits lower as you and your competitors battle for market share.

(Note: *The Marketing Game!* is designed to be more "forgiving" in the early periods when students are getting started. Initially, there is a lot of growth in the product-market, which means that firms can be relatively successful even if their strategies are somewhat flawed. However, as the game progresses, the growth slows and a good strategy is more and more important.)

STUDENT QUESTIONS ABOUT LEVEL 3

Q: At Level 3 do I have to introduce the second product?

A: No. Introduction of the second product is a marketing strategy decision that you should make based on careful analysis.

Q: What are the starting product features for the second product?

A: Unlike the situation with the first product, which was already in the market when you took over responsibility for marketing, there is not yet a second product under development. Thus, the "starting position" for the second product for the purpose of calculating R&D costs is 0 on the number of tasks feature, 0 on command similarity, and 0 on ability to customize.

Note that this means that development costs for the second product can be substantial. For example, a product with a level of 5 for all three attributes would have R&D costs of $400,000. For this reason, your firm may need to delay introducing a second product if it does not have the money to develop and market it.

Q: Can I do market research about the second product before introducing it?

A: Once you are allowed to move to Level 3, you can get marketing research reports on Product 2 in any period, regardless of whether or not you have introduced the second product. In the upper right section of the Marketing Plan Decisions screen, in addition to seeing the check boxes for Product 1 marketing research reports, you will also see a column of check boxes for Product 2 marketing research reports.

You may wish to request marketing research reports on the second product one period earlier than you plan to introduce it, so that you can use this information to support the introduction.

Q: If I don't introduce the second product as soon as we're allowed to move to Level 3, can I do so later?

A: Yes. You can introduce the second product at any time after you move to Level 3. Bear in mind, though, that you do face development costs and it is sensible to think about how long it might take you to recoup those costs once the product is on the market.

Q: If I want to spread out R&D costs for a second product over more than one period, can I do that?

A: Yes. As soon as we go to Level 3, you can manufacture a prototype of the product with a reduced feature set. For example, if your eventual product feature levels will be 5, 5, and 5, you could create a prototype at levels 2, 2, and 2 in one period. To do this, enter 2, 2, and 2 as your product features and specify a production order quantity of 1. In the next period, you can move the product features to 5, 5, and 5, thus spreading out the R&D costs across two periods.

QUESTIONS ABOUT ADMINISTERING THE GAME

Q: Should I give students a "practice round" of decisions before the real competition begins?

A: This is really a matter of personal preference. In general, we don't think a practice round is required, in part because students all start on a level playing field (not knowing everything they would like to know!) and in part because it may be better to add another "real" decision period. Students who get off to a poor start, or for that matter a good start, are not locked into a position by the first decision. The market is dynamic and the learning that takes place from feedback can be used to improve subsequent marketing plans. So, our general advice on this matter is that instructors using TMG for the first time should probably just have students start with decisions "that count". After getting some experience with the game, an instructor will probably have clearer opinions about the pros and cons of a practice round.

Q: What do I need to do to move to a higher level in TMG?

A: First, tell your students what level you will be moving to and remind them that they will need to enter the correct level when they run the TMGPlan program to create a plan decisions file for the right level. Second, tell them what additional materials to read (see Chapter 4). Then, before you run the decisions that the students submit, be sure to change the TMGSim setup (and save the revised file) to reflect the level you want to use. This takes only a second and you can do it immediately before you run the simulation from the Simulation Command Center.

You may also want to consider increasing the reserve (discretionary) budget available to the students, especially if you are moving to Level 3. If you decide to do this, tell the students what the reserve budget will be. Remind them that the new level will not show on the report for the previous period. Then, when you change the TMGSim setup to reflect the new level you should also change the level for the discretionary budget.

Q: Can I increase (decrease) a firm's budget?

A: Yes. The "adjustments" button on the Marketing Plan Decisions Form Screen in the TMGSim program allows you to modify a firm's budget. If you enter a positive amount, that will increase the budget. A negative amount will decrease a firm's budget. Note that you enter the amount of change (i.e., the increment), not what the final budget amount will be. Don't forget to save the plan file after you have entered the adjustment.

The decision whether to grant a budget increase and how much will depend on the particular situation and your philosophy. Some instructors require a firm to submit a written proposal requesting the additional budget and explaining how it will be used and the expected results. This approach can discourage firms from regularly asking for more money without thinking it through. When deciding how much of an increase to grant, one consideration is the budgets of other firms in the industry. One approach is to limit the amount of a budget increase so that the requesting firm is on a par with the average of other firms, or perhaps at a slight disadvantage.

Q: I gave some "consulting" advice to a firm and want to charge the firm for it. How can I do that? AND A firm came requesting a market research report which it hadn't originally purchased but, on second thought, decided it should have. Can I charge them for this "purchase"?

A: Consulting or additional market research reports can be charged to the firm using the "adjustments" button on the Marketing Plan Decisions Form Screen in the TMGSim program. To get to that screen, select the modify a plan button on the Main Screen and open the plan file you want to adjust. Simply enter the amount in the "Extra Market Research" input field. Of course, you must decide how much to charge. For buying market research reports after the fact, one approach is to charge the amount of the report plus a premium of 50% or more. Don't forget to save the plan file after you have entered the adjustment.

Q: Can I use a higher level of the game, but ignore some decisions?

A: Yes. *The Marketing Game!* is designed to be flexible. The sets of decisions in levels 1, 2, and 3 were chosen because they meet the needs and objectives of most instructors. However, it is impossible to anticipate all possible new topics and the order in which you will want to introduce them in the game. In particular, you may want to move from level 1 to level 2, but to ignore one (or more) decisions for a period or two. This is easy to do—just instruct students to use fixed values for those decisions. Typical fixed values (and those corresponding to the defaults used for lower levels) are 5% for sales commission rate, 10% for percent non-selling time, and a "blank" (no value) for advertising type. For example, suppose you want to move to level 2 but don't want to include decisions on sales commission rate and advertising type. Tell students to leave the advertising type input field blank, and to use a sales commission rate of 5%.

(Note: There is the possibility that this may confuse some students. One suggestion which may minimize confusion, is for you to make a copy of the appropriate decision form (blank copies are provided in Appendix D), fill in the "fixed" fields, and then make copies for the students to fill in with the rest of their decisions. Then, if students are submitting a plan file for their decisions, they can enter the numbers off of their form into the TMGPlan screen.)

Appendix D. *Blank Forms*

This appendix contains one copy of each of the blank forms which are included in the student text:

LEVEL 1 MARKETING PLAN DECISION FORM

LEVEL 2 MARKETING PLAN DECISION FORM

LEVEL 3 MARKETING PLAN DECISION FORM

BUDGET PLANNING FORM/STRATEGY PLANNING FORM

TEAM EVALUATION FORM

Marketing Plan Decisions Form – Level 1

Marketing Plan Decisions - Level 1

Channel 1   Channel 2   **General**

[ ] [ ]   Distribution intensity (% of dealers)

[ ] [ ]   Number of sales reps (0-100)

[   ]   Customer service budget
           ($0-$9,999,999)

Marketing Research

Product 1
1. Share by segment [ ]
2. Share by channel [ ]
3. Preferences   [ ]
4. Effectiveness   [ ]
5. Segment by channel [ ]
6. Shopping habits   [ ]

Industry and
Firm

[ ][ ]

Product 1

[   ]   Brand name (8 letters)

Features
[ ]   Special Commands (5-20)
[ ]   Error Protection (1-10)
[ ]   Ease of Learning (1-10)

[   ]   Production Order Quantity (> 99)

[   ]   Advertising Spending

[   ]   Wholesale Price
         ($75-$250)

Marketing Plan Decisions - Level 2

General

Channel 1 Channel 2

Distribution intensity (% of dealers)

Number of sales reps (0-100)

Percent non-selling time (0-50%)

Sales commission percent (5-15%)

Customer service budget
($0-$9,999,999)

Marketing Research

Product 1

1. Share by segment
2. Share by channel
3. Preferences
4. Effectiveness
5. Segment by channel
6. Shopping habits
7. Product positioning

Industry and Firm

Product 1

Brand name (8 letters)

Features
- Special Commands (5-20)
- Error Protection (1-10)
- Ease of Learning (1-10)

Production Order Quantity (> 99)

Advertising Spending

Type of Advertising (P,D,I,R, or C)

Channel 1   Channel 2

Sales Promotion

Wholesale Price
($75-$250)

Marketing Plan Decisions Form - Level 3

Marketing Plan Decisions - Level 3 -

General

Channel 1 Channel 2

Distribution intensity (% of dealers)
Number of sales reps (0-100)
Percent non-selling time (0-50%)
Sales commission percent (5-15%)
Customer service budget ($0-$9,999,999)

Marketing Research

Product 1 Product 2

1. Share by segment — 1.
2. Share by channel — 2.
3. Preferences — 3.
4. Effectiveness — 4.
5. Segment by channel — 5.
6. Shopping habits
7. Product positioning — 7.

Industry and Firm

☐ Click if you have a second product

Product 1

Brand name (8 letters)

Features
Special Commands (5-20)
Error Protection (1-10)
Ease of Learning (1-10)

Production Order Quantity (> 99)
Advertising Spending
Type of Advertising (P,D,I,R, or C)

Channel 1 Channel 2
Sales Promotion
Wholesale Price ($75-$250)

Product 2

Brand name (8 letters)

Features
Number of tasks (1-10)
Similarity of commands (1-10)
Ability to customize (1-10)

Production Order Quantity (>0)
Advertising Spending
Type of Advertising (P,D,I,R, or C)

Channel 1 Channel 2
Sales Promotion
Wholesale Price ($35-$200)

Marketing Budget Planning Form

******Financial Summary / Pro Forma ******

Industry: _____ Firm: _____ Period: _____ Brand name: _____

	Channel 1	Channel 2	Total
(1) Estimated Units Sold	_____	_____	_____
(2) Wholesale Price	$_____	$_____	
(3) Base Unit Cost	$_____	$_____	
(4) Gross Sales [(1) □(2)]	$_____	$_____	$_____
(5) Cost of Goods Sold [(1) □ (3)]	$_____	$_____	$_____
(6) GROSS MARGIN [(4) minus (5)]			$_____
EXPENSES:			
(7) Advertising			$_____
(8) Sales Force-Salary	$_____	$_____	$_____
(9) Sales Force-Firing Costs	$_____	$_____	$_____
(10) Sales Force-Commission	$_____	$_____	$_____
(11) Customer Service			$_____
(12) Sales Promotion	$_____	$_____	$_____
(13) R&D for Product Modifications			$_____
(14) Marketing Research			$_____
(15) TOTAL EXPENSES [sum of (7) to (14)]			$_____
(16) Net Contribution to Profit or Loss [(6) minus (15)]			$_____
(17) Total Spending against Budget [(15) minus (10)]			$_____

Marketing Strategy Summary Form

Industry: _____   Firm: _____   Period: _____

Target Market:

Product:

Place:

Promotion:

Price:

Competition:

THE MARKETING GAME! Team Evaluation Form

Student's Name:_____

Industry: _____   Firm: _____

Assume that you have $100 to divide among the members of your team (including yourself) based on each member's overall contribution to the group. The team member whose contribution was the greatest should receive the largest share of the $100. The member whose overall contribution was smallest would receive the smallest amount. In the space below, please write the names of your team – *including yourself* – and the dollars you feel they deserve:

<u>Name</u>	<u>Dollars</u> (Total = $100)
_____	_____
_____	_____
_____	_____
_____	_____
_____	_____
_____	_____

Now, use the following space to write a few sentences explaining the major strengths and weaknesses of each member of your team (*excluding* yourself):

Name:_____

Comments:_____
_____
_____
_____
_____
_____
_____

Name:_____

Comments:_____
_____
_____
_____
_____
_____
_____

Name:_____

Comments:_____

_____

_____

_____

_____

_____

_____

Name:_____

Comments:_____

_____

_____

_____

_____

_____

_____

Name:_____

Comments:_____

_____

_____

_____

_____

_____

_____

Next, consider your <u>overall</u> team effort – both the amount of effort as well as the <u>quality</u> of that effort. On a scale from 0 - 100, what does your team's total effort deserve? (In assigning a value to your team effort, don't be modest and don't be unrealistic):

Overall Team Effort (0–100): _____

Finally, refer back to the first question where you divided $100 among your team members and consider the number of dollars that you believe your team members will assign to you. On average, how many dollars will other team members give you, and why?

_____

_____

_____

_____

_____

_____

_____

Appendix E. *Sample Memos*

This appendix contains a sample memo that you can use to advise students about the level of the discretionary budget (reserve fund); the default value in the TMGSim setup is $200,000. There is also a memo concerning economies of scale in production (if you select that option in the TMGSim setup). There are files on the Instructor CD-Rom (in rich text format, which can be read by Word, WordPerfect and most other word processing programs) for each of these memos.

MEMO CONCERNING THE DISCRETIONARY (RESERVE FUND) BUDGET

MEMO CONCERNING ECONOMIES OF SCALE

M E M O R A N D U M

TO: Marketing Manager

FROM: Company President

RE: Discretionary Reserve Fund

In the years since the founding of this company, I've asked the marketing department to develop plans that were within the budget the firm has allocated to you. At times, I know this has meant that certain initiatives could not be pursued – because the financial resources weren't available. Now, the company has sufficient financial resources that I have decided to authorize a discretionary reserve fund for the exclusive use of the marketing department. This should give your division more flexibility in today's increasingly competitive market. Starting immediately, a reserve fund (that is, a discretionary budget) totaling $_____ is available that you can spend on marketing department budget items you feel are important for achieving your strategy objectives.

You may spend the reserve funds all at once, across several years, or not at all. Interest income at the rate of 6% on any unspent reserve funds will be added to your financial results.   If, and when, your reserve funds are depleted, you will be restricted to keep your spending within your annual budget.

Although you should carefully consider the likely benefits before drawing on these reserve funds, you do not need to formally justify (to my office) the spending of these funds. Rather, if the cost of implementing your plan exceeds your budget allocation, I will just assume that you want extra expense drawn from your discretionary reserve fund. Your future financial reports will automatically track and report the amount of remaining reserve funds.

M E M O R A N D U M

TO: Marketing Manager

FROM: Company President

RE: Production Cost Savings

After careful analysis by the production department and the v.p. of finance, the company has recently purchased and installed new state-of-the-art equipment which will reduce production costs. Specifically, the production department is confident that they can reduce unit production costs by 3 percent for each additional 100,000 units that are produced. Of course, the savings from scale economies may ultimately taper off, but that is likely to be quite some time in the future. These economies of scale depend on total units produced and will not be affected by changes in the specific product features.

From this point forward, your production summary report will include the total cumulative production using the new equipment. You can use this to forecast your unit production costs for the coming year. The unit product cost charged for each year will be based on the cumulative production volume at the end of the preceding year. For example, if your production summary reports a cumulative production volume of 50,000 units, then your unit product cost for the coming year will be the 'base' unit cost times 0.985 (i.e., the economies of scale amount to a 1.5% reduction from the base unit cost.)

Appendix F. *Feedback From Users*

We have worked hard to make *The Marketing Game!* an interesting and challenging learning experience for your students, and a game which is simple and free of hassles for you to administer. But we, like you, are marketers—and we encourage and welcome feedback from users of *The Marketing Game!* Are there aspects of the game or the manuals that are unclear? Do you have suggestions for what you would like to see in the next edition? Did you use an assignment or something else that worked especially well for you? Did you find a bug we need to address? Below we give various ways to reach us. Please contact us with your comments and suggestions using whatever approaches is easiest for you. Please let us know if you would like to be notified by if we become aware of typos in the manual or any bugs in the programs (we promise not to pass along your name to anyone else or hassle you with promotional hype).

By email: MasonC@bschool.unc.edu or Bill_Perreault@unc.edu

By phone: Charlotte at 919-962-3185 or Bill at 919-962-3171

By fax: (919)- 962-3187 (at Kenan-Flagler Marketing Department)

By mail: University of North Carolina
Kenan-Flagler Business School
CB 3490 – McColl Building
Chapel Hill, NC 27599-3490
United States

Appendix G. Installing the Software from a Floppy Drive

WHEN YOUR COMPUTER DOES NOT HAVE A CD-ROM DRIVE—USE THE TMGDISKS PROGRAM

If the computer you want to use to run *The Marketing Game!* does not have a CD-drive, you can use a floppy disk drive to install the programs (except for TMGTutor, because its video files are too large to fit on floppies).

Creating installation disks is simple—and you do it with **a few clicks in the TMGDisks program, which is in the root directory of the Instructor CD-Rom.** All you need is a few floppy disks (2 to 4, depending on which programs you want to install) and temporary access to a computer that does have a CD-drive so that you can run the TMGDisks program and have it copy some files from the CD-Rom to the floppies. As with the other TMG programs, **there is online help** with the TMGDisks program. And there's nothing to it.

The main thing to remember is that **you need to start with formatted 1.44 MB 3.5" floppy disks that don't have any files on them (including any system or hidden files)**; there will not be enough space on the disk to copy the installation files if the disks are not completely empty. It's also good to have labels for the disks so that it's easier to keep them straight!

Although the program is very simple and instructions are probably unnecessary, in the next section we give a step-by-step guide on how to start the program, create disks, and then, in the next section, do the same for installing the software from the newly created disks. After that we'll overview your options for creating combinations.

Keep in mind that everything in this appendix comes directly from the program help file, so there is no need to study it carefully or worry about the details. It's here if you want a "hard copy" overview.

STEP-BY-STEP INSTRUCTIONS FOR USING THE TMGDISKS PROGRAM

To use the TMGDisks program, follow the steps below:

- Insert the CD-Rom in the CD-drive of the computer that you will use to make the installation disks, and wait a moment while the computer loads the CD-Rom.
- In most cases, the welcome screen will appear automatically (after the computer takes a moment to load the CD); if the welcome screen does not appear, just skip to step 4.
- At the welcome screen, click exit—but leave the CD in the drive.
- Select the Start button on the Windows task bar (usually in the lower left corner of the screen), then select Run, then select Browse, then select the drive where the TMG_Instruc CD-Rom is loaded, then select the TMGDisks program (TMGDisks.exe)—don't select the help file by mistake—and then click the Open button and then click Ok.
- The TMGDisks program will start.
- Click the radio button to select drive A: or drive B: as the drive to which files will be copied. If you are not certain which to select, try A: first; the program will notify you if you select an invalid drive or have the disk in the wrong drive.
- Click the radio button to select which installation disk(s) you want. Note that there you can create installation disks for different combinations of software so you can just select what you need. You'll definitely need the TMGSim software (program and help file), so start with it.
- Format two floppy disks (without system files) and label them "TMGSim Software Disk 1" and "TMGSim Software Disk 2." If you are using disks that were previously formatted, make certain that they have no files on them (or there will not be enough space for the installation files).
- Select the Create Installation disk(s) button. Messages will appear when it is time to put in a new disk and to confirm that copying is complete. There are also error messages if the program detects a problem.
- Check the log window to confirm that all of the files copied have an "ok" designation that the file copied correctly. If any file has a "failed" designation, the installation disk is not complete and there was a problem copying the files. In that event, check the troubleshooting section.
- If you wish to make installation disk(s) for another program, repeat steps 7 through 10; in step 8 label the disk(s) with the name of the software you select in step 7 (and note whether one or two disks are required).
- Select the Exit button when you are finished.
- Now you're ready to install the software on the other computer, which is covered in the next section.

SETUP THE TMG SOFTWARE FROM THE INSTALLATION DISKS

After you have created the installation disks, all you have to do is start the setup process and the rest (including any instructions you need) is handled automatically. To install the software:

1. Load your newly created "TMGSim Software Disk 1" in the floppy drive of your computer.
2. Close any Windows programs that may be open on your computer.
3. Select the Start button at the Windows task bar, then select Run, then select Browse, then select the floppy drive in which you loaded the disk, then select setup.exe, then select the Open button, then select the Ok button. From that point, just follow the instructions that appear on the screen.
4. If you have another program to install, repeat the steps above, starting with disk 1 for any program.

TMG! SOFTWARE INSTALLATION DISK SETS

The TMGSim software and TMGftp software for *The Marketing Game!* are discussed in detail in Chapter 5 of the Instructor's Manual. The TMGPlan software is discussed in Appendix A of the text and also in Chapter 8 of the Instructor's Manual. All of the software is overviewed in the multimedia tutorials, which use videos played by the TMGTutor program. So, we won't try to repeat all of that here. Rather, we'll overview the choices you have with the TMGDisks program to create different (combinations of) installation disks.

You will need at least two formatted floppy disks—to install TMGSim and its help file, the main instructor software.

You may also want to install the other TMG programs (TMGPlan, TMGftp, or TMGtoXLS) or perhaps create a disk with the old (second edition) DOS version of the Plan. These programs (and their associated help files) are packaged in different ways to minimize the number of disks required – depending on what you want to install. The subsections below show the possibilities. In the TMGDisks program, to select the combination you want, just click the relevant radio button on the main screen.

[Note: The TMGTutor program cannot be installed from floppy disks. The video files used by TMGTutor are much too large to fit on floppies. However, if you want to check it out using someone else's computer, see the help file for TMGTutor about running the program from the CD-Rom without installing the software.]

The Student Software Combination: TMGPlan and TMGftp

The student software—requires 2 installation disks and installs both TMGPlan and TMGftp. TMGPlan is the program that students use to create plan files, decrypt and print password-protected report files, and create pro formas for a plan. You probably don't need to install TMGPlan because the TMGSim program includes all of the same features. But, some profs want to check out what the students are using.

The TMGftp software is what students use to upload and download files over the Internet (at the instructor's option) and that instructors use to create configuration files specific to the computer system at their schools.

The "student software" combination (TMGPlan and TMGftp) above saves a disk and a step--if you plan to install both TMGPlan and TMGftp. However, if you want to install one but not the other they are available separately as well.

TMGSim: The Main Instructor Software

TMGSim—requires two installation disks. You'll need this. It's the main instructor software to process decisions, create reports, etc.--and it also incorporates all of the features of the student TMGPlan program.

TMGPlan: by Itself

TMGPlan—requires two installation disks. The student combination of TMGPlan and TMGftp (above) saves a disk and a few minutes if you want both programs, but if you don't intend to use TMGftp you can use this installation to setup TMGPlan. See notes above concerning the combination package to decide if you want to install TMGPlan at this point.

TMGftp: by Itself

TMGftp—requires 1 installation disk. Here again, the "Student software" combination (TMGPlan and TMGftp) above saves a disk and a step--if you plan to install both TMGPlan and TMGftp. If you want TMGftp but not TMGPlan, this is for you.

TMGtoXLS: by Itself

TMGtoXLS—requires 1 installation disk. You will need this only if you want to do supplementary analysis of data from the Summary files.

DOSPlan—requires 1 installation disk. This is a self-extracting zip file with the student plan software from the second edition of *The Marketing Game!* You probably don't need this but it is here for completeness if you are in a situation where computers running Windows 95 (or later) are generally not available but students have access to DOS or Win 3.1 computers. See the readme.txt file in the folder on the CD-Rom (\DiskOnly\DOSPlan\Readme.txt) for a discussion of the limitations of this program and what is involved to use it with the new version of the instructor's software. We don't recommend this...but ultimately it's an instructor's choice.

Appendix H. TMGtoXLS and Exporting TMG Data to an Excel Spreadsheet File

INTRODUCTION

From a teaching standpoint, one of the clear advantages of *The Marketing Game!* is that it makes it quick and easy for an instructor to diagnose a firm's plan decisions. In designing the simulation, our objective has been to give instructors information that they need, while preserving parsimony. The standard instructor reports (for each period) and summary reports (which provide information across decision periods) were created to give instructors the information they need in a format that's time-efficient for the instructor to use.

On the other hand, instructors sometimes want to assemble all of the relevant data in a form that's specific to their own taste. Further, when teaching large classes it's often useful to do cross-industry evaluations and graphs like those discussed in Chapter 7. In addition, software applications like Microsoft Excel have become popular for manipulating and graphing data. In light of this, one of our objectives for this edition was to provide instructors with a simple way to put information created by the simulation into an easy-to-manage spreadsheet format. The TMGtoXLS program meets this need.

What Does the TMGtoXLS Program Do?

The TMGtoXLS program is a simple "utility" program that extracts information from the summary file (for all TMG industries, firms, and decision periods) and exports it to a single file formatted so that it can be directly read by the Microsoft Excel™ spreadsheet program (versions 5 and later). Most other popular software packages for statistical analysis, graphing, database management, and the like now provide the option of reading or importing data in this file format.

With extensive data available in an easy-to-manage form, an instructor has the option to work with whatever subset of the information is of most interest and with whatever software tools are most familiar.

USING THE TMGtoXLS PROGRAM

The TMGtoXLS.exe program file is installed along with the other software on the Instructor CD-Rom. There's virtually nothing involved to use it. All you do is:

1. After you've run one or more decision periods, click the Start button the task bar, select Program files, the TMG, then TMGtoXLS to start the program. (Note: If your TMGSim program (or TMGPlan program) is open, close it before starting TMGtoXLS).
2. When the main screen appears, use the drop down box to select the drive and folder where your SUMMARYi.TMG files are saved; normally this will be the folder you specified as the instructor master files folder in your TMGSim setup file. Check the drop down file list to confirm that the program is in the directory where the SUMMARYi.TMG files (where *i* stands for the letter code for each industry) are saved.
3. Click the Export to Summary.XLS button and then watch the status bar at the bottom of the screen for updates as the different industries are processed. When the message appears to confirm that the file has been created, click Ok.
4. The SUMMARY.XLS file will be in the folder with your other master files. Open it with Excel or whatever other software program you want to use.
5. Run the program again after a new decision period. The old SUMMARY.XLS file will be overwritten and a new file with the same name—but updated with the new information--will be saved.

As this suggests, all you need to do to run the program is to select the correct folder and then click the Export to SUMMARY.XLS button. There's nothing to it and creating the Excel format summary file takes only a few seconds.

It's useful to highlight a few caveats:
- The SUMMARYi.TMG files for all industries should be in the same folder on your hard drive. This is what's normal. However, if for some reason you have used floppy disks to store your instructor files for different industries, you will need to copy the SUMMARYi.TMG files to the hard disk. (The main reason for this is that Excel files can be large and if you have many industries or decision periods the files may not fit on a floppy disk).
- Before you run the TMGtoXLS program, be certain to close the TMGSim (or TMGPlan) program if either of them is open. The programs are configured so that they will NOT run at the same time. This is intentional! It prevents the possibility of two programs trying to open or access TMG files at the same time, which could corrupt a file or cause other problems.

- A description of the variables in the SUMMARY.XLS file and how they are structured is provided in the next section.

INFORMATION ABOUT THE SUMMARY.XLS FILE

The SUMMARY.XLS file is formatted as a standard Excel (version 5 or higher) file.

The First Row Is a Header Row of Labels

The first row in the file consists of a set of column labels that correspond to the values that appear in that column for all of the other rows in the spreadsheet. To conserve space, these labels tend to be short abbreviations for the variable name. At the end of this section we provide a complete list of all of the variables in the file as well as an annotated explanation of the abbreviated names. However, for now it's useful to know that the variables in the file include:

- identification information (the period, industry, firm id),
- all of each firm's marketing plan decisions for each period,
- key financial information (such as profit contribution earned and various types of expenses, such a product modification costs)
- and all of the diagnostic indices (discussed in Chapter 7 and developed in detail in Chapter 14).

Every Other Row Corresponds to a Firm and a Decision Period

After the first (header) row, every row of data in the datasheet corresponds to a record with information about one firm in one industry for a particular decision period. The rows are organized by firm within periods within industries. Thus, the first four rows of data will be for Firm A1, Firm A2, Firm A3, and Firm A4 (respectively) for period 1. The next four rows will be for Firms A1, A2, A3 and A4 for period 2, and so on until the last period run. After all of the records for one industry, the next row starts with the first firm in the next industry for the first period.

- **The Size of the File**

As this suggests, the total number of rows in the sheet (and the size of the file) depends on the number of industries and number of decision periods. Specifically, the total number of rows is:

Number of data rows = (# of industries) * (4 firms per industry) * (# periods per industry)

Thus, if you had five industries (that is, 20 firms) and had (so far) run decisions for 5 periods, the sheet would have 100 data rows plus a header (label) row. As this suggests, when the number of industries or decision periods is large, the file becomes quite large.

As a rough estimate, the file will require about 8kb of disk space for each industry for each period. Thus, the size of the SUMMARY.XLS file for the example above (5 industries, 5 periods) would be about 200kb.

THE VARIABLES IN THE FILE

General Information

Each row in the file includes exactly the same variables and they are in the same order. The variables are listed below in the order that they appear, starting from column 1 and continuing for 113 columns to the last column in the spreadsheet. This organization is a convenient one that facilitates manipulation of the data. At the same time, it is important to understand that this approach means that some of the variables for a particular row may not be very relevant to a particular firm in a particular decision period.

For example, every row includes all of the decision variables that it is possible for a firm to control at Level 3 of the game. However, the decisions that students actually make (say, if the game is run at Level 1) might be a subset of those decisions. Thus, some of the variables in a record that corresponds to a firm that in a particular decision period was run at Level 1 or Level 2 would be set to zero (or to whatever the "default" value is in the simulation model). Consider the sales force commission rate variable. At Level 1 the standard commission rate is 5 percent; but at Level 2 (and Level 3) students explicitly make a decision about what commission rate to set (and it may be higher or lower than 5 percent). In a row that corresponds to a firm's decisions in period 1 (run at Level 1) the commission percent variable would always have a value of 5. If, at a later period, the level of the game were increased to Level 2, the value of the commission variable would be specific to the decision made by each firm.

Keep in mind that when *The Marketing Game!* is run at a lower level you are really allowing only a subset of the simulation parameters to vary. In other words, firms in a decision period run at a lower level of the game are (or can be) different on some characteristics due to the decisions they make, but on characteristics related to decisions that they cannot control they will be the same. You will see this when you look at the values of variables in the file.

Variable Labels (Column Headers) and Explanations

The table below, which continues for several pages, lists all of the variables in the order that they appear in the file, along with a number that indicates each variable's position in the order, the abbreviated label used in the spreadsheet, and a brief explanation of what the variable is. (This information is in the help file as well, and that provides an easy way to get a printed copy of this information).

Note that there is a consistent pattern to the abbreviations. The labels for variables related to product 1 have the prefix P1_ and those related to product 2 have the P2_prefix. Variables that relate to Channel 1 or Channel 2 have the C1 or C2 suffix, respectively. Segments are referenced with the segment number; for example, S2 refers to segment 2.

Variable Order	Abbreviated Variable Label	Explanation
1	obs	A record number unique to each row, starting at 1
2	Period	The game decision period associated with the data
3	Indust	The industry the firm is in
4	Firm	The firm ID code (industry and number)
5	ProfitCont	Profit contribution earned by the firm in this period
6	NextBudget	Budget available for the next decision period
7	DistInt_C1	Distribution intensity goal (percent) in Channel 1
8	DistIntl_C2	Distribution intensity goal (percent) in Channel 2
9	Reps_C1	Number of sales reps in Channel 1
10	Reps_C2	Number of sales reps in Channel 2
11	NonSell_C1	Percent non-selling time for sales reps in Channel 1
12	NonSell_C2	Percent non-selling time for sales reps in Channel 2
13	Commission	Commission percent for sales reps
14	CustService	Spending on customer service
15	P1_Brandname	Product 1 (VRD) brandname
16	P1_Attrib1	Level for 1st attribute for Product 1
17	P1_Attrib2	Level for 2nd attribute for Product 1
18	P1_Attrib3	Level for 3rd attribute for Product 1
19	P1_UnitCost	Product 1 unit production cost
20	P1_R&DCost	Total cost of R&D for product modifications in this period
21	P1_AdDollars	Advertising dollars spent to support Product 1
22	P1_AdType	Type of advertising used to support Product 1
23	P1_SlsProm_C1	Dollars spent on sales (trade) promotion) in Channel 1
24	P1_SlsProm_C2	Dollars spent on sales (trade) promotion) in Channel 2
25	P1_ProdOrder	Production order quantity (demand estimate) for Product 1
26	P1_WPrice_C1	Wholesale price for Product 1 in Channel 1
27	P1_WPrice_C2	Wholesale price for Product 1 in Channel 1
28	P1_RPrice_C1	Retail price charged by dealers for Product 1 in Channel 1
29	P1_RPrice_C2	Retail price charged by dealers for Product 1 in Channel 2
30	P1_MktRes1	Firm purchased market research report 1 for Product 1 (Y=yes)
31	P1_MktRes2	Firm purchased market research report 2 for Product 1 (Y=yes)
32	P1_MktRes3	Firm purchased market research report 3 for Product 1 (Y=yes)
33	P1_MktRes4	Firm purchased market research report 4 for Product 1 (Y=yes)
34	P1_MktRes5	Firm purchased market research report 5 for Product 1 (Y=yes)
35	P1_MktRes6	Firm purchased market research report 6 for Product 1 (Y=yes)
36	P1_MktRes7	Firm purchased market research report 7 for Product 1 (Y=yes)
37	2ndProduct	Firm has a second product (true or false)
38	P2_Brandname	Product 2 (DVC) brandname
39	P2_Attrib1	Level for 1st attribute for Product 2
40	P2_Attrib2	Level for 2nd attribute for Product 2
41	P2_Attrib3	Level for 3rd attribute for Product 2
42	P2_UnitCost	Product 2 unit production cost
43	P2_R&Dcosts	Total cost of R&D for product modifications in this period

Variable Order	Abbreviated Variable Label	Explanation
44	P2_AdDollars	Advertising dollars spent to support Product 2
45	P2_AdType	Type of advertising used to support Product 2
46	P2_SlsProm_C1	Dollars spent on sales (trade) promotion) in Channel 1
47	P2_SlsProm_C2	Dollars spent on sales (trade) promotion) in Channel 2
48	P2_ProdOrder	Production order quantity (demand estimate) for Product 2
49	P2_WPrice_C1	Wholesale price for Product 2 in Channel 1
50	P2_WPrice_C2	Wholesale price for Product 2 in Channel 2
51	P2_RPrice_C1	Retail price charged by dealers for Product 2 in Channel 1
52	P2_RPrice_C2	Retail price charged by dealers for Product 2 in Channel 2
53	P2_MktRes1	Firm purchased market research report 1 for Product 2 (Y=yes)
54	P2_MktRes2	Firm purchased market research report 2 for Product 2 (Y=yes)
55	P2_MktRes3	Firm purchased market research report 3 for Product 2 (Y=yes)
56	P2_MktRes4	Firm purchased market research report 4 for Product 2 (Y=yes)
57	P2_MktRes5	Firm purchased market research report 5 for Product 2 (Y=yes)
58	P2_MktRes6	Firm purchased market research report 6 for Product 2 (Y=yes)
59	P2_MktRes7	Firm purchased market research report 7 for Product 2 (Y=yes)
60	ServiceIndx	Firm's customer service index (percent satisfied)
61	ServImpact	Index of customer service relative to industry
62	Exposure_C1	Index of how well sales for size matches distribution intensity goal in Channel 1
63	Exposure_C2	Index of how well sales for size matches distribution intensity goal in Channel 2
64	CallEffect_C1	Index for personal selling effectiveness in Channel 1
65	CallEffect_C2	Index for personal selling effectiveness in Channel 2
66	Effort	Index for sales rep effort (motivation)
67	Goodwill_C1	Index of sales (trade) promotion effectiveness in Channel 1
68	Goodwill_C2	Index of sales (trade) promotion effectiveness in Channel 2
69	SalesForce_C1	Index of overall sales force in Channel 1
70	SalesForce_C2	Index of overall sales force in Channel 2
71	P1_Awareness	Index for consumer awareness of Product 1
72	P1_AdEfficiency	Index for efficiency of advertising for Product 1
73	P2_Awareness	Index for consumer awareness of Product 2
74	P2_AdEfficiency	Index for efficiency of advertising for Product 1
75	ChanlPush_C1	Index of channel push in Channel 1
76	ChanlPush_C2	Index of channel push in Channel 2
77	P1_MkEff-S1C1	Index of marketing effort toward Segment 1 in Channel 1 for Product 1
78	P1_MkEff-S1C2	Index of marketing effort toward Segment 1 in Channel 2 for Product 1
79	P1_MkEff-S2C1	Index of marketing effort toward Segment 2 in Channel 1 for Product 1
80	P1_MkEff-S2C2	Index of marketing effort toward Segment 2 in Channel 2 for Product 1
81	P1_MkEff-S3C1	Index of marketing effort toward Segment 3 in Channel 1 for Product 1
82	P1_MkEff-S3C2	Index of marketing effort toward Segment 3 in Channel 2 for Product 1
83	P1_MkEff-S4C1	Index of marketing effort toward Segment 4 in Channel 1 for

Variable Order	Abbreviated Variable Label	Explanation
		Product 1
84	P1_MkEff-S4C2	Index of marketing effort toward Segment 4 in Channel 2 for Product 1
85	P1_MkEff-S5C1	Index of marketing effort toward Segment 5 in Channel 1 for Product 1
86	P1_MkEff-S5C2	Index of marketing effort toward Segment 5 in Channel 2 for Product 1
87	P1_MkEff-S6C1	Index of marketing effort toward Segment 6 in Channel 1 for Product 1
88	P1_MkEff-S6C2	Index of marketing effort toward Segment 6 in Channel 2 for Product 1
89	P2_MkEff-S1C1	Index of marketing effort toward Segment 1 in Channel 1 for Product 2
90	P2_MkEff-S1C2	Index of marketing effort toward Segment 1 in Channel 2 for Product 2
91	P2_MkEff-S2C1	Index of marketing effort toward Segment 2 in Channel 1 for Product 2
92	P2_MkEff-S2C2	Index of marketing effort toward Segment 2 in Channel 2 for Product 2
93	P2_MkEff-S3C1	Index of marketing effort toward Segment 3 in Channel 1 for Product 2
94	P2_MkEff-S3C2	Index of marketing effort toward Segment 3 in Channel 2 for Product 2
95	P2_MkEff-S4C1	Index of marketing effort toward Segment 4 in Channel 1 for Product 2
96	P2_MkEff-S4C2	Index of marketing effort toward Segment 4 in Channel 2 for Product 2
97	P2_MkEff-S5C1	Index of marketing effort toward Segment 5 in Channel 1 for Product 2
98	P2_MkEff-S5C2	Index of marketing effort toward Segment 5 in Channel 2 for Product 2
99	P2_MkEff-S6C1	Index of marketing effort toward Segment 6 in Channel 1 for Product 2
100	P2_MkEff-S6C2	Index of marketing effort toward Segment 6 in Channel 2 for Product 2
101	Cost:Firing	Total sales cost severance (firing) costs for the period
102	Cost:Service	Customer service expense
103	Cost:SlsPro_C1	Sales promotion expense in Channel 1
104	Cost:SlsPro_C2	Sales promotion expense in Channel 2
105	P1_Cost:COGS	Cost of goods sold for Product 1
106	P1_Cost:Transfers	Transfer costs (from overproduction) for Product 1
106	P1_Cost:MktRes	Total cost of market research for Product 1
108	P2_COGS	Costs of goods sold for Product 2
109	P2_Cost:Transfers	Transfer costs (from overproduction) for Product 2
110	P2_Cost:MktRes	Total cost of market research for Product 2
111	ExtraMktRes	Any adjustment by prof for extra marketing research costs
112	Fines	Any fine by prof to adjust outcome
113	BudgetChange	Any change from this period's budget based on an adjustment made by the instructor

Variable Order	Abbreviated Variable Label	Explanation
114	Total Costs	Firm's total costs in the current period

Creating a Subset of the File

The file includes a large number of variables so that you have access to what you want. However, the organization and structure is designed to make it easy for you to select a subset of the rows and/or columns if there are particular things that you want to focus on in a given graph or analysis. For example, all of the records for an industry are ordered together, and in general related sets of variables are (decision variables for product 1, for product 2, indices, expenses, etc.) are grouped together. With Excel (and other similar applications) it is easy to copy and paste a subset of the rows or columns from this overall file into a new worksheet. Similarly, you can sort by relevant criteria because there are variables that allow you to reorganize the records any way you want (for example, by period, by firm, before and after introduction of a second product, etc.). Note that if you rearrange the file and then want to return to the original order all you need to do is sort the records by the observation number in the first column.

SOME CONCLUDING COMMENTS

It's reasonable to ask why the TMGSim software doesn't automatically create the SUMMARY.XLS file in the same way that it automatically creates reports. In point of fact, we have created and tested a version of the program that does that. However, we have several reasons for offering TMGtoXLS as a separate program with this edition. First, as noted earlier, the SUMMARY.XLS files can be very large. That means that there are trade-offs in terms of instructor flexibility. The design of the new software means that it is most efficient for instructors when everything is run from a hard drive, and in that event file size is less of an issue. On the other hand, if instructors want to use floppy disks there are difficulties when it comes to accumulating all of the information from across all industries. As that implies, there is a sequencing effect. All industries need to have been run for the summary files to be available to create one consolidated XLS file, but there are reliability and error protection benefits that accrue by completing the processing one industry at a time.

A second issue concerns our desire to make all of the TMG software "bullet-proof"--so that instructors don't encounter any problems when running the simulation. Creating the routines to extract the XLS format files was complicated and, as you may be aware, attempting to "link" independent software with Microsoft products isn't always free of surprises. Because of this, we felt it was smarter not to have the routines to create the Excel files operating in the middle of the TMGSim procedures that run the simulation. An unexpected (and perhaps even untestable) "gotcha" in creating the XLS file could disrupt the basic